ECONOMIC DEVELOPMENT IN INDIA

ECONOMIC DEVELOPMENT IN INDIA

Dr Suman Kalyan Chaudhury

Dr Sukanta Sarkar

GenNext Publication

ISBN : 978-93-8022-298-1

Price : ₹ 990

First Published, 2016

Published by

GenNext Publications
5, Ansari Road
Daryaganj, New Delhi-110002
Phone: 9811692060
E-mail: gennext@hotmail.com

Printed at: G. Print Process, Delhi.

Cataloging in Publication Data—DK
Courtesy: D.K. Agencies (P) Ltd. <docinfo@dkagencies.com>

Economic development in India / Dr Suman Kalyan Chaudhury, Dr Sukanta Sarkar.
pages cm
Contributed articles.
Includes bibliographical references.
ISBN 9789380222981

1. Economic development—India. 2. Sustainable development—India. I. Chaudhury, Suman Kalyan, 1972- editor. II. Sarkar, Sukanta, editor.

HC435.3.E26 2016 DDC 338.954 23

Contents

Foreword

Date: 22/11/2015

I am glad to know that Dr Suman Kalyan Chaudhury and Dr Sukanta Sarkar have prepared edited book entitled *Economic Development in India* and the book is going to be published by the Gen-Next Publication, New Delhi, India. Eighteen papers of contributors have been concluded in this book. By reading the manuscript, I think most of the contemporary topics of economic development have been included in it. I am confident that this book will be very useful to the students and researchers of Planning, Sociology, Rural Development, Economics, Commerce, Developmental studies etc.

I wish academic endeavour of the authors of this book shall be fruitful and it will satisfy the academic queries of the readers.

With best wishes

Professor M A Rahman, PhD (USA)
Director, Centre for Global Environmental Culture (CGEC)
Coordinator, RCE Greater Dhaka and WWOOF Bangladesh
International University of Business Agriculture and Technology
Uttara Model Town, Dhaka, Bangladesh

Preface

Economic development is the sustained, concerted actions of policy-makers and communities that promote the standard of living and economic health of a specific area. It can be referred to as the quantitative and qualitative changes in the economy. The study of economic development was borne out of an extension to traditional economics that focused entirely on national product, or the aggregate output of goods and services. It is important so that our society can constantly grow and evolve, making new advancements in both technology and industry. Understanding economics is important for our society to continue its rapid development. The level of it in a country may be measured by considering levels of public welfare, education, health and liberty.

We desire to express our heartiest thank to Professor B.K. Panda, Department of Economics, Berhampur University, Odisha who despite his busy schedule and hectic academic engagements, all the time encouraged and supported us. We have also beholden to Dr N.G. Pendse, Department of Economics, Rani Durgabati University, Jabalpur who's erudite and scholarly tidbits for preparing such a vast work are still fresh in our mind. We also thanks to Dr Pradeep Kumar Pandey, Centre of Judicial Studies, Dibrugarh University, Assam; Dr Rakesh Joshi, Department of Economics, Saurashtra University, Gujarat; Dr D. Pulla Rao, Department of Economics, Andhra University; Dr Vibhuti Patel, Professor-cum-Director, Centre for Study of Social Exclusion and Inclusive Policy, SNDT Women's University, Mumbai; Dr Wakar Amin, Department of Social Work, University of Kashmir, J and K; Dr Shazia Manzoor, Assistant Professor, Department of Social Work, University of Kashmir, J & K; Dr Pallab Kanti Ghoshal, Department of Commerce, BBM College, Agartala, for their valuable suggestions and moral support.

We are heartily grateful to Professor R. Prasad, Department of Economics, Pandit Ravishankar Shukla University, Raipur; who always encouraged us to carry on this constructive work. Further, we express our heartily thankfulness to each and every person who directly/indirectly helped us in preparing this work.

It is hoped that this book will be very useful for Society in general and students of economics in particular. Comments and suggestions are most welcomed.

Dr Suman Kalyan Chaudhury
Dr Sukanta Sarkar

Introduction

Economic development is a term that economists, politicians, and others have used frequently in the twentieth century. The scope of economic development includes the process and policies by which a nation improves the economic, political, and social well-being of its people. Economic development has evolved into a professional industry of highly specialised practitioners.

Dr Suman Kalyan Chaudhury and Dr Sukanta Sarkar in their paper, "Corporate Governance in India: Challenges and Future Prospects" discuss about the growth of corporate governance in India. Corporate Governance has grown very rapidly in the last decade and is now viewed as an important attribute of the corporate sector. In terms of the legislative mechanisms, Indian government and industry constituted three committees to study corporate governance practices in the country and suggest measures for improvement based on what has globally recognised as "best practices".

According to Akanshya Patnaik and Dr Sunil Kumar Pradhan paper, "Green Marketing Strategies for Sustainable Development in the Present Era" green marketing strategy is no doubt a step towards sustainable development. But it can not be successful without its full-fledged Implementation. Government has gone for many green policies but any way it needs to be implemented as it is planned. It will take some time to make a complete green life style. The march had already begin by government and continued by business now it is the right time for all academicians and researchers to raise its awareness to that extent by which one day our dream of green planet will be successful in its true sense.

Dr B.K. Panda and Dr Sukanta Sarkar in their paper, "Rubber Plantation in Tripura: A Strategy of Aforestation" found that rubber based agro-forestry involves a complex and diverse cropping system that combines the growing of rubber and other agricultural crops in the area in a sustainable manner. Rubber has been identified as one of the thrust areas in Tripura, in view of its suitability to the terrain and the acceptability amongst the people.

In 1976, Tripura Forest Development and Plantation Corporation was set up to get a big leap for expansion of rubber mostly in denuded forest land. Dr Simanchala Das and Dr Suman Kalyan Chaudhury in their paper "Corporate Social Responsibility and Sustainable Development: A Case Based Approach" concluded that the case for demonstrating corporate responsibility is getting stronger as expectations among key opinion formers, customers and the public are increasing over. Priority has to be accorded to activities pertaining to inclusive growth of society with special attention to development of weaker sections of society and the backward districts of the country and environment sustainability.

Dr R. Mutharayappa in his paper, "Factors Affecting Adolescent Childbearing and Its Impacts on Maternal and Child Health in India" found that marriage of girls at young ages is declining. Secondly, girls given in marriage before 20 years of age are going down. This is because marriage of girls at young ages leads to teenage pregnancy and motherhood. Young women who become pregnant and give birth experience a number of health problems as well as social, economic and emotional problems. Women educational attainment, religion, standard of living and rural-urban differentials and caste group differentials in relative risk of being pregnant have not been found significant. However, among the social groups, scheduled caste women have been found to face an 18 per cent higher risk of being pregnant.

Dr Suman Kalyan Chaudhury and Dr Sukanta Sarkar in their paper, "Changing Scenario of Insurance Sector in India: An Analysis" found that insurance is the backbone of a country's risk management system. Risk is an inherent part of our lives. The insurance providers offer a variety of products to businesses and individuals in order to provide protection from risk and to ensure financial security. The Insurance Act of 1938 was the first legislation governing all forms of insurance to provide strict state control over insurance business.

G. Stephen, Dr Sudhir K. Jena and Dr Manaswini Patra in their paper, "Online Newspaper Reading Habits and Attitude in the ICT Environment: A Study of Alagappa University, Karaikudi" reveals that, both Tamil and English newspapers are frequently read by the under and post graduate students and faculties of Alagappa University, Karaikudi and they prefer international section to the national section for the purpose of keeping abreast of the day-to-day happenings in different parts of the world. The study also indicate that, in spite of their interest in newspaper reading, students are prevented from newspaper reading because of various socio-cultural, administrative and environmental problems. Concerned authorities of the university must take proper actions to make sure that students can read newspapers without facing any problem.

According to Dr Archana Sethi paper, "Urbanisation in India: Trends and Problems," urbanisation in India was mainly caused after independence, due to adoption of mixed system of economy by the country which gave rise to the development of private sector. Urbanisation is taking place at a faster rate in India. After the industrial revolution urban population all over the world is increasing. There is a rapid migration of rural people to urban areas for jobs and better living. As a result, the population in the towns and cities are increasing and rural population is dwindling. Dr Rakesh Joshi and Dr Sukanta Sarkar in their paper said that the Central Government has announced the availability of incentive funds for states to carry out appropriate agriculture market policy reforms. With the development process, significance of primary sector declines while that of secondary and tertiary sectors increases. A remarkable feature of the Indian macroeconomic story since independence has been the continuous rise in household savings over the decades. The reform process in India was initiated with the aim of accelerating the pace of economic growth and eradication of poverty.

Dr Ch. Sudipta Kishore Nandain his paper, "Correlation between Individual Governance Mechanism and Indian Companies Performance" summarising the results of the analysis of individual impact of governance facets on performance variables under a random effect model, no facets of governance impacts the EBITDA margin. Further, Board structure impacts negatively to the performance in terms of P/B ratio, Return on Equity, Sales growth and Dividend payout ratio. Dr D. Pulla Rao and Dr Sukanta Sarkar in their paper, "Growth and Progress of Indian Agriculture and Industrial Sector" agriculture is unquestionably the largest livelihood provider in India, more so in the vast rural areas. It also contributes a significant figure to the Gross Domestic Product. Small scale industries play a vital role in the development of economy, mainly in developing countries. Major problems faced by the small scale industries are: finance, raw material, idle capacity, technology, marketing, infrastructure, under-utilisation of capacity, and project planning.

Dr Biswajit Prasad Chhatoi in his paper, "Managerial and Operational Efficiency: A Study of Indian Cement Industry" pointed out that managerial and operational efficiency are central terms in assessing and measuring the performance of organisations, as well as inter-organisational arrangements such as strategic alliances, joint ventures, sourcing as well as outsourcing agreements. Managerial efficiency refers to efficient management of assets of an organisation whereas operational efficiency refers to profitability of the firm. Dr Rohini Prasad and Dr Sukanta Sarkar in their paper, "Problems and Prospects for Development of North-Eastern Region of India" found that India's north-east region is endowed with huge untapped natural resources and is acknowledged as the eastern gateway for the country's 'Look East Policy'. Agriculture provides livelihood to 70 per cent of the region's population. Rubber and bamboo are among the important agricultural produces which can attract a lot of investment opportunities. India's sensitive North Eastern region, especially Assam, is fast emerging as an epicentre of international jihadi networks.

Dr P.K. Ghoshal and Dr Sukanta Sarkar in their paper, "Women Empowerment and Development: A Study in India" concluded that women's empowerment has been an issue of immense discussions and contemplation over the last few decades world-wide. This as an agenda has been on top of the lists of most government plans and programmes as well. The empowerment of women would result in overall development of society both at micro and macro level. Dr Suman Kalyan Chaudhury, Manoj Kumar Panda and Professor A. K. Sahu in their paper, "Foreign Direct Investment in India: An Overview" found that the growth of FDI gives opportunities to Indian industry for technological upgradation, gaining access to global managerial skills and practices, optimising utilisation of human and natural resources and competing internationally with higher efficiency. FDI plays an important role in economic growth of an economy.

Dr D. Rajasekaran in his paper, "Growth and Composition of Population in Karnataka State Spatio-Temporal Analysis from 1991-2011" summarise the decadal growth how is different among the districts, the Hyderabad Karnataka region records highest growth rate comparatively to the Mysore region. The Mumbai region and remaining districts have registered moderate growth. The density is also varies among the districts, the southern, coastal, and the Mumbai region has high density, and remaining northern, Mysore region has moderate density, in the Malnad districts have registered low density.

About the Contributors

Dr Suman Kalyan Chaudhury: Faculty Member, Department of Business Administration, Berhampur University, Odisha.

Dr Sukanta Sarkar: Assistant Professor, Faculty of Management Studies, ICFAI University, Agartala, Tripura.

Akanshya Patnaik: Research Scholar, Department of Business Administration, Berhampur University, Odisha.

Sunil Kumar Pradhan: Faculty Member, Department of Business Administration, Berhampur University, Odisha.

Dr B.K. Panda: Professor, P.G. Department of Economics, Berhampur University, Ganjam, Odisha.

Dr Simanchala Das: Faculty Member, Global Institute of Management, Hanspal, Bhubaneswar, Odisha.

Dr R. Mutharayappa: Professor, Population Research Centre, Institute of Social and Economic Change, Bangalore, Karnataka.

G. Stephen: Research Scholar, DLIS, Alagappa University, Karaikudi, Tamil Nadu.

Dr Sudhir K. Jena: Librarian, Indian Institute of Management, Shilling, Meghalaya.

Dr Manaswini Patra: Librarian I/c, R.P. Padhy Central Library, Berhampur University, Odisha.

Dr Archana Sethi: Assistant Professor, Department of Economics, Pandit Ravishankar Shukla University, Raipur, Chhattisgarh.

Dr Rakesh Joshi: Associate Professor, Department of Economics, Saurashtra University, Gujarat.

Dr Ch. Sudipta Kishore Nanda: Lecturer, School of Commerce and Management Studies, Department of Commerce, Ravenshaw University, Cuttack, Odisha.

Dr D. Pulla Rao: Professor, Department of Economics, Andhra University, Andhra Pradesh.

Dr Jaydevi G. Rajyaguru: Assistant Professor, Siddharth Law College, Kamrej, Gujarat.

Dr Parmeshwari Rajyaguru: Assistant Professor, Department of Human Rights, Saurashtra University, Rajkot, Gujarat.

Dr Rohini Prasad: Professor and Dean of Social Science, Department of Economics, Pandit Ravishankar Shukla University, Raipur, Chhattisgarh.

Dr P.K. Ghoshal: Associate Professor, Department of Commerce, BBM College, Agartala, Tripura.

Dr Biswajit Prasad Chhatoi: Asst. Professor, School of Business Administration, Ravenshaw University, Cuttack.

Dr Farzana Alim: Professor and Chairman, Department of Home Science, Aligarh Muslim University, Uttar Pradesh.

Manoj Kumar Panda: Research Scholar, P.G. Department of Business Administration, Berhampur University, Odisha.

Dr A. K. Sahu: Professor, P.G. Department of Business Administration, Berhampur University, Odisha.

Dr N.G. Pendse: Professor, Department of Economics, Rani Durgabati University, Jabalpur, Uttar Pradesh.

Dr D. Rajasekaran: Associate Professor in Geography, Govt. Arts College, Bangalore, Karnataka.

Abbreviations

ACU	: Association of Common Wealth Universities
AFSPA	: Armed Forces Special Power Act
AICG	: Asian Institute of Corporate Governance
AIU	: Association of Indian Universities
AMA	: American Marketing Association
APW	: Assam Public Works
ASSOCHAM	: Associated Chambers of Commerce and Industry
ATTF	: All Tripura Tiger Force
BRO	: Border Road Organisation
BSE	: Bombay Stock Exchange
BSY	: Balika Samriddhi Yojana
CSR	: Corporate Social Responsibility
DCA	: Department of Company Affairs
DHD	: Dima Halam Daoga
DPE	: Department of Public Enterprises
ECGC	: Export Credit Guarantee Corporation
ECGI	: European Corporate Governance Institute
EDP	: Entrepreneurship Development Programmes
EIR	: East Indian Railway
EMS	: Environmental Management System
ETPs	: Effluent Treatment Plants
FDI	: Foreign Direct Investment
GDP	: Gross Domestic Product
GIC	: General Insurance Corporation
GIPR	: Great Indian Peninsular Railway
GNLA	: Garo National Liberation Army
GNP	: Gross National Product

GOI	: Government of India
GRI	: Global Reporting Initiatives
HALC	: Hynniewtrep Achik Liberation Council
HDFC	: Housing Development Finance Corporation
HRD	: Human Resource Development
ICDS	: Integrated Child Development Services
IDC	: Integrated Development Centre
ILO	: International Labour Organisation
IMDT	: Illegal Migrants (Determination by Tribunal) Act
IMY	: Indira Mahila Yojana
IRDA	: Insurance Regulatory and Development Authority
KLO	: Kamtapur Liberation Organisation
KNV	: Karbi National Volunteers
LIC	: Life Insurance Corporation
LPG	: Liberalisation, Privatisation and Globalisation
MGNREGS	: Mahatma Gandhi National Rural Employment Guarantee Scheme
MNC	: Multinational Corporation
MNCs	: Multi-National Corporations
MSMED	: Micro, Small and Medium Enterprises Development
NABARD	: National Bank for Agriculture and Rural Development
NCF	: National Creche Fund
NCW	: National Commission for Women
NDDB	: National Dairy Development Board
NDFB	: National Democratic Front of Bodoland
NEC	: North Eastern Council
NER	: North East Region
NFHS	: National Family Health Survey
NIAC	: New India Assurance Company
NIC	: National Insurance Company
NNC	: Naga National Council
NNP	: National Nutrition Policy
NSCN	: National Socialist Council of Nagaland
OBC	: Other Backward Communities
OECD	: Organisation for Economic Cooperation and Development

OIC	: Oriental Insurance Company
ONGC	: Oil and Natural Gas Corporation
PLDQ	: Purnapani Limestone and Dolomite Quarry
RMK	: Rashtriya Mahila Kosh
RPS	: Rubber Producers Societies
RRII	: Rubber Research Institute of India
RWDEP	: Rural Women's Development and Empowerment Project
SAIL	: Steel Authority of India Limited
SC	: Scheduled Castes
SD	: Sustainable Development
SDSETI	: Skill Development and Self Employment Training Institute
SEBI	: Securities and Exchanges Board of India
SEZ	: Special Economic Zone
SHGs	: Self Help Groups
SIDO	: Small Industries Development Organisation
SSIs	: Small-Scale Industries
ST	: Scheduled Tribes
TBL	: Triple Bottom Line
TCS	: Tata Consultancy Services
TFDPC	: Tripura Forest Development and Plantation Corporation
TIDC	: Tripura Industrial Development Corporation
TRPC	: Tripura Rehabilitation and Plantation Corporation
TTAADC	: Tripura Tribal Areas Autonomous District Council
UIIC	: United India Insurance Company
UK	: United Kingdom
UNDFW	: United Nations Development Fund for Women
US	: United States
VTI	: Vocational Training Institutes

Chapter 1

Corporate Governance in India: Challenges and Future Prospects

Dr Suman Kalyan Chaudhury and
Dr Sukanta Sarkar

"Unlike a drop of water which loses its identity when it joins the ocean, man does not lose his being in the society in which he lives. Man's life is independent. He is born not for the development of the society alone, but for the development of his self." **–B. R. Ambedkar**

Introduction

Governance refers to "all processes of governing, whether undertaken by a government, market, or network, whether over a family, tribe, formal or informal organisation, or territory, and whether through laws, norms, power, or language." Governance is a very general concept that can refer to all manner of organisations. Good governance is an indeterminate term used in international development literature to describe various normative accounts of how public institutions ought to conduct public affairs and manage public resources. These normative accounts are often justified on the grounds that they are thought to be conducive to economic ends, such as the eradication of poverty and successful economic development. Government is one of the actors in governance. Other actors involved in governance vary depending on the level of government that is under discussion. Good governance has eight major characteristics. It is participatory, consensus oriented, accountable, transparent, responsive, effective and efficient, equitable and inclusive and follows the rule of law. It assures that corruption is minimised, the views of minorities are taken into account and that the voices of the most vulnerable in society are heard in decision-making.

In the community of nations, governance is considered "good" and "democratic" to the degree in which a country's institutions and processes are transparent. Its institutions refer to such bodies as parliament and its various ministries. Good governance promotes equity, participation, pluralism, transparency, accountability and the rule of law, in a manner that is effective, efficient and enduring. Corporate governance became a pressing issue following the 2002 introduction of the Sarbanes-Oxley Act in the US, which was ushered in to restore public confidence in companies and markets after accounting fraud bankrupted high-profile companies such as Enron and WorldCom.

What is Corporate Governance?

Corporate governance refers to the system by which corporations are directed and controlled. The governance structure specifies the distribution of rights and responsibilities among different participants in the corporation (such as the board of directors, managers, shareholders, creditors, auditors, regulators, and other stakeholders) and specifies the rules and procedures for making decisions in corporate affairs. Corporate governance has also been defined as "a system of law and sound approaches by which corporations are directed and controlled focusing on the internal and external corporate structures with the intention of monitoring the actions of management and directors and thereby mitigating agency risks which may stem from the misdeeds of corporate officers."

India's SEBI Committee on Corporate Governance defines corporate governance as the "acceptance by management of the inalienable rights of shareholders as the true owners of the corporation and of their own role as trustees on behalf of the shareholders. It is about commitment to values, about ethical business conduct and about making a distinction between personal and corporate funds in the management of a company." In a narrow sense, corporate governance involves a set of relationships amongst the company's management, its board of directors, its shareholders, its auditors and other stakeholders.

History of Corporate Governance

The Mauryan period is regarded as the period of good governance. It was one of the largest empires in Ancient India and its administration was considered as one of the best administration over the entire world. The Mauryan King was the head of the state administration holding legislative, executive and judicial powers. Judicial system was well-organised and there was continued supervision and inspection process which was installed in every walk of administration. Secret services played a major role in maintenance of law and order in the kingdom. Local authority was controlled by Parishad who in turn used to report to king. Above all these it was

Chanakya's *Arthashastra,* written during the period of Chandra Gupta Maurya which made Mauryan Empire stronger in terms of administration. Arthashastra contains 6000 sutras divided into 15 chapters and 18 subchapter's instructions about administration, management, law and justice, economy, foreign policy etc. The key areas which can use the ancient period governance in present day situation are: (a) Learning on Leadership qualities and skills; (b) Selection or right person for right job; (c) Accountability and Delegation of Authorities and (d) System of Spy and Intelligence agency to control corruption and monitoring of work; and Social welfare ideas of king and his team.

The "corporate governance concept" dwells in India from the Arthashastra time instead of CEO at that time there were kings and subjects. During Vedic times kings used to have their ministers and used to have ethics, values, principles and laws to run their state but today it is in the form corporate governance having same rules, laws, ethics, values, and morals etc which helps in running corporate bodies in the more effective ways so that they in the age of globalisation become global giants. Need for corporate governance arises due to separation of management from the ownership. For a firm success, it needs to concentrate on both economical and social aspect. It needs to be fair with producers, shareholders, customers etc. It has various responsibilities towards employees, customers, communities and at last towards governance and it needs to serve its responsibilities at the best at all aspects.

Government regulations have required most Multi-National Corporations (MNCs) in India to operate through subsidiaries which are not 100 per cent owned by the parent. In the 70s, the government enacted a law limiting foreign ownership in most industries to 40 per cent while allowing 51 per cent in a few high technology areas. This law was liberalised in the 90s and now 51 per cent is permitted in most industries while 74 per cent or even 100 per cent ownership is allowed in some cases. In the 90s when the law permitted higher foreign ownership, these MNCs raised the foreign stake by issuing shares at very deep discounts to the market price. Corporate governance concept emerged in India after the second half of 1996 due to economic liberalisation and deregulation of industry and business.

Corporate Governance: Global Perspectives

Issues of corporate governance have been hotly debated in the United States and Europe over the last decade or two. In India, these issues have come to the fore only in the last couple of years. Naturally, the debate in

India has drawn heavily on the British and American literature on corporate governance. The corporate governance literature in the US and the UK focuses on the role of the Board as a bridge between the owners and the management. Corporate governance reforms in the US and UK have focused on making the Board independent of the CEO. The Compensation Committee of the Board has been strengthened to exercise greater control over CEO compensation following widespread complaints that top management pay is disproportionate to performance.

Established in 1999, the OECD-Asian Roundtable on Corporate Governance serves as a regional forum for exchanging experiences and advancing the reform agenda on corporate governance while promoting awareness and use of the OECD Principles of Corporate Governance. It brings together policy-makers, practitioners and experts on corporate governance from the Asian region, OECD countries and relevant international organisations. In 2012, the Asian Roundtable established a Taskforce on Enforcement to develop a good practices report on public enforcement and supervision in Asia. The Taskforce is currently engaged in conducting a survey of participating jurisdictions to determine the current practices and policies regarding public enforcement and supervision and identify the key challenges and obstacles. In 2014, the OECD is launching the OECD-Southeast Asia Programme on Capital Market Development and Corporate Governance of State-Owned Enterprises, with the financial support of the government of Japan.

Complementary to the Asian Roundtable on Corporate Governance, the new programme will initially focus on corporate governance and capital market development in Myanmar and Viet Nam. The South Asia Corporate Governance Programme work in selected countries in the region at differing levels of intervention, from work with firms, institutions, and economy-wide market-level interventions to improve the enabling environment for corporate governance. IFC provides advice to companies and banks on how to introduce and strengthen corporate governance practices based on international standards. The region has already been implementing a comprehensive Bangladesh Corporate Governance Project which aims to improve financial performance and operational efficiency by promoting better corporate governance practices among business enterprises in the country.

The Asian Institute of Corporate Governance (AICG) at Korea University is the primary research institute on corporate governance issues in Asia and other emerging markets. The AICG supports top-rated academic research, develops policy measures on corporate governance issues, and provides training programmes for corporate managers. First released in May 1999 and revised in 2004, the OECD Principles are one of the 12 key standards for international financial stability of the Financial Stability Board and form the basis for the corporate governance component of the Report on the Observance of Standards and Codes of the World Bank Group. The financial crisis revealed severe shortcomings in corporate governance. When most needed, existing standards failed to provide the checks and balances that companies need in order to cultivate sound business practices. The OECD launched an ambitious action plan to develop a set of recommendations for improvements in priority areas such as remuneration, risk management, board practices and the exercise of shareholder rights.

Corporate governance is an issue high on the agenda in Europe as well as in the UK. The European Commission is concerned about the gender imbalance on corporate boards and is consulting on ways to get more women on to listed company boards. The 13th European Corporate Governance Conference was held under the auspices of the Lithuanian Presidency of the Council of the European Union on 8-9 October 2013 in Vilnius. The Conference focuses on shareholders' engagement including topics on corporate governance in unlisted companies and state-owned enterprises. *The European Commission has adopted an Action Plan outlining future initiatives in the areas of company law and corporate governance.* The Action Plan announces 16 different actions to be taken by the Commission. Some of these will be proposals for new legislation; others could require soft law or an information campaign, but all are priority actions.

The EU corporate governance rules apply in principle to all EU companies listed on a stock exchange. Since most banks are listed on a stock exchange they will be covered by the actions announced in the Action Plan in the area of corporate governance. Harmonisation of the rules relating to company law and corporate governance, as well as to accounting and auditing, is essential for creating a Single Market for Financial Services and products. In the fields of company law and corporate governance, objectives include: providing equivalent protection for shareholders and other parties concerned with companies; ensuring freedom of establishment for companies throughout the EU; fostering efficiency and competitiveness of business; promoting cross-border cooperation between companies in different Member States; and stimulating discussions between Member States on the modernisation of company law and corporate governance. The European Corporate Governance Institute is an international scientific non-profit association. It provides a forum for debate and dialogue between academics, legislators and practitioners, focusing on major corporate governance issues and thereby promotes best practice.

Corporate governance gained importance with the occurrence of the Watergate scandal in United States. As a result of subsequent investigations, US regulatory and legislative bodies were able to highlight control failures that had allowed several major corporations to make illegal political contributions and to bribe government officials. The World Bank, involved in sustainable development was one of the earliest economic organisation to study the issue of corporate governance and suggest certain guidelines. The World Bank report on corporate governance recognises the complexity of the concept and focuses on the principles such as transparency, accountability, fairness and responsibility that are universal in their applications. Companies around the world are realising that better corporate governance adds considerable value to their operational performance:

1. It improves strategic thinking at the top by inducting independent directors who bring a wealth of experience, and a host of new ideas.
2. It rationalises the management and monitoring of risk that a firm faces globally.
3. It limits the liability of top management and directors, by carefully articulating the decision-making process.
4. It assures the integrity of financial reports.
5. It has long-term reputational effects among key stakeholders, both internally and externally.

Corporate Governance in India

The corporate governance plays a major role in the integrity of businesses and markets and helps in maintaining vitality, growth and stability and leads to increase in economic efficiency. In India, SEBI under its listing agreement Clause 49 has laid down rules and regulations for effective corporate governance and lot of research has been carried out to evaluate the corporate governance practices of the Indian corporate. At global level Organisation for Economic Cooperation and Development (OECD) has also framed principles of corporate governance which are non-binding and intended to assist member and non-member government to evaluate and improve the legal, institutional and regulatory framework of corporate governance. The principles of corporate governance as laid down by OECD can lead to examine the level of disclosure practices to corporate governance at global level of the Indian corporate.

A corporation is a congregation of various stakeholders, namely customers, employees, investors, vendor partners, government and society. In this changed scenario an Indian corporation, as also a corporation elsewhere should be fair and transparent to its stakeholders in all its transactions. This has become imperative in today's globalised business world where corporations need to access global pools of capital, need to attract and retain the best human capital from various parts of the world, need to partner with vendors on mega collaborations and need to live in harmony with the community. Unless a corporation embraces and demonstrates ethical conduct, it will not be able to succeed. Liberalisation and its associated developments, i.e. deregulation, privatisation and extensive financial liberalisation, have made effective Corporate Governance very crucial. Cases of frauds, malpractices can render capital market reforms desultory.

Corporate governance in India is evident from the various legal and regulatory frameworks and Committees set relating to corporate functioning comprising of the following:

1. Companies Act, 1956,
2. Monopolies and Restrictive Trade Practices Act, 1969 (replaced by new Competition Law),
3. Foreign Exchange Management Act, 2000,
4. Securities and Exchange Board of India Act, 1992,
5. Securities Contract Regulation Act, 1956,
6. The Depositories Act, 1996,
7. Arbitration and Conciliation Act, 1996,
8. SEBI Code on Corporate Governance,
9. CII Code of Desirable Corporate Governance (1998),
10. UTI Code of Governance (1999),
11. Kumar Mangalam Birla Committee on Corporate Governance (2000),
12. Naresh Chandra Committee (2002),
13. N.R. Narayanamurthy Committee (SEBI 2003).

Several Indian Companies like PepsiCo, Infosys, Tata, Wipro, TCS, and Reliance are some of the global giants which have their flag of success flying high in the sky due to good corporate governance. Corporate bodies have their aim, values, motto, ethics and principles etc which guide them to the ladder of success. Big and small organisations have their magazines, annual reports which reflect their achievements, failure, their profit and loss, their current position in the market. With increase in independence and free trade among countries and citizens across the globe, internationally accepted corporate governance standards are of paramount importance for Indian Companies seeking to distinguish themselves in global footprint. Shareholder primacy is embodied in the finance view of corporate governance, which is a special instance of the principal-agent framework in economic theory. While companies are encouraged to foster long-term relationships with stakeholders by taking their interests into account, there is no concomitant pressure to build into corporate governance, structures and processes that would ensure company accountability towards stakeholder groups.

India currently has two major stock exchanges—the National Stock Exchange, established in 1994, and the Bombay Stock Exchange (BSE), the oldest stock exchange in Asia, established in 1875. Until 1992, the BSE was a monopoly, marked with inefficiencies, high costs of intermediation, and manipulative practices, so external market users often found themselves disadvantaged. The economic reforms of the early nineties created four new institutions: the Securities and Exchanges Board of India, the National Stock Exchange, the National Securities Clearing Corporation, and the National Securities Depository. The Securities and Exchanges Board of India has introduced a rigorous regulatory regime to ensure fairness, transparency and good practice. For example, for greater transparency, the SEBI has mandated disclosure of all transactions where the total quantity of shares is more than 0.5 per cent of the equity of the company. Brokers must disclose to the Stock Exchange, immediately after trade execution, the name of the client and other trade details, and the Exchange must then disseminate this information to the general public on the same day.

The Securities and Exchanges Board of India has introduced a rigorous regulatory regime to ensure fairness, transparency and good practice. Brokers must disclose to the Stock Exchange, immediately after trade execution, the name of the client and other trade details, and the Exchange must then disseminate this information to the general public on the same day. The National Securities Clearing Corporation is the legal counter-party to net obligations of each brokerage firm, and thereby eliminates counter-party risk and the possibility of payments crises. The SEBI implemented the recommendations of the Birla Committee through the enactment of Clause 49 of the Listing Agreements.

Clause 49 may well be viewed as a milestone in the evolution of corporate governance practices in India. The key mandatory features of

Clause 49 regulations deal with the following: (i) composition of the board of directors; (ii) the composition and functioning of the audit committee; (iii) governance and disclosures regarding subsidiary companies; (iv) disclosures by the company; (vi) CEO/CFO certification of financial results; (vi) reporting on corporate governance as part of the annual report; and (vii) certification of compliance of a company with the provisions of Clause 49. The areas where Clause 49 stipulates specific corporate disclosures are: (i) related party transactions; (ii) accounting treatment; (iii) risk management procedures; (iv) proceeds from various kinds of share issues; (v) remuneration of directors; (vi) a Management Discussion and Analysis section in the annual report discussing general business conditions and outlook; and (vii) background and committee memberships of new directors as well as presentations to analysts.

In India, 'Corporate Governance' standards for listed companies are stipulated by Securities and Exchange Board of India through a special provision- Clause 49 of the Listing Agreement. India has become one of the fastest emerging nations to have aligned itself with the international trends in Corporate Governance. As a result, Indian companies have increasingly been able to access to newer and larger markets around the world; as well as able to acquire more businesses. The response of the government and regulators has been admirably quick to meet the challenges of corporate delinquency.

But, as the global environment changing continuously, there is a greater need of adopting and sustaining good corporate governance practices for value creation and building corporations of the future. Quality of corporate governance primarily depends on following factors, namely, integrity of the management; ability of the Board; adequacy of the processes; commitment level of individual Board members; quality of corporate reporting; participation of stakeholders in the management; etc. Since this is an important element affecting the long-term financial health of companies, good governance framework also calls for effective legal and institutional environment, business ethics and awareness of the environmental and societal interests.

Good corporate governance and transparency in actions of the management is key to a strong bond of trust with the Company's stakeholders. It is a continuous process and the Company relentlessly pursues it through full regulatory compliance, transparency, efficient operational practices, strong internal control and risk management systems and operating with fairness and integrity to enhance the interest of all its stakeholders.

Over the past few years, trust in political and business institutions in India has seen a sharp decline as a series of corruption scandals rocked both sets of institutions. The recent moves of India's capital market watchdog, Securities and Exchange Board of India to improve corporate governance norms of listed companies has seen as a welcome step in the direction of reform. Poor corporate governance standards in India have been a major grievance of domestic and foreign investors alike for long. India's national stock exchanges and SEBI have come under fire repeatedly from investor associations for not taking action against companies that failed to honour listing agreements. The lack of stringent disclosure norms and the absence of strong punitive action have loaded the die in favour of insiders and against minority shareholders. SEBI will soon come out with new corporate governance rules for the listed entities in the country. Its chairman said that the board will take up the proposals in its next board meeting and will announce them after board approval.

While SEBI had put out a discussion paper in January 2013, it was waiting for the Companies Bill to get passed before coming out with the new rules. The capital markets regulator touched upon the need for investors to be careful about the corporate governance norms followed by companies. There is an ongoing need for constant review and course corrections that would keep the country in the pink of health in terms of its corporate excellence by a judicious mix of legislation, regulation and suasion. This task needs to be constantly addressed with growing maturity and competitive compulsions. It should be possible to gradually reduce legislative interventions and increase regulatory compliance with and self-induced adherence to the best practices in this field. Till then, however, legislation and regulations to ensure at least certain minimum standards is inevitable. To facilitate such a graduation into better governance practices, globalisation has opened up an array of opportunities to Corporate India to emerge successful in its new tryst with destiny.

The Department of Company Affairs (DCA) appointed a study group on 15.5.2000 under the Chairmanship of the then Secretary DCA to suggest ways and means of achieving corporate governance. The study group appointed a task force. The study group recommended the setting up of an independent, autonomous centre for corporate excellence with a view to accord accredition and promotes policy research and studies, training and education and awards etc., in the field of corporate excellence through improved corporate governance.

The Department of Company Affairs also constituted on August 21, 2002 a high level committee, popularly known as Naresh Chandra committee, to examine various corporate governance issues and to recommend changes in the diverse areas such as the statutory auditor-company relationship, rotation of statutory auditors, procedure for appointment and determination of audit fees, restrictions, if necessary, on non-audit fees, independence of auditing functions, ensuring presentation of 'true and fair' statement of the financial affairs of companies, certification of financial statements and accounts, regulation of oversight functionaries, setting up an independent regulator and the role of independent directors. The Department of Company Affairs has set up a proactive standing company law advisory committee to advise on issues like inspection of corporates for wrong doings, role of independent directors and auditors and their liability, suggesting steps to enhance imposition of penalties.

Market regulator SEBI approved a series of decisions to increase transparency in corporate governance, a move that will have far-reaching implications for top honchos of India Inc. SEBI mandated that there should be more disclosures about the remuneration of senior executives and also asked companies to put in place a system to evaluate the performance of independent directors and other board members. The market regulator reiterated that there should be at least one woman director on the board of every company, something already mandated under the Companies Act. The regulator removed some of the contradictions in SEBI rules and the New Companies Act and, in some cases, the new provisions are even stricter for listed entities, lawyers said. These changes are effective October 1, 2014.

The SEBI board approved the proposal for a compulsory whistle-blower mechanism in every company and to expand the role of the audit committee. It prohibited offering stock options to independent directors, and asked companies to have separate meetings of independent directors and put in place a stakeholders' relationship committee. In addition, SEBI made regulations for related-party transactions stricter. It said that companies should seek prior approval of the audit committee for all material-related party transactions. Besides, they should seek the nod of shareholders for all material-related party transactions through a vote on a special resolution in which all the related parties should not participate. SEBI mandated that all companies should have nomination and remuneration committees, with the chiefs of such committees being independent directors on the board of the companies. The amendments propose to align the provisions of Listing Agreement with the provisions of the newly enacted Companies Act, 2013 and also provide additional requirements to strengthen the corporate governance framework for listed companies in India.

The SEBI board increased the minimum net worth of mutual funds to Rs 50 crore. It asked all the fund houses to invest at least one per cent of the amount raised in each open-ended scheme from their own corpus. As of now, of the 42 fund houses only a select few invest their own money in each of the funds they manage. SEBI board said that fund houses should launch long-term products that can serve as retirement plans (MFLRP) for investors besides giving additional tax incentive of Rs 50,000 under 80C of Income Tax Act. Alternatively, the limit of Section 80C of the Income Tax Act, 1961, may be enhanced from Rs 1 lakh to Rs 2 lakh to make mutual funds products (ELSS, MFLRP, etc) as a priority for investors among the different investment avenues. RGESS may also be brought under this enhanced limit.

The SEBI has stepped up its rules to protect small investors as well as to reduce the power held by so-called "promoters" of a company, or key stakeholders who have a disproportionate say on management appointments and day-to-day operations. In 2013, SEBI asked stock exchanges to beef up their compliance departments to ensure that companies make proper disclosures of market sensitive information, while a new insider trading law is also in the works. It proposed new measures aimed at helping India's mutual funds industry, including higher tax incentives for equity funds and a proposal to allow India's state-owned pension fund to channel money into mutual funds.

SEBI has recommended the implementation of several measures to the government, including additional tax sops on investment in long-term MF plans. It has proposed to the government to either provide an additional tax incentive on investment of Rs 50,000 in mutual fund-linked retirement plan under Section 80C of Income Tax Act or enhance the investment limit under Section 80C from Rs 1 lakh to Rs 2 lakh to make mutual funds as priority for investors. In a bid to improve transparency in the working of mutual funds, the regulator has increased the disclosure requirement by mutual funds. While fund houses will be required to disclose on AUM from different categories, they will also have to disclose break up of AUM from top 15 cities and below top 15 cities.

Corporate Governance in India: Challenges

The corporate governance code proposed by the Confederation of Indian Industry is modelled on the lines of the Cadbury Committee in the United Kingdom. On account of the interest generated by Cadbury Committee Report, the Confederation of Indian Industry, the Associated Chambers of

Commerce and Industry (ASSOCHAM) and the Securities and Exchange Board of India constituted Committees to recommend initiatives in Corporate Governance. The main objective of it was to develop and promote a code for Corporate Governance. The efforts for enhancement of corporate governance in India was mainly started by the constitution of the Committee on Corporate Governance in 2002 under Securities and Exchange Board of India, in order to evaluate the adequacy of existing corporate governance practices and further improve these practices.

Effective corporate governance enhances access to external financing by firms, leading to greater investment as well as higher growth and employment. Good corporate governance additionally lowers the cost of capital by reducing risk and creates higher firm valuation once again boosting real investments. It has the potential of significantly reducing the risk of nation-wide financial crises. There is a strong inverse relationship between the quality of corporate governance and currency depreciation.

Corporate governance practices in India are still evolving. It is a process of engaging shareholders and the management effectively to enhance the organisation's value. It involves participation of various stakeholders and management, communication, exchanging and validating ideas, and lots of debate and discussion. Corporate governance in India faces its own set of challenges which are set out below. There is a gap between corporate governance standards in the public sector and the private sector.

1. Although India has numerous regulations, their enforcement is quite weak.
2. There needs to be an objective debate in corporate India about what is required to be done to make Independent directors more effective.
3. There is substantial room for improvement in enhancing accountability.
4. The regulation and scrutiny of the audit profession in India could benefit from some objective introspection.

The Ministry of Corporate Affairs is concerned with the administration of the Companies Act for regulating functioning of the corporate sector in accordance with law. Regulators face a number of difficulties in tackling the problem of corporate governance abuses by the dominant shareholders. In many cases, it is difficult to decide how far the regulator should go in interfering with the normal course of corporate functioning. Shareholder democracy is not the essence of the corporate form of business at all. Shares are first and foremost ownership rights - rights to profits and assets. In some cases that is all there is to it. In other cases, shares also carry some secondary rights including the control rights - rights to appoint the Board and approve certain major decisions.

Corporate governance abuses perpetrated by a dominant shareholder pose another and far more difficult regulatory dilemma. Regulatory intervention would often imply a micromanagement of routine business decisions. Regulatory intervention must perforce be confined to a few clearly defined prohibitions and restrictions that require minimal exercise of regulatory discretion. The primary protection to minority shareholders is laid down in the Companies' Law. Some of these provisions are the regulatory equivalent of an atom bomb - they are drastic remedies suitable only for the gravest cases of misgovernance.

The SEBI had made it mandatory that all listed companies should create a mechanism for employees to report to the management concerns about any unethical behaviour, fraud or violation of the code of conduct. The regulator also asked companies to put in place a suitable mechanism for safeguards against victimisation of whistle-blowers and that they should have direct access to the Company's Audit Committee. Effective implementation is a way out to prevent corporate frauds.

The SEBI Regulations 2002 define 'insider" as any person who, is or was connected with the company or is deemed to have been connected with the company, and who is reasonably expected to have access to unpublished price sensitive information in respect of securities of the company, or who has received or has had access to such unpublished price sensitive information. As defined under the Act, the definition of insider information is driven by the notion that a person in a fiduciary position should not use the privileged information for his or her own advantage. The practical limitation of the 'person-connected' approach is chiefly the practical difficulties of ensuring that all people who trade on inside information are caught. It may be quite difficult for the prosecution to show the existence of a 'connection', even when they can show that the secondary insider in question has been dealing and using the information.

Conclusion

Corporate governance has grown very rapidly in the last decade and is now viewed as an important attribute of the corporate sector. As far as corporate governance is concerned, although there are detailed norms on paper in the form of Clause 49 of the listing agreement, what matters is their implementation in practice. There are limits to legislating on corporate governance as a lot depends on the integrity and ethical values of various corporate players such as directors, managers, promoters and other stakeholders. The Indian corporates are governed by the Company's Act of 1956 that follows more or less the UK model. In terms of the legislative mechanisms, Indian government and industry constituted three committees to study corporate governance practices in the country and suggest measures for improvement based on what has globally recognised as "best practices".

Significantly, most of the recommendations of the three committees—the SEBI-appointed Kumar Mangalam Birla Committee (2000), the government-appointed Naresh Chandra Committee (2003) and the SEBI's Narayana Murthy Committee are remarkably similar to those of England's Cadbury Committee and America's Sarbanes-Oxley Act, in terms of their approaches and recommendations. The Securities and Exchange Board of India has announced that it would release corporate governance rules for the listed entities in India. Further, the Parliament of India passed the Indian Companies Act, 2013 to improve the corporate culture in India.

Indian companies have a long way to go before adhering to corporate governance best practices, as their performance is below-par on parameters like rotation of auditors, attendance of directors and board composition. An analysis of the top 100 companies that form part of the Nifty and Junior Nifty indices shows that 10 per cent of these firms have board sizes of either more than 16 directors or less than seven directors. The Companies Act, 2013 prescribes a minimum of three and maximum of 15 directors on the board of a company and permits firms to appoint more than 15 directors after passing a special resolution. Average number of board meetings held by top 100 Indian Companies is seven. Corporate India has a long way to go before adhering to corporate governance best practices. The new Companies Act and initiatives from SEBI to improve corporate governance are steps in the right direction.

References

1. Action Plan on European company law and corporate governance (2013). Retrieved from http://www.eubusiness.com/topics/single-market/governance-3
2. Asian Institute of Corporate Governance (2013). Retrieved from http://www.aicg.org/
3. Avinash Mohapatra (2011). Corporate Governance in India: evolution and challenges ahead, Retrieved from http://www.dfdl.com/images/stories/Articles/News/Corporate_Governance_in_India.pdf
4. Chakrabarti, Rajesh; Megginson, William L.; Yadav, Pradeep K. (2007). Corporate governance in India, CFR working paper, No. 08-02. Retrieved from http://www.econstor.eu/bitstream/10419/41393/1/582127289.pdf

5. Chapter 1, Introduction to Corporate Governance. Retrieved from http://shodhganga.inflibnet.ac.in/bitstream/10603/1558/10/10_chapter1.pdf

6. Corporate governance (2013). Retrieved from http://en.wikipedia.org/wiki/Corporate_governance

7. Corporate Governance: Future Prospects. Retrieved from http://business.gov.in/corporate_governance/future_prospects.php

8. Company law and corporate governance (2013). Retrieved from http://ec.europa.eu/internal_market/company/index_en.htm

9. Corporate governance of state-owned enterprises in Asia (2013). Retrieved from http://www.oecd.org/daf/ca/corporategovernanceofstate-ownedenterprisesinasia.htm

10. Corporate Governance: South Asia (2013). Retrieved from http://www.ifc. org/wps/wcm/connect/Topics_Ext_Content/IFC_External_Corporate_Site/Corporate+Governance/Advisory_Services_Regional_Programs/South Asia/

11. Corporate Governance: Introduction. Retrieved from http://www.newage-publishers.com/samplechapter/001167.pdf

12. Dr Anshul Sharma and Pooja Gupta (2012). Corporate governance in India: Evoluation and Challenges, International Journal of Multidisciplinary Management Studies, Vol. 2 Issue 5, Retrieved from http://zenithresearch. org.in/images/stories/pdf/2012/May/EIJMMS/9_EIJMMS_MAY12_ VOL2_ISSUE 5.pdf

13. Dr S.K.Chaudhury, S.K. Das, D. Mishra (2011). Corporate governance practice in some selected Indian financial institutions, European Journal of Business and Economics, Volume 05, p. 40

14. Governance, Global issue, United Nations. Retrieved from http://www.un.org/en/globalissues/governance/

15. Issues and Challenges of Corporate Governance in India. Retrieved from http://liba.edu/beacon/archives/beacon07/corporateindia.htm

16. Jayanth Rama Varma, Corporate Governance in India: Disciplining the Dominant Shareholder. Retrieved from http://www.iimahd.ernet.in/~jrvarma/papers/iimbr9-4.pdf

17. Jayanth Rama Varma , Corporate Governance in India: Disciplining the Dominant Shareholder, Retrieved from http://www.iimahd.ernet.in/~jrvarma/papers/iimbr9-4.pdf

18. Mr. CmAaN Raveendranth Kaushik, Corporate governance: its origin in ancient India. Retrieved from http://www.driems.ac.in/mba/Download/6%20CORPORATE%20GOVERNANCE%20-%20ITS%20ORIGIN%20IN%20ANCIENT%20INDIA.pdf

19. OECD-Asian Roundtable on Corporate Governance (2013). Retrieved from http://www.oecd.org/daf/ca/oecd-asianroundtableoncorporategover-nance.htm

20. OECD Principles of Corporate Governance (2013). Retrieved from http://www.oecd.org/corporate/oecdprinciplesofcorporategovernance.htm

21. Prabhash Dalei, Paridhi Tulsyan and Shikhar Maravi (2012). Corporate Governance in India: A legal Analysis, International Conference on Humanities, Economics and Geography (ICHEG, 2012) March 17-18, 2012 Bangkok

22. Rujita TR (2012). Challenges to corporate governance: issues and concerns, International Journal of Marketing, Financial Services & Management Research, Vol.1 Issue 12, Retrieved from http://indianresearchjournals.com/pdf/IJMFSMR/2012/December/8.pdf
23. Smriti Sharma,Pravin Sexena and Dr N.K. Saxena (2011). Corporate Governance Practice of Indian Companies – An Assessment of OECD Principles at Global Perspective.
24. Sonali Soni (2011). Corporate Governance in India – Past, Present and Future, Retrieved from http://www.indiacsr.in/en/?p=2630
25. The Economic Times (Oct 18, 2013). India Inc performance below par on corporate governance. Retrieved from http://articles.economictimes. indiatimes.com/2013-10-18/news/43178328_1_corporate-governance-new-companies-act-directors
26. The Financial Express (Feb 14, 2014). Sebi tightens corporate governance norms, loosens mutual fund policy. Retrieved from http://indianexpress.com/article/business/banking-and-finance/sebi-tightens-corporate-governance-norms-loosens-mutual-fund-policy/
27. The model of governance. Retrieved from http://my.safaribooksonline.com/book/-/9788131758458/2dot-the-theory-and-practice-of-corporate-governance/c2s5_xhtml
28. The fight for corporate governance in India (2013). Retrieved from http://www.livemint.com/Opinion/hxFqnfbyCG5fRWD6PuiGfP/The-fight-for-corporate-governance-in-India.html
29. The Indian Express (January 12, 2014). SEBI chief: New norms for corporate governance soon. Retrieved from http://indianexpress.com/article/business/market/sebi-chief-new-norms-for-corporate-governance-soon/
30. The Practice of Corporate Governance in India (2009). Retrieved from http://indiacorplaw.blogspot.in/2009/06/practice-of-corporate-governance-in.html
31. The Times of India (Feb 14, 2014). Sebi tightens corporate governance norms, Retrieved from http://timesofindia.indiatimes.com/business/india-business/Sebi-tightens-corporate-governance-norms/articleshow/30359220.cms
32. What is good governance? Retrieved from http://www.unescap.org/pdd/prs/ProjectActivities/Ongoing/gg/governance.asp

Chapter 2

Green Marketing Strategies for Sustainable Development in the Present Era

Akanshya Patnaik and Dr Sunil Kumar Pradhan

"Gender equality is more than a goal in itself. It is a precondition for meeting the challenge of reducing poverty, promoting sustainable development and building good governance." ***–Kofi Annan***

Introduction

The terrified picture of tomorrow's environment has created an insight today for government and NGOs. This vigorous effort of the government to minimise the negative effect of human on environment created a concern in the society. As per (Doyle 1992, Vandermerwe and Oliff, 1990) the increase of consumer concern with regards to restitution of ecology leads to demand for eco-friendly products in countries around world. Keeping eye on the changing need and wants of environment and society, business began to change its behaviour a product by which it can satisfy the unlimited human desires without adversely effecting the environment. This eco-friendly way of satisfying the consumer needs is called Green Marketing. Several experts interpret it in various ways but the motto is same that is satisfying all our needs and wants without damaging our natural resources. This growing consciousness of human being towards the most precious assert of the whole world "Environment" also created a glint within me for an intense survey of this topic. This thesis mostly focuses on the growing concern of the competitive business world towards the protection of the environment and the changing behaviour of human beings towards eco-friendly products.

The topic on Green Marketing first raised in an American Marketing Association (AMA) held workshop in 1975. The proceeding of the workshop came out with the first book on green marketing entitled *Ecological Marketing.* The idea of meeting current economic needs without compromising the ability of future generations to meet their own needs was first proposed in the Brundtland report, named "Our Common Future" in 1987. There are numerous thoughts given by various experts. Green marketing definition can be little unclean as anything from green product development to advertising campaign goes in it. Green Marketing is a relative concept, as different people and countries will have different perceptions of what it constitutes according to their perceptions which will change over time (Peattie, 1995). It is called by various names like sustainable marketing, environmental marketing, green advertising, eco-marketing, organic marketing, all of which point to similar concepts.

McDaniel and Rylander (1993) have coined the term green marketing to depict marketer's efforts to develop strategies targeting the eco-friendly consumer. Environmental marketing, more popularly known as green marketing or sustainable marketing can be defined as the effort by a company to design, promote, price and distribute products in a manner which promotes environmental protection. Peattie (1995) and Welford (2000) defined green marketing as the management process responsible for identifying, anticipating and satisfying the requirements of customers and society in a profitable and sustainable way. Peattie (2001), described evolution of Green marketing in three phases.

1. The first phase was termed "Ecological" green marketing. During this period all marketing activities were concerned to solve environment problems and provide remedies for such problems.
2. The second phase was "Environmental" green marketing and the focus shifted to clean technology that involved designing of innovative new products, which takes care of pollution and waste issues.
3. The third phase was "Sustainable" green marketing. It came into prominence in the late 1990s and early 2000.

Prakash (2002) argues that the relationship between the marketing discipline, the public policy process and the natural environment is of great importance. The development and marketing of products designed in a manner that is sensitive or responsive to ecological concerns (American Marketing Association, 2007).

Global Scenario in Green Marketing

Green is the buzzword that is gaining popularity among the current generation. A number of businesses right from private entities such as Coca-cola without any promotion or campaign silently contributing a lot to prevent the environmental dilemma. Coca-cola has modified their packaging and invested large sum of money in various recycling activities to minimise its environmental impact. Wal-Mart also trying to push the concept of organic food to public entities like Indian finance minister Arun Jaitely came out with a token fund of Rs 75 crore to uplift green vehicles like electric cars. The London governments' congestion charges are all aimed at improving the environment by promoting 'Green' products and issues. Eighty seven per cent of people from various nations like Brazil, Canada, China, France, Germany, India, the UK and the US have shown an interest in reducing their impact on the environment, according to a survey by (McKinsey, 2007).

However, showing interest and actually acting on the interest are two different deeds. This fact is proved by a survey that was conducted on a global scale, which was repeated in 2008 with the help of BBC World, which showed that not a lot of people were actually doing something to move their lifestyle to a green lifestyle. Over the years there has been a subtle shift from practicing environmental marketing practices as a result of compulsion identified as a result of legislations and pressure from environmental groups to genuine efforts to improve sustainable marketing plans and behaving in an eco-responsible manner (Polonsky and Rosenberger, 2001).

Green Responsibility

There are some companies who are environmentally responsible where as they are not interested to promote the fact of their responsible behaviour like Coca-cola, Walt Disney World has an extensive waste management programme and corresponding infrastructure. Some companies recalled their products when they found that their products were either not performing at the desired efficiency level or were unsafe for consumer use or were harming the environment. It is mostly seen in automobile sectors. Automobile industries are constantly seeking to produce environment-friendly vehicles. In 1990's Toyota with a view of greener vehicle lunched Pirus, the world's first mass produced hybrid car, was a major step towards environment safety. Toyota came with a claim of twice fuel efficiency than any other conventional cars and 90 per cent cleaner than the Japanese regulation specifications.

Company sources revealed that continuous work is going on leaner and cleaner power train technologies basically focusing on recycled materials. Toyota is one of the companies who initiated fuel cell technology and secured a global Patent for its NOX catalytic system, a major breach in controlling pollution. Johnson & Johnson is the most socially responsible organisation in the world that recently began switching much of its energy dependency over to solar power. Today, Johnson and Johnson is the second largest user of solar power in the United States. IKEA company giant retail in furniture world, also engage in small motor vehicles and home accessories plans to double its investment in renewable energy and hit 100 per cent clean energy by 2020. It has an exceptional record of investment in solar and wind energy.

Green Products/Production

There is no extensive agreement on what exactly makes a product green. Some general guidelines include that a green product: (a) Not responsible for a health hazard to people or animals; (b) Efficient in use of resources during manufacture, use and disposal; and (c) Does not integrate materials derived from endangered species or threatened environments.

IKEA one of the multinational group of companies that designs and sells ready-to-assemble furniture (such as beds, chairs and desks), appliances, small motor vehicles and home accessories. Being the largest furniture retailer it always tries to make use of lumber for its affordable price furniture. The company's secret is it uses sustainable forestry techniques for stylist range of furniture with minimal effect to planet. NIKE as a footwear giant not only provides its customer to walk with recycled aluminum and underground energy storage. It also enforces strict emission standards at all its factories, and has been successful in reducing its overall carbon footprints by approximately 80 per cent since last 90's. Moreover, it offers greenest soccer shoes around.

Green Pricing

Shell decided to consider the costs of prevention, control, abatement or elimination of releases into the air and water as well as handling and disposal of wastes at operating facilities as ordinary part of business. Such expenditure amounted to 800 million pounds in 1996 and 700 million pounds in 1997. In 1997 annual report, Shell gave details of the various measures it had taken to protect the environment.

Green Promotion

Toyota is working with the Japanese government to implement a concept where people purchase "transportation" without owning a car. Consumer can buy access to Toyota's electronic fleet of automobiles for short distances. In this way Toyota establishes as a leader in electronic-

combustion and reducing pollutants from environment. Shell refineries were among the first to receive ISO 14001 certification from sound environmental management systems.

Environmental responsibility is promoted by the organisations like body soap. No doubt this kind of behaviour serves as a competitive advantage but also this philosophy has direct impact upon corporate culture and its value. Reliance Fresh try to promote red cloth bags with a concept "GO GREEN WITH RED". Similarly, Big Bazaar with a new strategy of promotion with another eco-friendly idea "Bring Junk and get extra discount on your shopping". "The Great Xchange" 14th Feb to 29th March. Bring junk, get exchange coupons, shop to redeem on any new product.

Green Packaging

Green marketing has become a unique way of creating awareness and promoting brand value. Burger King and Mc Donald's no longer Styrofoam cartons for packaging an effort to decrease waste in landfills. Brocato International markets shampoo and hair conditioner in biodegradable bottles to reduce negative effects on environment. Procter & Gamble markets Sure Pro & Old Spice in eco-friendly pump-spray packages that do not rely on aerosol propellants. Many other firms who have introduced eco-friendly pump sprays include S.C Johnson (Pledge furniture police) and Reckitt and Coleman Household products (Woolite rug cleaner).

Consumer Response

Early researches and surveys basically projected to shift the consumer attention to green product. Later study and survey mainly intended to change the consumer consumption habit in relation to environment safety. Now-a-days no doubt we can notice an inclined consumer mass towards this green concept, green product in a complete sense a green life style. But still talking about the overall consumer attitude in purchasing green product is still confusing. Consumers from developed country like USA and Western Europe were found to be more conscious about environment, relates issues and steps taken (Curlo, 1999). Eighty seven per cent of people from various nations like Brazil, Canada, China, France, Germany, India, the UK and the US have shown an interest in reducing their impact on the environment, according to a survey by (McKinsey, 2007).

Many investigations have found that there is a significant relationship between demographic characteristics, cognitive psychology, personality and attitude and activities that help to protect the environment. As per the evaluation by (Pickett *et. al,* 1994) the results showed that the influence of psychological and social factors is more powerful than demographic factors on consumer's green behaviour. There is an overall believe that due to these factors, people show different behaviour, and therefore have a positive effect on consumer response and decision towards purchase. Another study shows that environmental knowledge is one of the variables which effect consumer response. Still there is confusion regarding what variables lead to consumer purchase decision. If we talk about overall response of consumer towards these green revolution here the evaluation is some how positive, but talking about their adoption in their real day-to-day life is unsatisfactory.

Conclusion

Green marketing strategy is no doubt a step towards sustainable development. But it can not be successful without its full-fledged implementation. Government has gone for many green policies but any way it needs to be implemented as it is planned. Similarly, some business has also came with green strategies and green products it must be a inspiration for all other who had still not implemented these green concept. Now it is the right time for academician and researchers to spread the awareness regarding environment concern among mass. Consumers need to open their eyes and mind before adopting a lifestyle or purchasing a product.

It will take some time to make a complete green life style. The march had already begin by government and continued by business now it is the right time for all academicians and researchers to raise its awareness to that extent by which one day our dream of green planet will be successful in its true sense.

References

1. Allen Tracy, (2007). Could Green Marketing be a suitable competitive advantage for retailers with in South Africa?, Research Report, Gordon Institute of Business Science, University of Pretoria, South Africa.
2. American marketing association. Available at http:// www.marketing-power.com/ mg-dictionary-view 1332.php (accessed on 21/07/2007).
3. Bhattacharya, Saurabh. (2011). Consumer Attitude towards Green Marketing in India. The IUP Journal of Marketing Management, 62-70.
4. Chamorro, A., Sergio Rubio, S., and Miranda, Francisco J. (2009). Characteristics of Research on Green Marketing. Business Strategy and the Environment, 18, 223-239. http://dx.doi.org/10.1002/bse.571
5. Curlo, E. (1999). Marketing strategy, product safety, and ethical factors in consumer choice. Journal of Business Ethics, 21(1), 37-48. http://dx.doi.org/ 10.1023/A:1005973306941

6. Curtin, Emily (2006-09-14). "Lower East Side Green Market". January 2008.
7. Dodds, John (May 21, 2007). "Green Marketing 101" 2008.
8. D'Souza, Clar. (2004). Eco-label programmes: a stakeholder (consumer) perspective. Corporate communication. An International Journal, 9(3), 179-188.ns:
9. Doyle, J. (1992). Hold the Applause: A Case Study of Corporate Environmentalism. The Ecologist, 22(3), 84-90.
10. Earth day from Wikipedia, http://en.wikipedia.org/wiki/Earth_Day
11. Earth Day: The History of a Movement, http://www.earthday.org/earth-day-history-movement
12. E notes MBA : The Best References for MBA, http://www.enotesmba.com/2013/02/green-marketing-concept.html
13. F. Belz K. Peattie Sustainability Marketing: A Global Perspective. John Wiley & Sons, 2009.
14. Granzin KL, Olsen JE. Characterising participants in activities protecting the environment: A focus on donating, recycling, and conservation behaviors. J Public Pol Mark. 1991;10(2):1–27.
15. Green Marketing from Wikipedia, http://en.wikipedia.org/wiki/Green_marketing
16. Harrison, E.B. (1993). Going green: How to communicate your company's environmental commitment. Homewood, IL: Richard, D. Irwin, Inc.
17. Henion, K. E., and Kinnear, T. C. (1976). Ecological Marketing, American Marketing Association. Chicago.
18. Introduction of green marketing, http://www.ginnifilaments.com/eCom/pdf/investor/Code%20of%20Conduct.pdf
19. Jacob Cherian, Jacob Jolly (2012, September 20). Green Marketing: A Study of Consumer's Attitude towards Environment Friendly Products. Asian Social Science, Vol.8, No.12, November 28, 2014, http://dx.doi.org/10.5539/ass.v8n12p117
20. Kumar V, Kumar S and Haleem A (2011). " Barriers to Implement Green Supply Chain Management in Automobile Industry using Interpretive Structural Modelling Technique: An Indian Perspective", Journal of Industrial Engineering and Management, Vol. 4, No. 2, pp. 231-257.
21. Lee, K. (2008). Opportunities for green marketing: young consumers. Marketing Intelligence & Planning, 26(6),
22. 573-586. http://dx.doi.org/10.1108/02634500810902839
23. Lee, K. (2009). Gender Differences in Hong Kong Adolescent Consumers Green Purchasing Behavior. Journal of Consumer Marketing, 26(2), 87-96. http://dx.doi.org/10.1108/07363760910940456
24. Linda Lear, George Washington University, Rachel Carson and the Awakening of Environmental Consciousness in Wilder & American Identity, http://nationalhumanitiescenter.org/tserve/nattrans/ntwilderness/essays/carson.htm, 19 Nov 2014.
25. Mckinsey. (2007). Mckinsey and Company Inc.

26. Michael D Watkins and Max H. Bazerman, "Predictable Suprises: The Disasters You Should Have Seen Coming", Harvard Business Review, March 2003, Vol 81, Issue 3 and "Royal Dutch Shell", Global Strategic Management, Case Studies on Fortune 500 Companies, Transworld University, Vol.VI, The ICFAIAN Foundation.

27. Mintel, R., and Stamatiou, E. (2006). Green Roofs– A 21st Century Solution to the Urban Challenges of Green Space, Air Pollution, Flooding and Energy Conservation, WSEAS International Conference Vouliagmeni, Greece. Journal WSEAS Transactions on Energy, Environment, Ecosystems and Sustainable Development, 2(6), 909-918.

28. Nervi Giorgea. "Green Market Research anyone? A study on Green Market Research practice among companies," ESA Report no. 2008:13; ISSN: 1404-8167.

29. "Our Common Future" Report of the World Commission on Environment and Development, 1987.

30. Pickett GM, Kangun N, Grove SJ. An Examination of the Conserving Consumer: Implications for Public Policy Formation in Promoting Conservation Behavior. The Harvard Press; 1994.

31. Peattie, K. (1995). Environmental marketing management. Great Britain: Pitman publishing.

32. Planet save, "Green your Life".

33. http://planetsave.com/2013/06/21/10-companies-with-eco-conscious-production-processes/

34. Polonsky, M.J. and Mintu-Wimsatt, A.T. (Eds) (1995). Environmental Marketing: Strategies, Practice, Theory and Research, the Haworth Press, New York, NY.

35. Prakash, A. (2002). Green Marketing, public policy and managerial strategy.

36. Rahbar, E., and Wahid, N. A. (2011). Investigation of green marketing tools' effect on consumers' purchases behavior. Business Strategy Series, 12(2), 73-83.

37. Ramanakumar, K.P.V, Manojkrishnan,C.G, Suma, S.R. (2012). "Consumer Attitude Towards Green Products of FMCG Sector: an Empirical Study", International Journal of Research in Commerce and Management, Vol. 3, No. 2, ISSN 0976-2183.

38. Shamdasani, P., Chon-Lin, G. and Richmond, D. (1993). Exploring green consumers in an oriental culture: role of personal and marketing mix. Advances in Consumer Research, 20, 488-493.

39. Vandermerwe, S., and Michael, D. O. (1990). Customers Drive Corporations Green. Long Range Planning, 23(6), 10-16. http://dx.doi.org/10.1016/0024-6301(90)90096-M.

40. World Environment Day from Wikipedia, http://en.wikipedia.org/wiki/World_Environment_Day.

Chapter 3

Rubber Plantation in Tripura: A Strategy of Afforestation

Dr B.K. Panda and Dr Sukanta Sarkar

"A grateful heart is a beginning of greatness. It is an expression of humility. It is a foundation for the development of such virtues as prayer, faith, courage, contentment, happiness, love, and well-being."

-James E. Faust

Introduction

The rubber plantation sector in India is a century old. Ever since its introduction on a commercial scale in the south-western coastal state of Kerala in 1902, the plantation sector has made rapid progress. This is evidenced by increase in area, production and productivity. In India, natural rubber is cultivated mostly in all parts of Kerala. Initial plantings of rubber were done by Europeans who encouraged the domestication of the crop in this part of the world to meet its industrial demand and the bulk of the crop used to be exported during the pre-independence period (Rubber Plantation Kerala, 2012). Plantation sector is not just a foreign exchange earner but a key sector in India's inclusive growth strategy because of its role in employment generation, livelihood of small and marginal growers, backward communities, balanced regional development and addressing environmental issues. The long-term vision shall be to build a system of production and innovation that is competitive and inclusive through modernising plantation sector (Joseph and George, 2011).

Rubber is found in the fluid of some specific plants but it can also be produced synthetically. Synthetic rubber is produced through the process of polymerisation of various monomers. Naturally, rubber is produced by the process of tapping of the plant called Hevea Brasiliensis. The rubber tree is a native of the Amazon River basin in South America. The ideal rubber growing regions should be eight degree North of Equator, 10 degree

South of Equator, high temperature, altitude not beyond 400 m and high humidity. The rubber industry produces wide range products like auto tyre, auto tubes, automobile parts, footwear, belts, cables and wires, battery boxes etc. Block rubber, Preserved Latex, Crepes and sheets are some forms in which rubber is produced and used. India is the fourth largest producer of Natural Rubber, after Thailand, Indonesia and Malaysia.

Table 3.1: Country-wise Export of Natural Rubber (In Thousand Tonnes)

Country	*2000*	*2001*	*2002*	*2003*	*2004*	*2005*	*2006*	*2007*
Thailand	2166	2042	2354	2574	2637	2632	2772	2704
Indonesia	1380	1497	1502	1661	1875	2025	2287	2379
Malaysia	430	345	430	510	680	666	619	413
Vietnam	254	270	278	303	340	445	474	520
Liberia	105	107	109	107	115	111	101	115
India	13	4	44	58	71	60	71	29
Cambodia	39	38	40	41	41	41	60	53
Sri Lanka	33	32	36	35	40	32	46	49
Nigenia	36	30	24	22	29	25	28	29
World	**4989**	**5108**	**5155**	**5639**	**6174**	**6416**	**6877**	**6740**

Source: 'Rubber Bulletin' of the International Rubber Study Group.

Thailand is the world's largest producer of natural rubber. India is the fourth largest producer of natural rubber in the world. In the year 2011, India produced 890 thousand tonnes of natural rubber, up from 851 thousand tonnes in the previous year. India contributes eight per cent of the world natural rubber production. Other major producers include Vietnam and China contributing seven per cent each to the world production. China being the fastest growing economy of the world is also the world's largest natural rubber consuming country (Natural Rubber, 2013).

What is Rubber Plantation?

The rubber plantations can be categorised into two types i.e. those with immature plants and others with mature trees. A rubber plant takes almost seven years of growth to mature for tapping and start yielding. A mature healthy tree can be tapped for about 22 years. When the yield starts decreasing beyond a certain level due to aging, the trees are usually cut and the area replanted. The period of effective yield can vary from 16 to 22 years. The yield from natural rubber trees will be available only after seven years from the year of cultivation. The impact of a price change can be experienced only after seven or more years. But a sudden response from the rubber growers for a change in price of rubber can be noticed in the care given to rubber trees (Rubber Plantation Kerala, 2012).

Rubber plantation agriculture has evolved as an estate-based system in the tropical Asian countries since the early 1900s, mostly under the patronage of Western colonialism. The total area planted to rubber all over the world has grown by 1.71 per cent per annum, showing an almost three-fold increase during the last four decades, that is, from 3.88 million hectares (ha) in 1961 to 11 million ha in 2006 (Viswanathan, 2010).

Afforestation

Afforestation is the establishment of a forest or stand of trees in an area where there was no forest. Afforestation and reforestation refer to establishment of trees on non-treed land. Reforestation means establishment of forest on land that had recent tree cover, whereas afforestation refers to land that has been without forest for much longer. A variety of definitions differentiate between these two processes. As forests grow the trees absorb CO_2 and hold it within their biomass (trunk, branches, leaves and roots). Since non-forest is converted to forest, planting additional trees boosts forests and their ability to store carbon. Many governments and non-governmental organisations directly engage in programmes of afforestation to create forests, increase carbon capture and sequestration, and help to anthropogenically improve biodiversity (Afforestation, 2015).

Significance of Afforestation

India is an emerging or developing country whereas the controlling of Carbon emission is very much challenging for the policy makers. Nowadays afforestation is very much necessary in India to maintain the biodiversity in the environment. There are two ways i.e. afforestation and reforestation, the development of new forest on a non-forest land is called afforestation but reforestation means the reestablishment of the forest cover by either naturally or artificially. Considering the need of afforestation in India, many government, private and NGOs are engaged to create new forests through afforestation method to maximise the carbon capture or control the soil erosion (Patra, 2014).

Table 3.2: Main Functions of the Forests

Functions	*Benefits*
Productive functions	Production of various types of wood, fruits and a wide range of compounds such as resins, alkaloids, essential oil, latex and pharmaceutical substances.
Protective functions	Provides habitats for various organisms conservation of soil and water, prevention of drought, shelter against wind, cold, radiation, noise, sounds, smells and sights.

Regulative functions	Absorption, storage and release of gases (most importantly carbon dioxide and oxygen), water, minerals, elements and radiant energy. All such functions improve the atmospheric and temperature conditions and enhance the economic and environmental value of the land. Forests also effectively regulates floods and drought and all the bio-geochemical cycles.

Source: http://download.nos.org/333courseE/9.pdf

Afforestation restores ecological balance of all ecosystems, maintain biological diversity, and act as catchments for all soil and water, conservation, prevent floods and future of tribal people. It shall assist in achieving 33 per cent of land to be covered by forest in future. Massive afforestation programme will help fast in growing indigenous and exotic species for production and protection of forestry on suitable land including waste land (Tripathi, 2014). Ecological studies have shown that forests help to maintain the optimum level of rainfall for agricultural purposes, for constructing dams and hydro-electric projects etc. They play a paramount role in checking the floods and soil erosion. They are also important for wild life, human recreation and preservation of balanced environment. Above all, forests bring clouds and clouds bring rain and rain brings our harvest. It is interesting to note that one-third land is required as forests in any country to maintain ecological balance. Otherwise the whole atmosphere with its dust, smoke, noise and bustle will choke the human society (Sharma, 2014).

Afforestation helps in addressing the environmental issues of the world, especially. in preventing further global warming and reversing the effects of global warming. It helps in avoiding desertification. It helps in addressing the environmental issues of the world in preventing further global warming and reversing the effects of global warming. It helps in avoiding desertification. A shrinking forest cover coupled with over exploitation of ground water has accelerated erosion along the slopes of the lower Himalayas and Aravali hills, making them prone to landslides.

Forests enhance local precipitation and improve water holding capacity of soil, regulate water cycle, maintain soil fertility by returning the nutrients to the soil through leaf fall and decomposition of litter. Forests check soil-erosion, landslides and reduce intensity of flood and droughts. Forests, being home of wildlife are important assets of aesthetic, touristic and cultural value to the society. Forests have profound effect on the climate. Forest absorbed carbon dioxide from the atmosphere and help in balancing carbon dioxide and oxygen in the atmosphere (Deforestation, 2012).

With the increasing demand for wood fuels and building materials, this process helps to meet these demands without cutting down the natural forests. Deforestation can lead to the depletion of trees in water catchments and riverside zones. Afforestation ensures trees and plants that hold the soil in these sensitive areas remain protected. Many countries have introduced the practice of planting trees along with agricultural crops in croplands. The benefits of this practice, which is called agro-forestry, are: (a) It provides a supply of timber, fruit, and fodder for cattle apart from crop production; (b) It prevents soil erosion; (c) It enables better retention of water; and (d) It shields crops from excessive wind and sun damage (Cosmato, 2010).

Deforestation in Tripura

Deforestation is the permanent destruction of forests in order to make the land available for other uses. In recent history large-scale destruction of the forests began with the British who wished to utilise the timber and the natural resources for the expansion and continuation of the empire. Vast tracks of forest were chopped to create the vast railway network that crosses India today. The main aim was the fast, cheap and efficient transport of inexpensive raw materials to the ports from the hinterlands of the country for export to Britain's industries and to ensure the fast movement of security forces to maintain the hold over the empire.

Many environmental historians hold the opinion that the large-scale destruction of the forests in India is rooted in the commercially oriented forest use and ownership policies of the British government and these have continued in their essence for several years even in post-independence India. In certain parts of the country; particularly the rainforest regions of the north-eastern states bordering China and Burma and the remote islands of the Andaman and Nicobar, a lot of the forests have been fed into the plywood mills (Sekhsaria, 2012).

The Border Road Organisation (BRO) under the Defence Ministry has paid Rs 6 crore to the Tripura Forest Department as penalty for deforestation of vast areas in the State for construction of border. Domestic elephants and their owners are bearing massive losses in Damcherra village in Tripura due to rampant deforestation and toughening of the Indian Forest Act. Mahouts and elephant owners say the profitable business which involved pachyderms carrying and loading wooden logs does not find much work anymore and dwindling of forests is leading to severe food crisis in the wild and even the elephant owners have difficulty making both ends meet (ANI News, May 25, 2015).

The most common reason for deforestation is cutting of wood for fuel, lumber and paper. Another important cause relates to the clearing of forest land for agriculture, including conversion to crop land and pasture. The expanding agriculture is one of the most important causes of deforestation. Man has always modified the natural ecosystems in such a way that environment becomes more favourable for crop growth whether using traditional or modern methods of agriculture. Hunting and gathering has been the main form of sustenance practiced in the earlier periods of human history. Shifting cultivation or Jhoom farming is a 12000-year old practice and a step towards transition from food collection to food production.

Firewood has been used as a source of energy for cooking, heating etc. Almost 44 per cent of the total global wood produced fulfils the fuel requirements of the world. Wood, the versatile forest produce, is used for several industrial purposes, such as making crates, packing cases, furniture, match boxes, wooden boxes, paper and pulp, plywood, etc. 1.24 lakh ha of forest have been cut for various industrial uses. Often urbanisation and developmental activities lead to deforestation. The process of deforestation begins with building of infrastructure in the form of roads, railway lines, building of dams, townships, electric supply etc. Thermal power plants, mining for coal, metal ores and minerals are also important causes of deforestation (Deforestation, 2012).

Currently, Tripura needs 2.3 metric tons of bamboo annually but this requirement wills more than double within the next five years. So, to cope with the growing demand, we have decided to expand bamboo cultivation to 50,000 hectares of additional land. Bamboo provides raw material for making handicrafts, incense sticks and clubs wielded by security personnel. The dip in bamboo production over the past two decades can be attributed to large scale deforestation and smuggling. The state government will involve small and marginal indigenous farmers to cultivate the 50,000 acres earmarked for bamboo plantations. Restriction on rubber monoculture beyond 25 per cent of a state's land has infused a new sense of urgency in bamboo cultivation under government sponsorship. Bamboo has even made some cultural crossovers. The Bengalis of the state have eagerly adopted bamboo-based dishes like godhak and boiled and spicy bamboo shoots (The Telegraph, September 6, 2012).

Shifting cultivation was assessed by the FAO to be one of the causes of deforestation. In Tripura, comparison of the current forest cover (Satellite data of Nov 2006-Jan 2007) with the previous assessment (satellite data of

Nov 2004) shows a loss of 100 sq. km of forest cover. With reduction in jhum cycle from 20–30 years to 2–3 years, the land under shifting cultivation looses its nutrients and the top soil. With reduction in crop yield, the families start moving to other virgin areas. Frequent shifting from one land to the other has affected the ecology of these regions. The area under natural forest has declined; the fragmentation of habitat, local disappearance of native species and invasion by exotic weeds and other plants are some of the other ecological consequences of shifting agriculture.

Rubber Plantation in India

The rubber growing regions in India can be classified under two major zones, traditional and non-traditional, on the basis of agro-climatic conditions. Rubber cultivation in India has been traditionally confined to hinterlands of southwest coast, mainly in Kanyakumari district of Tamil Nadu and Kerala. Kerala and Tamil Nadu together constitute the traditional rubber growing regions in the country.

Non-traditional Regions are hinterlands of coastal Karnataka, Goa, Konkan Region of Maharashtra, hinterlands of coastal Andhra Pradesh and Odisha, the northeastern states, Andaman and Nicobar Islands etc, where rubber is now being grown. In recent years among non-traditional region, Tripura has become one of the most thrust areas for Rubber growing because of its well acceptance worldwide. Tripura was declared the "Second Rubber Capital of India" by the Rubber Board (Natural Rubber, 2013). Historically plantations in India, as in other developing countries, were promoted as a means of foreign exchange earner to overcome its acute shortage (Thapa, 2012).

Rubber covers a sizeable portion of the area in the plantation sector of Kerala. During 1980-81 the total cropped area in Kerala was 1717000 hectares, of which 396000 hectares (14.8 per cent) was under rubber. Subsequently, the area under rubber increased and during 2001-02 it came to 475000 hectares. Natural rubber is cultivated in all the districts in Kerala. But the area and production of natural rubber is unevenly distributed in Kerala. Rubber trees will not grow in places located above 1000 meters from the sea level. The coastal district, Alappuzha and hilly district Wyanad produce least quantity of natural rubber in Kerala. In Alappuzha, the density of population is highest and the scope of plantation crops is limited (Rubber Plantation Kerala, 2012).

Table 3.3: Statewise Area and Production of Natural Rubber in India during 2006-07

State/Territory	*Total Area (ha)*	*Per cent Share*	*Production (Tonnes)*	*Per cent Share*
1. Traditional Region				
(a) Kerala	502740	81.72	783275	91.84
(b) Tamil Nadu	19233	3.13	24020	2.82
Sub Total	**521973**	**84.85**	**807225**	**94.65**
2. Non-traditional Region				
(a) North Eastern States				
Tripura	37846	6.15	18705	2.19
Assam	15890	2.58	4932	0.58\
Meghalaya	5331	0.87	3967	0.47
Nagaland	2486	0.4	660	0.08
Manipur	1859	0.3	139	0.02
Mizoram	525	0.09	88	0.01
Arunachal Pradesh	446	0.07	114	0.01
Sub Total	**446**	**10.47**	**28605**	**3.35**
(b) Other States				
Karnataka	26035	4.23	16125	1.89
Andaman & Nicobar Islands	729	0.12	236	0.03
Goa	772	0.13	317	0.04
Maharashtra	171	0.03	76	0.01
Odisha	500	0.08	89	0.01
West Bengal	526	0.09	132	0.02
Andhra Pradesh	111	0.02	20	0
Sub Total	**28844**	**4.69**	**16995**	**1.99**
Grand Total (India)	**615200**	**100**	**852895**	**100**

Source: Rubber Board (Kerala).

India's natural rubber production has been increasing steadily over the past decade. The production grew at the rate of 4.8 per cent in the year 2011-12. India produced 904 thousand tonnes in 2011-12 compared to 862 thousand tonnes in 2010-11. Consumption too has been rising steadily. It grew at the rate of 1.8 per cent in 2011-12 and more than 6.8 per cent in 2009-10. Consumption grew from 525 thousand tonnes in 1995-96 to 964 thousand tonnes in 2011-12 (Natural Rubber, 2013). The consumption of natural rubber in India is increasing year after year. The area of application ranges from aero tyre to toy balloons. The industry employs over 2,50,000 people. After 1990 the price of natural rubber in India and in the international market remained more or less the same (Rubber Plantation Kerala, 2012).

From 1980, the Rubber Board has given equal importance to replanting and new planting and promoted both alike under common integrated schemes. These are called Rubber Plantation Development schemes.

One of the reasons for the effectiveness of the Board's extension machinery has been constant rapport with the grower community. The Board launches a campaign every year on a theme of topical importance. Individual small growers in North Eastern region who have constructed biogas plants of suitable size in their own land for treating the effluent generated in their processing sheds and control environmental problems, will be considered for financial assistance at a rate of 50 per cent of the cost of the construction limited to a maximum of Rs 5000 per unit (Rubber Plantation Development Scheme, 2012).

The Brahmaputra valley region of India has become an alternate area for cultivating rubber trees since 1960s. The price of natural rubber remains high, which prompts farmers to take up rubber tree cultivation in Brahmaputra valley as a livelihood option. Rubber tree plantations provide valuable ecosystem services in the marginal and 'jhummed' barren lands, where it is predominantly grown in the Brahmaputra valley. According to the directives of the Government of India, the Rubber Board has taken up a target to bring 5000 ha/year area under rubber plantation. Any approach of mapping suitable land area based on scientific study will certainly help reaching out the target (Ray *et. al.,* 2014).

The Rubber Board is a statutory body constituted by the Government of India, under the Rubber Act 1947, for the overall development of the rubber industry in the country. A consideration of the post-war natural rubber scenario prompted the Government of India to pass the Rubber (Production and Marketing) Act, 1947 to provide for the overall promotion and development of the sector under its guidance and control. As envisaged in the Act, the Indian Rubber Board was set up as the statutory organisation responsible for assisting the government in implementation of the various provisions of the Act. The Act which came into force on 18 April 1947 has since undergone many amendments.

The Rubber Production and Marketing (Amendment) Act of 1954 which took effect on 1 August 1954 made some important changes in the constitution of the Board now renamed as The Rubber Board. The Rubber Research Institute of India (RRII) established in 1955 is located on a hillock in the eastern suburb of Puthuppally, Kottayam, eight kilometres from the town. There are nine research disciplines, seven Regional Research Stations, two Hevean Breeding Sub-stations and a Central Experimental Station attached to the RRII. The Institute is headed by the Director (Research). The Department headed by the Rubber Production Commissioner is responsible for planning, formulation and implementation of schemes for improvement and expansion of rubber cultivation and production (Rubber Board, 2015).

Rubber Plantation in Tripura

Tribal populations are prominent in the North-Eastern region. Rubber cultivation has already attracted large scale participation of tribal's is proving to be an effective means of weaning away the 'jhumiyas' to settled cultivation. Considering this situation, the Rubber Board in collaboration with the Tribal Welfare Department of the Government of Tripura is implementing a series of block planting programmes in which large blocks of tribal areas are planted with rubber initially engaging beneficiaries as wage earners.

The plantation on attaining maturity will be parcelled out and handed over to the beneficiaries and they will be collectively helped to produce and market the rubber from their individual holdings. Where compact blocks of tribal lands are not available, the tribal families in each hamlet are being helped to raise rubber plantation in their individual land holdings under the group planting programme. Along with rubber, energy plantations are also being raised on as much of fringe lands as feasible for ensuring ecology improvements and availability of fuel wood to the tribal families (Rubber Plantation Development Scheme, 2012).

Rubber is an important commercial crop in Tripura. Government of Tripura earns large amount of revenue from this cash crop. Kerala and Tripura are the two states which are known for rubber cultivation. A rubber plant has to grow for about seven years before it can be tapped on a regular basis. Rubber based agro-forestry involves a complex and diverse cropping system that combines the growing of rubber and other agricultural crops in the area in a sustainable manner. Rubber has been identified as one of the thrust areas in Tripura, in view of its suitability to the terrain and the acceptability amongst the people.

A significant number of persons and families in Tripura continue to depend on forests and jhum or shifting cultivation as their main source of cultivation. Almost 10 per cent forests area in under jhum in the State. Jhum has an intimate relationship with forest use, not only in terms of habitation and cultivation of tracts, but also because the forestry sector provides important supplementary income and inputs in daily lives of tribal people residing in forested areas. Jhum cultivation has become unproductive owing to frequent exposure of soil as evident from the reduction of jhum cycle to the present day two to three years from earlier five to six years. The Government of Tripura has taken innovative approaches towards the development of tribal livelihood systems. The number of families involved in four major plantation schemes clearly shows that raising rubber plantations has been one of the important means of jhumia rehabilitation.

The history of rubber in Tripura dates back to 1963 when the State Forest Department, with the technical support of the Rubber Board, introduced rubber to Tripura. In 1976, Tripura Forest Development and Plantation Corporation was set up to get a big leap for expansion of rubber mostly in denuded forest land. This effort took momentum with the opening of a Rubber Board Field office at Agartala in 1967, which now upgraded to the level of Zonal Office under a Joint Rubber Production Commissioner with a Nucleus Rubber Estate and training centre, four Regional Offices at Agartala, Udaipur, Dharmanagar and Ambassa and a Regional Research Station aiming allocation specific R&D. The Rubber Board, through its plantation development schemes, took the rubber concept out of estate sector and domesticated the crop for the rural masses. Today, the vast majority of the rubber plantations in Tripura are owned by small to marginal growers.

Table 3.4: Year-wise Extension in Area of Rubber Plantation in Tripura

Year of Planting	*Planting Area (in Ha)*
1976-77	574
1981-82	3,590
1986-87	10,085
1991-92	17,860
1996-97	23,936
2001-02	30,575
2006-07	35,760
2011-12	57,620
2012-12	61,231

Source: Rubber Board, Tripura.

India's second Rubber Park has been set up in Tripura at Bodhjungnager, which is jointly promoted by Tripura Industrial Development Corporation and Rubber Board with an estimated cost of Rs 23 crore. Rubber Park will provide all infrastructure facilities for promoting rubber-based industries in the State. The TFDPC Ltd. is the major producer of rubber in the State and it functions under the administrative control of State Forest Department. A rubber mission has been set up by Government of Tripura for better coordination of all the agencies involved in taking up rubber plantation and marketing of rubber. The Rubber Mission aims at assessing the resource potential through GPS mapping.

TRPC Ltd. was registered on the 3rd February, 1983 under the Companies Act, 1956 with the objective to economically rehabilitate shifting cultivators (jhumia), tribal landless and small farmers principally through rubber plantation. Tribal Welfare is the administrative department of the corporation. The first phase of TRPC project for creation of 1200 ha. of rubber plantation for 800 shifting cultivators was supported by bank loan under NABARD refinance scheme channelled through a consortium of tree banks, State Bank of India, United Bank of India and Tripura Gramin Bank.

TRPC received a loan of Rs 173.82 lakh under the World Bank Aided Rubber Project for raising 1000 ha of rubber plantation for tribal small farmers owning un-arable uplands; and against that 924 ha of rubber plantation was created for 720 beneficiaries during 1993-94 to 2000-01. The most successful story in the rubber cultivation in Tripura is the establishment of marketing set up. The wide network of rubber dealers, spread over most of the areas, ensures for the growers, the countries best farm gate price of an agriculture commodity. The increased global demand also contributed to price stability. Two other factors, which were of prime effectiveness, are regular market intervention by the Rubber Board-promoted companies and the bargaining capacity built up by the Rubber Producers' Societies (Economic Review of Tripura, 2013-14, 2015).

Benefits of Rubber Plantation

The period of gestation of rubber is about seven years. After the commencement of taping proper processing and profitable disposal of the crop create problems to the small growers. The system of grading is always manipulated by buyers and it often results in lack of realisation of fair selling price. The middlemen marketing chain also creates harm to the interest of the small holders. Low profitability is one of the problems faced by the Small Rubber Growers.

Rapid rise in the wages of labours and increase in the price of fertilisers are the problems faced by the small rubber growers. In 1986, the Rubber Board promoted formation of small voluntary associations of small growers registered under the Charitable Societies Act called the Rubber Producers Societies (RPS) in 1986. RPS assists in transfer of new technologies to members. It assists common marketing of member's rubber grade-wise and at remunerative prices. There are economic as well as social benefits which are expected to get from the RPS. Members of RPS would get fair price for their products. It would create co-operative spirit and communal harmony as member would be from different castes and culture. The help from Rubber Board to cooperatives includes organisational assistance, share participation, working capital loans etc (Hameedu, 2014).

Tapping is the process of collecting latex from rubber plants. Those labours who involve in this work are identified as rubber tapper. Tapping work is normally done in early morning. Rubber sheet is the primary input of rubber industry. In rubber factory different types of goods are produce by using rubber sheets. In those factories large quantity of unemployed tribal's can get their work. Rubber seed is a minor source of non-edible oil.

The oil content ranges from 14-16 per cent of the total weight of seeds. Rubber seed cake can be used up to 20 per cent of the total weight of cattle feed. Rubber wood has emerged as a substitute source of timber. Processed rubber wood can be used in furniture panelling, flooring and household articles. Rubber tree is a rich source of nectar. It is found at the extra-floral nectar glands at the end of the petiole where the leaflets join. About 15 hives can be placed in a hectare of rubber. Common people can collect branches of the broken trees which they can be used as fuel. In every year during March-April all leafs of trees are generally falls and it also use as fuel in rural areas. In this way this will reduce pressure on forest for collecting firewood.

Rubber Plantation Insurance

The scheme is applicable to both mature and immature plantations. The policy is issued for a period of seven years from the last day of the month of planting for immature plants. Compensation will be available from the second year onwards, which is calculated on the basis of replacement cost of the plant plus present value of future returns arising out of the loss / death of the plant. For mature plantations, cover will be provided for blocks of 3/2/1 year(s) from the eighth year of planting. Fire, Lightning, Riot, Strike and Malicious Damage, Bush Fire, Forest Fire, Flood, Storm, Tempest, Inundation, Land Slide, Rock Slide, Earthquake and Drought provided the Block /Taluka concerned is declared as drought affected by the competent authority of the State Government.

The policy is extended to cover the loss or damage caused by road/ rail/vehicles and wild animals. Losses due to diseases and insect-pest are excluded from the scope of cover. In the case of destruction of 75 per cent of trees and above per hectare, the loss will be treated as total and the insured will be paid compensation as per the policy. Compensation for the remaining unaffected trees in the affected holding will be paid on production of a certificate from the Rubber Board / Surveyor certifying that the balance trees have been cut and that the entire land is ready for re-planting (Rubber Plantation Insurance, 2013).

Conclusion

Deforestation is the permanent destruction of forests in order to make the land available for other uses. The most common reason for deforestation is cutting of wood for fuel, lumber and paper. Another important cause relates to the clearing of forest land for agriculture, including conversion to crop land and pasture. Rubber is an important commercial crop in Tripura. Government of Tripura earns large amount of revenue from this cash crop. Kerala and Tripura are the two states which are known for rubber cultivation. A rubber plant has to grow for about seven years before it can be tapped on a regular basis.

Rubber based agro-forestry involves a complex and diverse cropping system that combines the growing of rubber and other agricultural crops in the area in a sustainable manner. Rubber has been identified as one of the thrust areas in Tripura, in view of its suitability to the terrain and the acceptability amongst the people. In 1976, Tripura Forest Development and Plantation Corporation was set up to get a big leap for expansion of rubber mostly in denuded forest land. TRPC Ltd. was registered on the 3rd February, 1983 under the Companies Act, 1956 with the objective to economically rehabilitate shifting cultivators, tribal landless and small farmers principally through rubber plantation. Tribal Welfare is the administrative department of the corporation.

References

1. Afforestation (2015), Retrieved from https://www.google.co.in/?gws_rd=ssl#q=afforestation
2. ANI News (May 25, 2015). Fate of domestic elephants at stake in Tripura, Retrieved from http://www.aninews.in/newsdetail2/story169910/fate-of-domestic-elephants-at-stake-in-tripura.html
3. Cosmato, D. (2010). Afforestation: Meaning, Importance and Current Efforts, Retrieved from http://www.brighthub.com/environment/science-environmental/articles/91133.aspx
4. Deforestation (2012). Retrieved from http://download.nos.org/333courseE/9.pdf
5. Economic Review of Tripura 2013-14 (2015). Directorate of Economics and Statistics; Planning (Statistics) Department; Government of Tripura, Agartala; www.destripura.nic.in; www.ecostat.tripura.gov.in
6. Hameedu, M. (2014). Role of rubber producers societies in Kerala, International Journal of Current Research and Academic Review, 2 (2), pp. 159-166.

7. Joseph, K. and George, P. (2011). Structural Infirmities in India's Plantation Sector: Natural Rubber and Spices, National Research Programme on Plantation Development (NRPPD) Centre for Development Studies, Trivandrum, pp. 1-22.
8. Natural Rubber (2013). Retrieved from http://www.nmce.com/files/study/rubber.pdf
9. Patra, H. (2014). Importance of afforestration in India, Retrieved from http://www.importantindia.com/10926/importance-of-afforestation-in-india/
10. Ray, D., Behera, M., and Jacob, J. (2014). Indian Brahmaputra valley offers significant potential for cultivation of rubber trees under changed climate, Current Science, 107 (3), p. 461.
11. Rubber Board (2015). Retrieved from http://en.wikipedia.org/wiki/Rubber_Board
12. Rubber Plantation Development Scheme (2012). Retrieved from http://mal.rubberboard.org.in/acts/subsidy_schemes.pdf
13. Rubber Plantation Insurance (2013). Retrieved from http://www.aicofindia. com/AICEng/General_Documents/Product_Profiles/Rubber_Ins.pdf
14. Rubber Plantation Kerala (2012). Retrieved from http://shodhganga. inflibnet.ac.in/bitstream/10603/6550/10/10_chapter%202.pdf
15. Sekhsaria, P. (2012). Deforestation in India: overview and propose case studies, Retrieved from http://enviroscope.iges.or.jp/modules/envirolib/upload/1508/attach/1ws-9-pankaji.pdf
16. Sharma, R. (2014). Short paragraph on importance of forest, Retrieved from http://www.importantindia.com/16261/short-paragraph-on-importance-of-forest/
17. Thapa, N. (2012). Performance and Innovation System: A Study of Plantation Sector in India, pp. 1-8.
18. The Telegraph (September 6, 2012). Bamboo's bond with Tripura- Additional 50000 hectares earmarked to boost production.
19. Tripathi, S. (2014). Short paragraph on afforestation, Retrieved from http://www.importantindia.com/12473/short-paragraph-on-afforestation/
20. Viswanathan, P. (2010). Emerging Smallholder Rubber Farming Systems in India and Thailand: A Comparative Economic Analysis, pp.1-13.

Chapter 4

Corporate Social Responsibility and Sustainable Development: A Case Based Approach

Dr Simanchala Das and Dr Suman Kalyan Chaudhury

"Education is not a tool for development - individual, community and the nation. It is the foundation for our future. It is empowerment to make choices and emboldens the youth to chase their dreams."

– ***Nita Ambani***

Introduction

Over the years, the concept of corporate social responsibility has gained unprecedented momentum in business and strategy. The global trend towards assessing the social and environmental impact of business decisions results in incorporating CSR practices in their business strategies. It is a company's continuous commitment to operate in an economically, socially and environmentally sustainable manner, while recognising the interests of its stakeholders. This commitment is beyond statutory requirements. It is closely linked with the practice of sustainable development. Further, it extends beyond philanthropic activities and reaches out to the integration of social and business goals. These activities need to be seen as those which would, in the long-term, help secure a sustainable competitive advantage. The argument is not that competitive gains for the corporation can be directly traced to the social benefits of its philanthropic activity. Rather, CSR can contribute to the competitive context within which the company operates.

Corporate Social Responsibility has become a worldwide concept whereby organisations consider the interests of society by taking responsibility for the impact of their activities on customers, employees, shareholders, communities and the environment in all aspects of their operations. It is one of the most important global issues with serious challenges and implications on almost all sectors. Surging economies, including India, are coping with issues related to poverty, child rights, community welfare etc and are a hotbed for an innovative CSR scenario which is still shaping up.

As a consequence of rising globalisation and pressing ecological issues, the perception of the role of corporates in the broader societal context within which it operates, has been altered. Stakeholders (employees, community, suppliers and shareholders) today are redefining the role of corporate taking into account the corporate's broader responsibility towards society and environment, beyond economic performance, and are evaluating whether they are conducting their role in an ethical and socially responsible manner. As a result of this shift, many forums, institutions and corporates are endorsing the term Corporate Social Responsibility.

The objective of this paper is to: (a) Review and evaluate corporate social responsibility initiatives undertaken by SAIL and its unit RSP; (b) Explore the relationship between CSR and sustainable development in the context of various CSR activities of the SAIL and RSP; and (c) Find out the degree of social and economic performance of SAIL in general and RSP in particular through its sustainable development practices.

Review of Literature

Corporate Social Responsibility is a widely used term in business literature, which can be interpreted as continuous commitment of a business to behave ethically and to contribute to economic development while improving the living standards of the workforce and their families as well as the community. It is a concept whereby companies integrate social and environmental concerns in their business operations and in their interaction with their stakeholders on a voluntary basis (European Commission, 2001). CSR is defined in many ways and no universally accepted definition is in place.

Hill (2006) explained that CSR is a set of practices that form a part of good management or business practices much of it is about transparency and disclosure. Many organisations find that in actuality they already do much of what is considered CSR but often do not have formalised systems to report on those activities. Hussain and Hussain (2005) provided a constructive picture between consumer's perception and organisation's spending pattern on different CSR activities. They also figured out whether consumers expect to incorporate only brand name, or only company name or both brand and company name while organising CSR activities.

Carroll (1991) viewed the 1980s as a shift to more empirical research applying his proposed four-dimensional pyramid model responsibility. He suggested that CSR includes four kinds of responsibilities or dimensions: economic, legal, ethical and philanthropic. In 1979, he offered a conceptual model that comprehensively describes essential aspects of corporate social performance. Mohr, Webb and Harris (2001) viewed corporate social responsibility as a company's commitment to minimising eliminating any harmful effects on society and maximising its long-term beneficial impact. The latest literature tradition to have impacted our understanding of corporate social responsibility is that of sustainable development.

It was the Brundtland Commission (1987) that for the first time systematically emphasised the link between poverty, environmental degradation, and economic development. Its definition of sustainable development, as meeting the needs of the present, without compromising the ability of future generations to meet theirs, extends the responsibility of firms both inter and intragenerationally. Firms are expected to consider traditionally unrepresented stakeholders such as the environment and as well as future generations. Although many CSR authors have taken up the notion of a triple bottom line (Elkington, 1997), there remain important tensions between the CSR and the sustainable development debate (i.e. Dyllick and Hockerts, 2002). Most of the studies on CSR typically focus on limited aspects (Maignan, Ferrell, and Ferrell, 2005). This means that an integrative framework has yet to be offered for the development and implementation of CSR in a fashion that is soundly integrated to the organisation's strategy, structure, and culture (Bhattacharya and Sen, 2004; Smith, 2003).

Studies show that while managers appear to have increasingly come to see the need to integrate or fit corporate philanthropic activity with the company's core mission and strategy, the actual practice of such strategic philanthropy seems to be weak. Some reliable evidence exists for a positive relationship between philanthropic activity and firm reputation as well as financial performance. There are important methodological problems with most of the studies, such as small, non-representative samples of firms and low response rates, which limit what we are able to say about American corporations in general.

The lack of consensus in the literature on how to measure various aspects of the phenomenon is another obstacle to overcome. Despite the growing importance of CSR communication, organisations still have to learn how to communicate their CSR. In fact, in spite of the research on

CSR being 50 years old, there is still no common definition of CSR (Gobbels, 2003). This field of study is not only theoretically and conceptually poor, but is also empirically unexplored (Hopkins, 1999). The CSR reporting and disclosure methods, despite their popularity, have several drawbacks as a measure of CSR practices. For example, corporate social reporting may lag behind actual involvement and might not be an accurate reflection of corporate behaviour (Hung and Ramasamy, 2004; Keeler, 2002). There is also a concern that the information provided by corporations in their annual reports and websites could be driven by publicity motives (Tsang, 1998).

Sustainable Development

The term sustainable development was used for the first time at the United Nations Conference on the Human Environment in Stockholm in 1972. A working definition of SD was coined in 1987 with the publication of 'Our Common Future', popularly known as the Brundtland Report of the World Commission on Environment and Development. The Commission's definition, since widely adopted, was: "Development as the means to satisfy the needs of present generations without compromising the resources of future generations". Sustainability, the Commission argued, includes not only economic and social development, but also a commitment to the needs of the poor and recognising the physical limitations of the earth.

The World Business Council for Sustainable Development states that corporate social responsibility is the continuing commitment by business to behave ethically and contribute to economic development while improving the quality of life of the workforce and their families as well as of the local community and society at large. It is not just obeying the law. It implies serious business where organisations have to be seen as partners in their communities and not just as profit centres promoting the interest of their shareholders but as businesses having obligation towards various 'stakeholders'.

Although in India, sustainability reporting is not mandatory, low but significant, subsidiaries of transnational companies as well as local Indian companies have started reporting on CSR. SAIL, Tata Chem and NLC were the winners of the FICCI-SEDF CSR Awards function held on 7th May 2007. Tata Steel had ranked among the top 100 companies in Standard and Poor's, 'The Global Reporters 2004 Survey of Corporate Sustainability Reporting'. The prominent CSR reporting standards are accountability's AA1000 standard, based on John Elkington's triple bottom line reporting;

Global Reporting Initiative's Sustainability Reporting Guidelines; Social Accountability International's SA8000 standard and the ISO 14000 environmental management standard. In India companies like Tata group, Dr Reddy's Laboratories, Ford India Limited, Paharpur Business Centre, Jubilant Organosys, ITC, etc are largely using GRI guidelines while reporting.

CSR has a significant role to play in controlling the perils of uncontrolled development, satisfying the needs of the present generation and at the same time ensuring that the resources of future generations is not jeopardised. Although, the 'beyond charity and legal obligations' agenda of sustainability may be challenging it is meaningful to integrate social, environmental and ethical concerns into business processes. It is proving prudent to embark on 'green policies'. The findings of the research conducted by the UK's Institute of Business Ethics, which compared companies in the FTSE 250, provided strong evidence that companies committed to ethical behaviour perform better financially over the long-term than those lacking such a commitment.

The year 2013 marks the beginning of a new era for corporation in India. The new Companies' Bill has been approved by the Parliament and the President of India has given assent to it. This Act aims to improve the transparency and accountability of corporate sector in India. The Acts among other aspects provides for certain change in norms of CSR. CSR is now accepted as a means to achieve sustainable development of an organisation. It needs to be accepted as an organisational objective. Under this Act, the prescribed plan of companies is required to outlay a portion of their profit on CSR activities. Business can no longer be limited to using resources by indulging in activities that increase their profit only.

The Companies have to be socially responsible corporate citizens and contribute to greater common social good. Ultimately, the aim of social responsibility is all about integrating the three objectives: economic, environmental and social within the framework of company operations and growth. Though the philanthropy is a fore runner to the concept of CSR, it's much more than the philanthropy. An organisation can accomplish sustainable development, if the CSR becomes an integral part of its business process. CSR impacts almost every operational area of a company. The Companies Act 2013 intends to inculcate the philosophy of CSR among Indian companies.

The research methodology used for the paper is mainly qualitative. The data have been collected mainly from the secondary source.

The company bulletin, Annual Reports, Sustainability Reports, news clippings have been referred. Besides, various books, articles, research papers published in various journals have been extensively studied for a complete review of literature.

Study of SAIL and RSP

SAIL reaffirms its commitment to contributing towards a clean and sustainable environment and continually enhancing its environmental performance as an integral part of its business philosophy and values under the banner of Corporate Environmental Policy and is also committed to continuously promote sustainable development, encompassing environmental, societal and economic aspects related to its business activities under Sustainable Development Policy. In addition to these, the company is committed to continuously improving its social responsibilities, environment and economic practices to make a positive impact on the society and to this effect; Corporate Social Responsibility Policy has been formulated.

SAIL's focus on social responsibility remains unwavering. The pivotal role of education, health, income generation and Sustainable Development is the cornerstone of Corporate Social Responsibility and SD initiatives. Department of Public Enterprises (DPE), Ministry of Heavy Industries and Public Enterprises, Government of India released the guidelines for SD in 2011 and made SD as one of the compulsory parameters in MoU of CPSEs. In accordance, the following SD projects were taken up during the year for implementation at SAIL Plants and Mines:

1. Water Management- Water Foot Print and Water Accounting Study at four SAIL Steel Plants: BSP, DSP, BSL and RSP.
2. Life Cycle Assessment- Carbon Foot Print Study of Steel Products at BSP.
3. Bio-diversity Conservation- CO Mitigation Strategy (Afforestation) and Bio-diversity Conservation at two Bolani Iron Ore Mine.
4. Sustainability Training across SAIL covering all strata of SAIL employees.
5. Publication of SD Performance Report (SDPR), 2011-12.
6. Water Management- Rain Water Harvesting in CRM Zone-II Complex at BSL.
7. Installation of Solar Power Plant at Bhilai Niwas of BSP.

The SD initiatives include innovative projects such as carbon and water foot print study at SAIL plants, biodiversity conservation at Bolani Iron Ore Mine, rain water harvesting and sustainability training exceeding 10000 man-hours across the Company, including exclusive interaction for SAIL Board of Directors with Global Reporting Initiative sustainability experts.

SAIL in general and Rourkela Steel Plant in particular recognises that its business activities have direct and indirect impact on the society. The Company strives to integrate its business values and operations in an ethical and transparent manner to demonstrate its commitment to sustainable development and to meet the interests of its stakeholders. The Company is committed to continuously improving its social responsibilities, environment and economic practices to make positive impact on the society. SAIL firmly believes that people must be at the centre of its development debate - what really counts is how they participate in economic growth and how they benefit from it. Accordingly, the focus of this study is on addressing SAIL's Triple Bottom Line (TBL) - economic, environmental and social performance in its areas of operation.

Human skill and agency would be important not just in raising productivity, but also in devising ways and means of dealing with environmental and other challenges. SAIL is dedicated to making sustainable steel. The Company believes that this is its core contribution to a more sustainable society and to all its stakeholders. Behind this belief is SAIL's underlying commitment to Sustainable Development and its inherent focus on TBL performance. Achieving this in practice requires that economic growth supports social progress and respects the environment, that social policy underpins economic performance, and that environmental policy is cost-effective.

SAIL's role as a responsible corporate citizen in nation building has not gone unrecognised. The company has won prestigious awards, honours and accolades in this sphere such as:

- SCOPE Meritorious Award for Corporate Social Responsibility and Responsiveness for the year 2008-09, presented by the President of India, Smt Pratibha Devi Singh Patil.
- Annual FICCI Awards 2008-09 in the category of The Vision Corporate Triple Impact - Business Performance: Social and Environmental Action and Globalisation Award, presented by Finance Minister of India, Sh. Pranab Mukherjee.
- Business world-FICCI-SEDF CSR Award for the year 2006 presented by the then President of India, Dr A.P.J. Abdul Kalam.

- FICCI Award for Rural and Community Development (2006-07) presented by Prime Minister Dr Manmohan Singh.
- CSR Award of the Ministry of Rural Development, Government of India.
- Golden Peacock Award - for CSR to Bhilai Steel Plant of SAIL for three consecutive years.
- CSR Award of Tamil Nadu Government for the year 2007-08 and 2008-09 to Salem Steel Plant of SAIL.

Rourkela Steel Plant has received the following awards

1. Award in three categories viz. Best CSR Practices, Women's Empowerment and Support and Improvement in Quality of Education was awarded to RSP at the World CSR Congress and World CSR Day held at Mumbai in Feb.' 2014 during Global CSR Excellence and Leadership Award Presentation Ceremony.
2. Certificate of Commendation was awarded to RSP in the 'CII ITC Sustainability Award 2013' for significant achievement in the journey towards Sustainable Development.
3. Greentech Environment Award (Gold) for the year 2012-13 by Greentech Foundation at Chandigarh on 29th-30th January, 2014.
4. Golden Peacock Environment Management Award 2012.
5. CII-EXIM Bank Award 2012-13 for strong commitment towards excellence in November, 2013.
6. CSR Leadership Award in the Think CSR Forum jointly organised by Telfa's, the Times of India and Think Foundation in August, 2013.
7. Champion's Award for Employee Engagement in June, 2013 by INSAAN.
8. Srishsti Good Green Governance Award, 2011 received 4th times in a row in June' 2013.
9. Ispat Suraksha Puraskar-2010 for no fatal accident in two areas, namely, Coal, Coke and Chemicals Zone and the Blast Furnace, Slag Granulation Plant, Sinter Plants and Raw Materials Department Zone by Joint Committee on Safety, Health and Environment of the Steel Industry in June, 2013.

Socio-economic Development

Steel Authority of India Limited - the Maharatna Steel Company, has adopted a balanced approach towards inclusive growth, consistent with socio-environment. The Company, during 2013-14, continued to focus on helping the downtrodden, the underprivileged with its development oriented CSR projects in the area of Medical and Healthcare, Education, livelihood generation etc.

Medical and Health care

Specialised and basic healthcare facilities either completely free or at very nominal charges are being provided to needy and underprivileged living in the vicinity of Pants/Units through 57 Primary Health Centres, 21 Hospitals, seven Reproductive and Child Health Centres and seven Super-Specialty Hospitals created by SAIL. More than 38.61 million people have benefited so far by availing the healthcare facilities being provided by SAIL. Seven health centres (Kalyan Chikitsalaya) have been established exclusively for BPL families at Plants location which provide free OPD facilities and medicines to poor and needy families. Over 90,000 people were treated at these Kalyan Chikitsalayas in 2013-14. SAIL has continuously been providing basic medical services to the rural populace residing in its peripheral villages. Around 3000 medical camps were organised during 2013-14 in the vicinity of its Plants/Units to provide medical facilities to such people in their neighbourhood itself. More than two lakh people received the medical facilities in these camps in 2013-14.

SAIL has created infrastructure for enhancing availability of safe drinking water for people living in far-flung areas, by installing over 7625 water sources. By virtue of these facilities created by SAIL, 42.70 lakh people have gained access to drinking water through improvement in availability of potable water resources at rural and water deficit locations. In order to promote sanitation and hygiene in peripheral villages, RSP has completed the project 'Comprehensive Water and Sanitation Facilities' in five peripheral villages – Chutiatola, Dumerjore, Ushra Colony, Baniguni and Jagdishpur benefiting 621 households.

Education

The Company firmly believes that only an enlightened and well informed citizen can play a constructive role in the progress of society. Company owns and maintains over 129 schools in its Steel townships for providing modern education to more than 59,000 children, besides actively providing assistance to over 629 schools with over 92,000 students. Seven Special Schools (Kalyan Vidyalaya), exclusively for BPL families established at Steel Plants locations, are providing free education, mid-day meals, uniform including shoes, text books, stationery items, school bags, water bottles and transportation to around 1,600 students. Scholarships to deserving undergraduate and postgraduate engineering students, adoption of tribal children from Maoist insurgency affected areas, nearly extinct Birhore tribes, sponsoring youth for Industrial Training and Nursing course, etc. are some of the major steps taken for uplifting poor, OBC, SC, ST, etc. Saranda Suvan Chhatravas – a fully residential complex at Kiriburu Mines has been set up for providing education and residential facilities to students belonging to areas affected by Maoist insurgency.

SAIL in association with Akshya Patra Foundation is providing Mid-Day Meal to students of government schools in and around Bhilai and Rourkela. Under this scheme, healthy and nutritious meal is being provided to more than 73000 students of around 550 government schools every day. SAIL has carried out construction of new roads/pathways and also undertaken repairs of damaged road/pathways in rural areas thereby providing connectivity for facilitating reach of education and healthcare amenities to over 77.04 lakh people across 435 villages.

Developing the Rural Livelihood and Conservation of Energy

In order to bridge the disparity between rural and urban areas and bring about holistic development of both physical and social infrastructure, 79 villages have been developed as "Model Steel Villages" across the country (in eight states). To promote renewable sources of energy, Solar street lights were installed and Solar Lanterns and smokeless chullahs have been distributed among the poor and needy in different parts of the country.

People of remote forest areas are deprived of basic infrastructural i.e. medical care, education and other essential requirements of livelihoods. The dense reserve forest of Saranda wherein SAIL's mines are situated is one of such deprived region where people face real hardships of life. Being a responsible corporate entity and to bring the marginalised masses of this remote forest area to the mainstream of development, SAIL in association with Ministry of Rural Development, Government of India has undertaken a developmental plan for the benefit of habitants of Saranda forest region. Under the Saranda Development Plan, SAIL has distributed bicycles, transistors, solar lanterns (seven thousand each) to the people of the region and established an Integrated Development Centre at Digha village in Saranda forest, West Singhbum District, Jharkhand consisting of a Hospital, Anganwadi Centre, Bank, Forest and Agriculture office, Ration shop, Community Hall, Accommodation Complex for civil official and a Community kitchen.

Rehabilitation Initiatives

SAIL, as a responsible corporate citizen, supported the rehabilitation initiatives for the people affected by Flash Floods in Uttarakhand and Phylin cyclone in Odisha by contributing one Crore and 20 Crore, respectively.

Vocational Training and Skill Development

Vocational training has been provided in areas such as Improved agriculture, Mushroom cultivation, Goatery, Poultry, Fishery, Piggery, Achar/Pappad/Agarbatti making, Welder, Fitter and Electrician Training, Sewing and embroidery, Smokeless chullah making etc. as a means to livelihood in a dignified manner. Vocational Training Centre for rural and unemployed youths – 'Bhilai Ispat Kaushal Kutir' and 'Swayamsiddha' at Bhilai, Skill Development and Self Employment Training Institute (SDSETI) at Durgapur, Garment Technician Training at Salem, JHARCRAFT centre at Bokaro and Self-employment centre "KIRAN" at Kiriburu Ore Mines are benefitting common masses by way of financial inclusion/SHG/training for income generation and then empowering them to be part of main-stream. Besides running Vocational Training Institutes (VTI), SAIL is supporting vocational training of the local youth at other ITIs/ITCs/ VTIs. RSP, ISP and RMD supported ITI/ITC training of more than 700 youths at ITC, Bargaon, (under the rehabilitation/prevention programme for the left wing extremists) and ITCs at Rourkela.

People living in the peripheral area of SAIL's plants/ units are taught skills that will help them to merit more than two square meals a day. These programmes promote rural savings and credit, natural resource management, village infrastructure development, increased agricultural productivity through better management of resources and intensive cropping, and skill development and enhancement of the community. During the last three years, SAIL has provided vocational training to around 44,000 people in and around SAIL Plants/units.

Promoting Art and Culture

For promoting the local art and culture, Chhattisgarh Lok Kala Mahotsav and Gramin Lokotsav are being organised every year. To promote local culture and games, Gramin Lokotsavas and Gramin Athletics Competition were organised by SAIL at different locations throughout the year. SAIL's efforts as a responsible corporate citizen in Nation building have been recognised at various forums in the form of numerous awards and accolades received by the Company which are tabulated along with other awards in Awards and Accolades Section reported earlier.

Developing the Weaker Sections of the Society including the SCs and STs

The Company follows Presidential Directives on Reservation for Scheduled Castes (SCs) and Scheduled Tribes (STs) in the matter of recruitments and promotions. As on 31st March, 2014, out of total manpower of 97897, 15.95 per cent belong to SC category and 13.77 per cent belong to ST category. SAIL steel plants and units including mines are located in economically backward regions of the country with predominantly SC/ST population. SAIL has contributed to the overall development of civic, medical, educational, recreational and other facilities in these regions. SAIL has undertaken several initiatives for the socio-economic development of SCs/STs and other weaker sections of the society which are mainly as under:

1. No tuition fee is charged from SC/ST students studying in the Company-run schools, irrespective of whether they are SAIL employees' wards or non-employees' wards.
2. Free medical health centres for poor have been set up at Bhilai, Durgapur, Rourkela, Bokaro, Burnpur (Gutgutpara) providing free medical consultation, medicines, etc. to the peripheral population mainly comprising of SC/ST and weaker sections of society.
3. SAIL Plants have adopted 15 children from nearly extinct Birhor Tribe. They are being provided free education, boarding, lodging and medical facilities for their overall growth.
4. Villagers are given free outdoor and indoor treatment in the SAIL hospitals located at Kiriburu, Gua and Chiria Mines after recommendations by Manki/Munda (Local Tribal Village Heads) of the peripheral villages.

Creating Sustainable Income

SAIL's efforts in the area of CSR are targeted to adding value for enriching lives and ensuring a strong future for the beneficiaries. Imparting them with skills that help them lead a better life and sustain their respective generations is a key focus towards creating communities that are in complete control of the time to come. Development of such families through workshops and skill enhancement training programmes has been a major entrepreneurial gesture of the company. SAIL is constantly working to identify various areas where training and help to the communities can be imparted so as to make them self-sustaining units that can generate incomes for themselves.

Environmental Management

Environment management at SAIL addresses control of pollution through clean-up as well as cleaner technologies, use of research and development to prepare environmental-friendly products and operation of facilities with the least impact on the environment. All environmental programmes at SAIL Plants and Units attend to critical issues such as resource optimisation, environmental protection, mitigation of adverse environmental impacts, if any, as well as smooth operational and maintenance programmes for environment and pollution control. In order to minimise adverse impact on environment, the Environment Management Division, as nodal agency, facilitates the environment management and pollution control activities in and around the Steel Plants and Mines of SAIL located across the country. With spending of about 5000 crore on pollution control schemes, SAIL is marching ahead with its massive modernisation-cum-expansion programme, installing more efficient and environment-friendly state-of-the-art technologies.

Implementation of EMS linked to ISO 14001

Effective environment management plays a key role in the efforts of steel industry to operate in a sustainable manner. SAIL has embraced the Environmental Management System enthusiastically, to continually improve the environmental performance and increase the operating efficiencies with concomitant economic advantages. SAIL has progressively introduced Environment Management System certification in its Plants and Mines, resulting in improvement in waste management, water and energy conservation, noise reduction, control of stack and fugitive emissions, improved housekeeping etc. SAIL has also introduced ISO 14001 in its CMO warehouses which establishes its commitment towards greening of supply chain. EMS linked with ISO-14001:2004 have been implemented at CFP, Chandrapur and two Warehouses of CMO at Ahmedabad and Ghaziabad, during the year 2013-14.

Improvement in Environmental Footprints and Operational Efficiency

SAIL Plants have taken various initiatives to reduce environmental footprint and enhance operational efficiency by improving operational discipline and minimise emissions. This has led to improvement in environmental parameters as well as in techno-economic efficiency, enabling us to produce greener and more environmental friendly steel.

Here are some major improvements:

1. SAIL Plants recorded the best ever Specific Energy Consumption of 6.59 Gcal/tcs, with an improvement of one per cent over 2012-13. This was achieved, as a result of higher volume of Crude Steel being produced through energy efficient CC route (up by three per cent over last year).
2. SAIL achieved the lowest ever Particulate Matter (PM) Emission
3. Load (0.86 kg/tcs), Specific Water Consumption (3.66 m^3/tcs) and Specific Effluent Discharge (2.18 m^3/tcs) during FY' 2014.
4. SAIL Plants have also reduced their CO Emission levels to 2.692 T/tcs which is their lowest ever emission, showing significant improvement over previous years.

Improvement in Air and Water Pollution Level

SAIL Plants are effectively maintaining the air pollution control devices and regularly upgrading them in order to maintain the norms which are becoming stricter day by day. Due to the continuous efforts, the specific Particulate Matter (PM) emission load from the major stacks has been reduced by more than 44 per cent in the last five years.

Water pollution level at the steel Plants are taken care of by effective utilisation of the installed Effluent Treatment Plants (ETPs) at the various shops, rejuvenation of the existing water re-circulation systems and recycling of used water for other operational purposes. The treated effluent from the ETPs, are then let out through the outfalls outside the plant boundary only after meeting the stipulated norms of effluent discharge. The specific effluent load at the discharges has been reduced by more than 35 per cent in the last five years. The integrated steel plants have also initiated actions towards achieving zero effluent discharge. PM Emission Load has reduced to 0.86 kg/tcs from 1.55 kg/tcs in 2009-10, which is a reduction of more than 44 per cent in the last five years.

New Initiatives on Environment during 2013-14

1. A project has been taken up, jointly with BSL, SAIL and the South Eastern Railways for utilisation of weathered LD Slag of BSL as rail track ballast.
2. Under R&D Master Plan of SAIL, a project on Laboratory Scale Study for Development of Technology for Dry Granulation of

LD/BOF Slag (Hydro-mechanical study) is in progress. The technology is being developed in association with IIT, Kharagpur.

3. Carbon sequestration project through afforestation at RSP.
4. (Technology Mission-3) under R&D Master Plan is in progress. M/s TFRI, Jabalpur and SAIL are jointly working on this project.
5. For Gainful Utilisation of Municipal Solid Wastes, a comprehensive Municipal Solid Waste Management Model has been prepared for implementation at the steel plant townships.

Plantation

SAIL realises the role of plantation in overall environment management initiatives. Extensive afforestation programme has been consistently followed in all the plants and mines over the last few decades. The green belt developed by afforestation adds not only to aesthetic environment but also helps in watershed management, soil protection, erosion control, landslide stabilisation and developing windbreaks. About 2.05 lakh saplings have been planted in and around the SAIL plants and mines during the year 2013-14. A cumulative of 183.9 lakhs saplings have been planted since inception.

Eco-Restoration of Degraded Lands

A project on restoration and rehabilitation of degraded ecosystems is under execution at the Purnapani Limestone and Dolomite Quarry (PLDQ). 172.92 acres of mined out area has been successfully restored so far to productive ecosystems at PLDQ, by planting more than 3.23 lakhs saplings. Pisciculture has been put into practice in five abandoned quarries filled with water. During 2013-14, a similar project has been initiated at the Bolani Ores Mines, for restoration of a total area of 75 acres.

Awards and Accolades in respect to Environment Protection

1. Award for "Best Practices in Training and HRD-2012" from Indian Society for Training and Development, Hyderabad Chapter.
2. "Greentech Environment Gold Award" in the field of eco-friendly steel making.
3. Awards under three categories - Best CSR Practices, Concern for Health and Women Empowerment in the World CSR Day Global CSR Leadership and Excellence Awards.
4. Greentech Environmental Excellence Gold Award 2012 in Metal and Mining sector, instituted by the Green Tech Foundation, New Delhi.
5. Srishsti Good Green Governance Award, 2012.

Environmental Performance of Rourkela Steel Plant

These are the performance of RSP towards environmental activities.

1. Repair of recuperator in reheating furnace of Hot Strip Mill.
2. Replacement of 2 nos. aluminium blades with FRP ones in cooling tower fans of CCD.
3. Thermal insulation of steam lines (1500 Sq. m).
4. Digitalisation of F-2 Motor in Hot Strip Mill.
5. Commissioning of 8 nos. ETPs in Coal Chemical Department.
6. Replacement of 16 nos. of 250 W SV lamps (street lights) by 90 W LED lights in Sinter Plant II.
7. Joint safety inspections conducted for precommissioning activities at project sites. Safety inspections by team of senior personnel and visit of safety personnel on Sundays, holidays and during odd hours.
8. Introduced revised 'Zero accident recognition' and 'Safety champion' schemes and 'Suraksha Chakra' scheme covering employees of total plant.
9. Workshop on Welding Safety with use of ELCB and RCCB and use of VRD and hands on training for welders organised. Special session on BBS organised for all HoDs and Project Managers. Interaction session with FR dress user group of SMS-I arranged.
10. Health check up for contractor workers deployed inside the plant.
11. Provision of safety alert through public announcement system in major project area. Audio message and alarm system installed at level crossings. Undertaking drives for Road Safety w.r.t. limit of speed to 20 Km/hr and surprise checking by DSOs.

Sustainable Performance Highlights 2012-13

Economic

1. 55 billion INR worth of projects commissioned; the highest for any year since inception.
2. 8.26 billion INR dividend paid.
3. 0.53 billion INR utilised in CSR activities.
4. 86.37 billion INR employee wages and benefits.

Environment

1. Particulate matter emission brought down to 0.88 kg/tcs from 1.01 kg/tcs in 2011-12.

2. Specific Effluent Discharge reduced to 2.22 m^3/tfs from 2.26 m^3/tfs in the previous year.
3. Specific Water Consumption reduced to 3.73 m3/tcs from 3.86 m^3/tcs in 2011-12.
4. Carbon dioxide intensity brought down to 2.75 T/tcs from 2.81 T/tcs over the past year.
5. Total Solid Waste Utilisation enhanced to 91 per cent from 86 per cent (2011-12).

Social

1. LTIFR and LDR reduced by 36 per cent and 58 per cent respectively during the last three years (2010-2012).
2. More than 21 lakhs people benefitted from the health services provided by SAIL during the year.
3. Students under BPL category provided education through 7 nos. Kalyan Vidyalaya (special schools) at five integrated steel plants.
4. Mid-day meals provided to over 22,000 students in different schools of Bhilai every day through Akshya Patra Foundation.
5. 18.76 million INR generated from orders obtained by women engaged in Mahila Samaj.
6. Solar Lanterns and Smokeless Chullahs distributed amongst the poor and needy in different parts of the country.

Table 4.1: Plant-wise Financial Performance (Profit before Tax) (in Crores)

Plant/Unit	*2013-14*	*2012-13*
Bhilai Steel Plant (BSP)	2084.84	2048.22
Durgapur Steel Plant (DSP)	415.60	552.66
Rourkela Steel Plant (RSP)	212.20	363.37
Bokaro Steel Plant (BSL)	202.01	307.50
IISCO Steel Plant (ISP)	-653.05	-158.73
Alloy Steels Plant (ASP)	-92.59	-119.53
Salem Steel Plant (SSP)	-375.55	-419.73
Visvesvaraya Iron & Steel Plant (VISP)	-122.68	-116.67
SAIL Refractory Unit (SRU)	3.00	9.76
Chandrapur Ferro Alloys Plant (CFP)	-77.65	-38.74
Raw Materials Division/Central Units*	1628.42	812.55

(Contd...)

SAIL: Profit Before Tax (PBT)	3224.55	3240.66
SAIL: Profit After Tax(PAT)	2616.48	2170.35

*including interest earned on deposits and retained in the books of Corporate Office The Profit After Tax (PAT) of SAIL during the financial year 2013-14 has increased by 446 crore.

Source: SAIL's Corporate Sustainability Report (2012-2013).

Table 4.2: Socio-economic Performance

Key Economic Indicators (In billion INR)	*2010-11*	*2011-12*	*2012-13*
Gross Turnover (Direct Economic Value Generated)	470.41	503.48	493.50
Net Turnover	427.19	456.54	439.61
Cost of Material Consumed including Bought out Goods	202.52	230.26	212.02
Employee Wages and Benefits	76.23	79.32	86.37
Payments to Providers of Capital			
- Interest (Finance Cost)	4.75	6.78	7.48
- Interest (Capital-Expenditure During construction)	6.08	8.68	8.00
- Dividends	9.91	8.26	8.26
- Community Investments (CSR Exp.)	0.68	0.61	0.53
- Contribution to Government / Exchequer for Taxes& Duties Including Dividends	111.68	110.08	121.22
Operating Profit (EBITA)	75.44	60.91	42.18
Profit After Tax	49.05	35.43	21.70
Retained Profits	31.80	23.60	9.01

Source: SAIL's Corporate Sustainability Report (2012-2013).

Gross Turnover of SAIL Stood at INR 493.50 billion for the year 2012-13 as compared to INR 503.48 billion for the year 2011-12. There has been steady increase in the wages and benefits offered to SAIL Employees and it has grown to INR 86.37 billion for 2012-13. The community investments made by SAIL as a part of its corporate social responsibility has seen a decline for past few years due to tough market situation resulting in lowers profits. SAIL made community investments of INR 0.53 billion during the year 2012-13. The Investment was INR 0.61 billion for 2011-12 and INR 0.68 billion during 2009-10.

Conclusion

The case for demonstrating corporate responsibility is getting stronger as expectations among key opinion formers, customers and the public are increasing over the years. Policies in the area of SD and CSR have to focus on the interrelation among different factors that hinder community well being. Such linkage is possible only when different departments in the government can take an integrated approach in policy development. Sustainable development for India will require a multi-disciplinary approach, spanning departments and regions and considering a long-term impact. India needs to build evidence sensing and participatory mechanisms as well as intra and extra-organisational capacity building to make CSR more robust and useful in achieving its goal of sustainable development.

Priority has to be accorded to activities pertaining to inclusive growth of society with special attention to development of weaker sections of society and the backward districts of the country and environment sustainability. Activities on capacity building, skill development, infrastructural development, education, promotion of heritage, art, culture and music, providing sanitation and healthcare facilities, promoting renewable energy, scholarship to under-privileged school children etc. may be chosen for creating a better linkage between SD and CSR. Activities like promoting research and excellence in the core area of operations of the company may also be chosen as this will lead to more reliable and secure environmental sustainability in the long run. Thus, CSR can be an effective tool for sustainable development.

References

1. Annual Report (2010-11), (2011-12), (2012-13), (2013-14) Ministry of Steel, Government of India.
2. Brundtland Commission. (1987). Our Common Future. Brussels: World Commission on Environment and Development.
3. Carroll, A.B. (1991). "The Pyramid of Corporate Social Responsibility: Toward the Moral Management or Organisational Stakeholders", Business Horizon, p. 9.
4. Dyllick, T., and Hockerts, K.(2002). Beyond the business case for corporate sustainability. Business Strategy and the Environment, 11: pp.130-141.
5. Elkington, J. (1997). Cannibals with Forks: The Triple Bottom Line of 21st Century Business. Oxford: Capstone.
6. European Commission (2006). "Implementing the Partnership for Growth and Jobs: Making Europe a Pole of Excellence on Corporate Social Responsibility", COM 136, Brussels.
7. Göbbels, M. (2003). "AA1000 and SA8000 compared: A systematic comparison of contemporary accountability standards", Managerial Auditing Journal 18 (1): pp. 53-8.
8. Hill, I. (2006), "How Finance Can Help Move CSR up the Agenda", The Cost and Management, Vol. 34, No. 6, November – December, pp. 5-9.
9. Hopkins, M. (1999). The Planetary Bargain: Corporate Social Responsibility Comes of Age, London: Macmillan.
10. Hussain B., and M. Hussain (2005), "Corporate Social Responsibility: Do Customers Get What They Expect?" Journal of Business Studies, Southeast University, ISSN- 1815- 3267 Vol. 1, No. 1, July-December, pp. 133-139.

11. Maignan, I. and Ferrell, O. (2003). 'Nature of Corporate Responsibilities: Perspectives from American, French, and German Consumers' Journal of Business Research, 56: 55- 67.
12. Mohr, L.A., D.J. Webb, and K.E. Harris (2001). "DO Consumers Expect Companies to be Socially Responsible? The Impact of Corporate Social Responsibility on Buying Behavior", Journal of Consumers Affairs, p. 45.
13. SAIL Sustainability Report (2012-13), (2013-14).
14. SAIL CSR Bulletin (2011-12).
15. http://en.wikipedia.org/wiki/Green_economy accessed on 12.6.14.
16. http://www.guardian.co.uk/world/2011/nov/08/australia-senate-passes-carbon-tax accessed on 14.6.14
17. http://ec.europa.eu/enterprise/policies/sustainable-business/corporate-social-responsibility/index_en.htm accessed on15.6.14.

Chapter 5

Factors affecting Adolescent Childbearing and Its Impacts on Maternal and Child Health in India

Dr R. Mutharayappa

"Sustainable development is the pathway to the future we want for all. It offers a framework to generate economic growth, achieve social justice, exercise environmental stewardship and strengthen governance."

– Ban Ki-moon

Introduction

Adolescent pregnancy is widely recognised as a complex and serious problem in India. Early childbearing appears to have negative effects beyond socio-economic and cultural factors (UNICEF, 2008). In some cases, the mother's age directly affects birth outcomes; in other cases, the mother's age influences other relevant factors that in turn affect her social, economic and physical well-being and that of her child. Studies conducted on adolescent pregnancy show that teenage pregnant women, especially those under the age of 19 years, suffer more complications like maternal morbidity and mortality and often give birth to premature and low birth weight babies (Bhagat, 2002).

Miscarriages, stillbirths and neo-natal deaths are more frequent among adolescent mothers. Biological vulnerability for adverse outcomes among younger mothers may persist due to physical immaturity and exacerbation of the effect of chronic malnutrition and scarce nutrients from the mother to foetus (Raj *et.al,* 2010). Factors such as early age at marriage, illiteracy, poor economic conditions and cultural issues are the main reasons for adolescent childbearing. This can be reduced with early and regular prenatal care (Alam, 2000). Generally, adolescents neglect their physical health regardless of pregnancy. Secondly, poor eating habits and poor healthcare

are relatively common among this age group (Raja *et. al.*, 2009). Lack of education and inadequate access to healthcare may also prevent adolescents from resorting to good antenatal care and skilled delivery care (Sivaram, *et.al,* 1995).

Studies conducted on adolescent childbearing show that adolescent pregnant women are at increased risk for domestic violence. A study conducted on teenage pregnant women revealed that 26 per cent of mothers aged 17 years or younger and 23 per cent of mothers aged 18 and 19 years experienced violence (Covington *et. al.*, 2001). Among teens who reported physical violence, over 50 per cent reported being injured in the abdominal area. While the majority of teens reported being battered by their husbands, about 25 per cent reported attacks by a relative, including mother (9.6 per cent), father (6.5 per cent) and brother (6.5 per cent) (Gessner and Perham, 1998). Adolescents who reported severe pre-natal violence were significantly more likely to deliver pre-term than those reporting other violence or no pre-natal violence (Covington *et. al*, 2001).

There is evidence to show the vulnerability of adolescent child-bearing. However, studies that analysed the factors responsible for adolescent childbearing and its implications for maternal and child healthcare are less. This is important because proper care during pregnancy and safe delivery can reduce maternal and child morbidity and mortality. Concerted efforts are, therefore, needed to provide useful information to planners and policy-makers to design appropriate strategies to bring about an improvement in maternal and child welfare. An attempt has been made in the present analysis to highlight factors affecting adolescent pregnancy and its effect on maternal and child health in India.

The focus of the study is: (a) to examine the extent of adolescent childbearing; (b) to study the factors affecting adolescent childbearing; and (c) to highlight the implications of adolescent childbearing on maternal and child health.

Data for the present study has been taken from the National Family Health Surveys (NFHS-1, NFHS-2 and NFHS-3) conducted during 1992-93, 1998-99 and 2005-06. The NFHS surveys were carried out in all the major states of India. For NFHS-1, as many as 89,777 ever-married women aged 13-49 years in 24 states were interviewed. For NFHS-2 and NFHS-3, about 91,000 ever-married women aged 15-49 years across 26 states, and 124,385 women aged 15-49 from 29 states were interviewed, respectively (IIPS and Macro International, 2007). In these surveys, the extent of adolescent pregnancies and problems of maternal and child health were measured more directly on a larger scale.

In all the NFHS surveys, women were asked about their current age, age at marriage, age at first childbirth and number of children both living and dead. NFHS-2 collected information from women about their two most recent births in the three years preceding the survey and for NFHS-3 the most recent births in the five years preceding the survey. For the present study, the problems relating to the most recent births have been taken. In all the surveys, the mother was asked if at any time of pregnancy she had experienced any of the following pregnancy-related problems: blurred vision, convulsions other than from fever, swelling of hands and feet, excessive fatigue, anaemia, and vaginal bleeding.

Women who had childbirths were asked if they had massive vaginal bleeding or very high fever at any time during the two months after delivery. Thirdly, in order to understand morbidity conditions during pregnancy, the survey asked whether respondents have taken any antenatal care during pregnancy, frequency of such care, place of delivery and problems during delivery. From this data, the extent of teenage pregnancies and problems during pregnancy and delivery has been analysed. In addition, socio-economic and demographic characteristics have been analysed to assess whether socio-economic variables had any effect on adolescent childbearing and its impact on maternal and child healthcare.

Characteristics of Adolescent Women

The National Family Health Surveys have collected information from women aged between 15 and 49 years. Of those surveyed, adolescent women aged 15-19 years accounted for 10.13 per cent in NFHS-1, 9.09 per cent in NFHS-2 and 5.50 per cent in NFHS-3. This indicates that marriage of girls at young ages is declining. The number of girls given in marriage before the age of 20 years is going down because pregnancy and motherhood at a very young age causes a number of health problems besides social, economic and emotional problems. In addition to higher levels of pregnancy, complications among young mothers, physiological immaturity and inexperience associated with childcare practices affect maternal and infant health. The information collected from women for the NFHS surveys varies between 1992-93 and 2005-06.

In NFHS-1, all ever-married women were included but during NFHS-3, unmarried women were also covered to understand reproductive health, nuptiality and gender relation; for the present study, only married women have been considered. For the present analysis, the number of ever-married women in the age group of 15-19 years in 1992-93 was 9,094. In 1998-99, it was 8,276 and in 2005-06 it was 6,842.

Data provided in Table 5.1 shows the demographic characteristics of adolescent women in the age group of 15-19 years. Over the period, the number of women in early marriage has reduced while the number of women marrying at 18 years and above has increased. For instance, the proportion of women at the age of 15 years was around eight per cent during NFHS-1 and it reduced to around six per cent in NFHS-3. However, for the age group of 19 years, it increased from 29 per cent in NFHS-1 to 33 per cent at NFHS-3. During the 1990s, the age at marriage was much below the legal age for marriage and more than two-thirds of women had got married before the age of menarche. Although the proportion reduced further in 2005-06, around 30 per cent of women had married before reaching the age of 15 years.

During NFHS-1, only 11 per cent of the women married before reaching the legal age and it increased slightly to around 16 per cent in 2005-06. The number of women who married before the legal age for marriage remained the largest group in India. Among the adolescent married women, around 47 per cent had at least one child at the time of survey in 1992-93 but in 2005-06, around 44 per cent of them had a child at the time of survey. Although adolescent pregnancy has reduced, more than two-thirds of women are bearing the burden of adolescent fertility and it is a major concern for a developing country like India. Interestingly, Table 5.1 shows that in 1992-93 around 12 per cent of women had two or more children, and it increased to 13 per cent in 1998-99, but reduced to around 10 per cent in 2005-06.

Table 5.1: Percentage of married women age 15-19 years by demographic characteristics

Demographic characteristics	*NFHS-1 N=9094*	*NFHS-2 N=8276*	*NFHS-3 N= 6842*
Age in single year			
15	7.4	7.9	5.8
16	12.6	14.1	11.0
17	18.6	18.6	16.6
18	32.4	30.3	33.3
19	29.0	29.1	33.3
Age at Marriage			
<15	43.0	29.5	29.6
15	19.1	21.0	19.2

(*Contd...*)

16	15.7	20.1	19.2
17	11.0	15.1	16.5
18	8.9	11.5	12.5
19	2.2	2.7	3.1
Current Marital Status			
Currently Married	97.8	97.9	98.3
Widow/Divorced/Separated	2.2	2.1	1.7
Ever had given Birth			
Yes	47.4	47.5	43.7
No	52.6	52.5	56.3
Children Born			
0	52.6	52.5	56.3
1	35.2	34.7	33.3
2	10.4	11.0	9.0
3 & Above	1.8	1.9	1.4
Total	**100.0**	**100.0**	**100.0**

Data provided in Table 5.2 shows the socio-economic characteristics of married women aged 15-19 years in India. Geographically, around 15.6 per cent of the adolescent women were found in urban areas from 1992-93 to 2005-06. The percentage of adolescent women from non-poor caste groups like Other Backward Classes and Others has decreased whereas that of Scheduled Castes and Scheduled Tribes has increased. Similarly, around 15 per cent of women belonged to Scheduled Castes and Scheduled Tribes in 1992-93 and it has increased to 23 per cent in 2005-06; the percentage of Other Backward Classes and Others that was around 75 per cent in 1992-93 decreased to around 65 per cent in 2005-06. Considering religion, over the period, the proportion of Hindu women decreased while that of Muslim women increased by around two per cent. Secondly, it can be observed from Table 5.2 that in 1992-93 around two-thirds of women in the age group of 15-19 years were illiterate.

This percentage has come down to around 53 in 1998-99 and 42 in 2005-06. The proportion of women with secondary level education and above increased from 14 per cent in 1992-93 to 25 per cent in 1998-99 and to around 36 per cent in 2005-06. The economic status of women during NFHS-2 shows that around 40 per cent of women had low standard of living and it reduced to around 28 per cent at the time of NFHS-3. During NFHS-1, data had not been collected on standard of living, and so we could not compare the standard of living of adolescent women in 1992-93. The working status of the women increased during NFHS-2, but decreased at the time of NFHS-3. During NFHS-1, around 25 per cent of adolescent women were working, and this has increased to around 29 per cent during NFHS-2 but reduced to around 23 per cent during NFHS-3.

Table 5.2: Percentage of married women aged 15-19 years by socio-economic characteristics

Socio-economic Characteristics	*NFHS-1 N=9094*	*NFHS-2 N=8276*	*NFHS-3 N= 6842*
Place of Residence			
Urban	15.1	14.7	16.1
Rural	84.9	85.3	83.9
Social Group			
Scheduled Caste	14.8	21.2	23.8
Scheduled Tribe	9.8	10.4	10.4
OBC	NA	34.9	42.5
Other	75.5	32.1	22.8
Religion			
Hindu	83.3	82.4	82.0
Muslim	13.2	14.6	15.2
Christian	1.1	1.4	1.1
Sikh	0.8	0.7	0.5
Other	1.5	0.9	1.2
Education			
Illiterate	67.1	53.4	41.9
Primary	18.6	18.8	21.2
Secondary	14.3	25.6	36.3
Higher	0.0	2.2	0.6
Household Standard of Living			
Low	NA	39.8	28.1
Medium	NA	50.1	32.8
High	NA	10.1	20.0
Dejure Resident	NA	NA	19.0
Working Status			
Yes	24.5	28.7	22.7
No	75.4	71.2	77.2
Total	**100.0**	**100.0**	**100.0**

Extent of Adolescent Women who had a Child

It is interesting to look at the data of adolescent women who had a child by region and inter-state variations. The data show that about 47 per cent of adolescent women had a child in 1992-93, which was almost the same during 1998-99 but reduced to about 44 per cent in 2005-06. Over a period, the percentage of adolescent women who had children reduced but it is still very high in the country. When we look at the data on regional variations among adolescents, it is the Northern region where the proportion of adolescent mothers was less during different NFH Surveys. It varies from about 40 per cent in 1992-93 to 38 per cent in 2005-06. The Western region had the maximum number of adolescent mothers in the age group of 15-19 years. These data are shown in Table 5.3.

Table 5.3: Percentage of Married Women who got Child among Adolescents by Regions

Region	NFHS-1		NFHS-2		NFHS-3	
	Per cent	*N*	*Per cent*	*N*	*Per cent*	*N*
North	40.5	884	38.9	653	38.1	675
Central	42.6	2502	47.1	2600	42.1	1756
East	45.3	2304	45.6	1940	45.2	2398
Northeast	61.3	318	50.6	257	49.3	225
West	57.5	1086	52.4	1084	47.9	722
South	51.2	2000	49.8	1742	42.1	1066
Total	**47.4**	**9094**	**47.5**	**8276**	**43.7**	**6841**

An interesting picture emerges when we look at the data on interstate variations for women aged 15-19 years which has been provided in Table-4. NFHS-1 found that the proportion of adolescent mothers was maximum in Assam (62 per cent), followed by Maharashtra and Karnataka (60 per cent). On the other hand, the same survey (NFHS-1) found fewer

Table 5.4: Percentage of Married Mothers in the Age Group of 15-19 years by States

States	NFHS-1		NFHS-2		NFHS-3	
	Per cent	*N*	*Per cent*	*N*	*Per cent*	*N*
Andhra Pradesh	49.5	975	49.8	851	40.9	509
Assam	62.5	261	49.8	205	48.2	168
Bihar	40.6	1172	43.5	1057	42.4	1073
Gujarat	47.1	261	47.8	276	45.4	218
Haryana	49.8	203	42.1	107	33.0	106
Himachal Pradesh	39.3	28	36.4	11	37.5	8
Jammu	36.4	22	50.0	26	50.0	16
Karnataka	58.9	518	54.5	475	48.0	371
Kerala	37.8	119	25.8	97	26.8	56
Madhya Pradesh	43.4	901	48.4	900	37.6	399
Maharashtra	60.7	825	54.0	806	49.2	502
Odisha	49.5	291	49.3	217	44.0	216
Punjab	42.6	94	42.4	59	31.7	63
Rajasthan	35.8	489	37.9	422	39.8	437
Tamil Nadu	49.2	388	50.0	320	37.7	130
West Bengal	50.4	841	47.7	665	49.2	778
Uttar Pradesh	42.2	1601	46.4	1700	43.4	1201
New Delhi	45.7	46	28.6	28	45.5	22
Total	**47.4**	**9094**	**47.5**	**8276**	**43.7**	**6841**

adolescent mothers in Rajasthan and Jammu (36 per cent) followed by Kerala (38 per cent). However, during NHFS-2 (1998-99), the maximum proportion (54 per cent) of adolescent mothers was found in Karnataka and Maharashtra, and least in Kerala (26 per cent) and Delhi (29 per cent). During NFHS-3, the maximum proportion of adolescent mothers was found in Jammu (50 per cent), West Bengal (49 per cent) and Maharashtra (49 per cent). The lowest number of adolescent mothers was found in Kerala (27 per cent), Punjab (31 per cent) and Haryana (33 per cent).

Data provided in Table 5.5 reveals the percentage of adolescent women currently having children, currently pregnant and pregnant for the first child. Around 48 per cent of adolescent women had children at the time of NFHS-1 and it reduced to 43.7 per cent at the time of NFHS-3 but the reduction was very less. Adolescent women currently pregnant were about 19 per cent in NFHS-1 and it increased to around 20 per cent in 2005-06. Women who were pregnant for the first child in NFHS-1 were about 23 per cent and this percentage increased to 25 per cent during NFHS-3.

Table 5.5: Percentage of Adolescent Women currently having Children, Currently pregnant and Pregnant for first child

	NFHS-1		*NFHS-2*		*NFHS-3*	
	Per cent	*N*	*Per cent*	*N*	*Per cent*	*N*
Adolescent women currently having children	47.4	9094	47.5	8276	43.7	6842
Adolescent women currently pregnant	18.8	8886	18.8	8276	19.9	6842
Adolescent women pregnant for first child	23.0	4642	23.6	4347	25	3854

Adolescent Maternal Health-care

Promotion of maternal and child health-care has been one of the important objectives of the family health programme and important elements of this programme include provision of antenatal care, encouragement of institutional deliveries, management of reproductive tract infections, sexually transmitted diseases etc. Antenatal care (ANC) refers to pregnancy-related healthcare, which is usually provided by a doctor, an ANM or any healthcare professional. Ideally, ANC should monitor a pregnancy for signs of complications, detect and treat pre-existing and concurrent problems of pregnancy, and provide advice and counselling on preventive care, diet during pregnancy, delivery care, postnatal care and related issues.

The Reproductive and Child Health Programme recommends that as part of antenatal care women should receive at least three antenatal check-ups which should include periodic monitoring of weight and blood pressure, abdominal examination, immunisation against tetanus, and management of iron and folic acid prophylaxis to control anaemia (Ministry of Health and Family Welfare, 2005: IIPS and Macro International, 2007). The National Family Health Survey has collected data from women regarding problems during pregnancy and their antenatal healthcare, their problems during pregnancy and treatment taken and the place of delivery. For the present study, we concentrate on ever married adolescent women aged 15-19 years who were pregnant and had given birth before the NFHS surveys.

As mentioned earlier, about 47 per cent of adolescent women during NFHS-1 and NFHS-2, and 43.7 per cent during NFHS-3 had given birth during the surveys. Of this, about 18 per cent were currently pregnant and 23 per cent of adolescent women were pregnant for the first child. But more than half of the women in NFHS-1 and about two-thirds of adolescent women in NFHS-2 and nearly 78 per cent of women in NFHS-3 had taken ANC when they were pregnant. To avoid complications during pregnancy, the timing and frequency of ANCs are very important. The surveys show that over the period, the ANC visits within the first trimester increased from 34 per cent during NFHS-1 to around 50 per cent during NFHS-3.

However, the percentage of women who had taken ANC in the third trimester decreased from 21 per cent in NFHS-1 to 10 per cent in NFHS-3. Secondly, the main objective of the Safe Motherhood as well as Reproductive and Child Health programmes is to encourage deliveries in hygienic conditions and supervised by trained health professionals. This is because institutional delivery reduces the risk of maternal death as well as risk of death of newborn. However, institutional delivery depends upon availability and accessibility of delivery services in areas where the mother resides. Data provided in Table 5.6 shows around 23 per cent of women were delivering in institutions while 77 per cent of women gave birth at home. More importantly, fewer women were using PNC services in the country. During NFHS-2, only 29 per cent of women had utilised PNC services, which increased to 35 per cent in NFHS-3.

Table 5.6: Percentage of Adolescent women who had ANC, place of delivery and post-natal care for the last childbirth

		NFHS-1	*NFHS-2*	*NFHS-3*
Women who had ANC		54.2	61.6	77.9
Place of delivery	Home	76.8	69.4	62.4
	Institution	23.2	30.6	37.6
Women who had post-natal care		-	28.8	35.0

Pregnancy Complications among Adolescent Women

This section explains the complications during pregnancy and post-delivery complications among adolescent women and the linkages with other obstetric care in India. Data in Table 5.7 depicts the complications during pregnancy for NFHS-2 and NFHS-3. During NFHS-2, more types of complications during pregnancy were collected. Overall, during NFHS-2, around 37 per cent of women aged 15-19 years reported that they did not have any complications during pregnancy. However, the maximum number of complications reported was about night blindness (about 22 per cent), followed by blurred (around 19 per cent) vision and convulsions (11 per cent).

Around two per cent of women had reported anemia and less than one per cent reported vaginal bleeding during NFHS-2. In NFHS-3, less serious complications were reported besides convulsions, swelling, fatigue and vaginal bleedings. As shown in the Table, about 12 per cent of adolescent women had reported that they did not have any complications during their pregnancy but around 50 per cent reported excessive fatigue, followed by swelling (23 per cent). Around three per cent reported vaginal bleeding.

Table 5.7: Percentage of adolescents who had pregnancy complication during last child birth

Type of complications	*NFHS-2*		*NFHS-3*	
	Per cent	*N*	*Per cent*	*N*
No Complications	37.2	1387	12.1	362
Night Blindness	21.6	803	NA	NA
Blurred vision	18.9	703	NA	NA
Convulsions	11.4	425	11.7	349
Swelling	6.4	240	23.4	698
Excessive Fatigue	2.9	109	49.9	1493
Anaemia	1.4	51	NA	NA
Vaginal Bleeding	0.2	10	2.7	82
Total	**100.0**	**3728**	**100.0**	**2984**

In the NFHS surveys, a woman who gave birth in the year preceding the survey was asked if she had massive vaginal bleeding or very high fever — both symptoms of possible postpartum complications — at any time during the two months after delivery. Women reported massive vaginal bleeding for 14 per cent of births and very high fever for 15 per cent of births. Both complications were more common among rural mothers rather than urban mothers. The likelihood of massive vaginal bleeding did not vary much by mother's age or birth order. Very high fever was more likely to be reported for first few births.

Table 5.7: Percentage of adolescent women who experienced post-delivery complications

Type of complications	*NFHS-2*		*NFHS-3*	
	Per cent	*N*	*Per cent*	*N*
Vaginal Bleeding	14.0	3728	14.1	2984
High Fever	14.1	3728	15.6	2984
Any one of them	15.2	3728	17.0	2984
Both	6.5	3728	6.4	2984
Not at all	78.3	3728	76.6	2984

The likelihood of having massive vaginal bleeding did not vary much by place of delivery, but very high fever was much more common for home delivery than for institutional births. Data also show that around seven per cent of women faced both types of problems, namely vaginal bleeding and high fever whereas around 15-17 per cent of women experienced only one problem. Overall, 21 to 23 per cent of women faced some kind of problem after delivery.

Determinants of Adolescent Childbearing and Its Linkages

To understand the demographic, socio-cultural, economic and regional variation of adolescent childbearing, pregnancy with first child and maternal healthcare multivariate analysis has been worked out. On demographic characteristics, age of women and age at marriage, socio-cultural and economic characteristics of social groups, education, religion and standard of living are considered. On spatial characteristics, place of residence and region are selected. The age of women considered as adolescent is 15-19 years, and hence to delineate the effect of different factors some modifications have been done. Similarly, women's age and age at first marriage have been clubbed into less than 18 years and 18 years and above.

Education has been categorised into illiterate, primary and secondary and above. Standard of living index is not available for NFHS-1 and at the time of NFHS-3, not de jure resident has also been considered as a separate category, but for better comparison of NFHS-2 and NFHS-3, not de jure resident category has not been considered here. Further, within religion, only Hindus and Muslims have been considered. The binary logistic regression is modelled to observe the determining factors of adolescent childrearing and adolescent maternal healthcare. The relative risk of being an adolescent mother, healthcare behaviour, and odds ratio have been worked out.

Determinants of Adolescent Childbearing

We have worked out the parameters of adolescent childbearing in the country between 1992-93 and 2005-06 using demographic, individual and social and economic components of their regulator and it has been presented in Table 5.9. Between NFHS-1 and NFHS-3, demographic variables like age of women and first age at marriage have been found highly significant in shaping the adolescent childbearing behaviour in the country. Age of marriage shows high variability when controlling for economic factors like standard of living of the households. However, data is not available for NFHS-1, and so it has not been presented for 1992-93.

Similarly, at the time of NFHS-1, the probability of childbearing was very high among the women who got married below the age of 18 years (OR: 9.5, $p>0.005$) but the relative risk reversed at the time of NFHS-2 and NFHS-3, when the women who were getting married above the age of 15 years were at highest risk. It was found that education plays a major role in shaping demographic behaviour in the country, and an attempt was made here to observe its effect in determining childbearing behaviour. It has been found that in NFHS-2 and 3, the risk of childbearing was high among women who were illiterate, and as the education level increases the risk reduces and it is highly significant. However, in NFHS-1, the risk was found high even among women who were highly educated compared to women who had primary or no education. Considering the standard of living, it was found that women who had low standard of living had 28 per cent more risk ($p> 0.005$) of childbearing compared to women with high standard of living. Though the caste of the women was not found significant across the periods, the lower castes like scheduled castes and scheduled tribes were at higher risk compared to the rest. Place of residence and regional pattern also have been found significant in shaping childbearing in the country.

Table 5.9: Determinants of Adolescent Childbearing by Background Characteristics

Characteristics	*NFHS-1*		*NFHS-2*		*NFHS-3*	
	Exp β	*p Value*	*Exp β*	*p Value*	*Exp β*	*p Value*
Age of Women						
18 years & Above®						
<18 years	0.288	0.000	3.989	0.000	4.178	0.000
Age at Marriage						
18 years & Above®						
<18 years	9.557	0.000	0.102	0.000	0.056	0.000
Educational Attainment						
Secondary & Higher ®						
No Education	0.656	0.000	1.591	0.000	1.285	0.002
Primary	0.741	0.000	1.471	0.000	1.124	0.186
Religion of Women						
Muslim®						
Hindu	0.682	0.000	1.380	0.000	1.244	0.024
Standard of Living index						
High®						
Low	@	@	1.281	0.014	1.228	0.033
Medium	@	@	1.149	0.136	0.999	0.993
Social Group of Women						
Other®						
SC	0.845	0.013	1.028	0.727	1.354	0.004
ST	0.740	0.000	1.057	0.552	1.156	0.248
OBC	@		0.834	0.006	1.056	0.549
Place of Residence						
Urban ®						
Rural	1.178	0.018	0.839	0.021	0.894	0.223
Regions						
South®						
North	1.841	0.000	0.555	0.000	0.933	0.605
Central	1.762	0.000	0.837	0.014	1.138	0.207
East	1.450	0.000	0.747	0.000	1.144	0.174
Northeast	0.686	0.008	1.053	0.754	1.562	0.024
West	0.732	0.000	1.119	0.222	1.482	0.002
Constant	0.910	0.661	0.943	0.808	1.124	0.695

@ Data Not Available on SLI for NFHS-1 and also for OBC caste group.

Determinants of Adolescent Pregnancy

Data provided in Table 5.10 shows the determinants of pregnancy at the time of survey among adolescent women, and here we have also tried to observe the determinants during 1992-93 to 2005-06. Demographic variables like age and marriage age have been found significant for NFHS-1 and NFHS-3 but not for NFHS-2. It has been found that women who get married before the age of 18 years are at higher risk of being pregnant (OR: 1.26, $p<0.02$) compared to those who married after 18 years of age. Educational attainment, religion, standard of living and rural-urban differentials and caste group differentials have not been found significant for the risk of being pregnant under the model. However, among social groups, scheduled caste women have been found to be at higher risk of being pregnant (18 per cent in NFHS-2 and 10 per cent in NFHS-3).

Table 5.10: Determinants of Adolescent Pregnancy with First Child

Characteristics	*NFHS-1*		*NFHS-2*		*NFHS-3*	
	Exp β	*p Value*	*Exp β*	*p Value*	*Exp β*	*p Value*
Age of Women						
18 years & Above®						
<18 years	0.649	0.000	0.940	0.421	1.416	0.001
Age at Marriage						
18 years & Above®						
<18 years	1.266	0.026	1.138	0.437	0.814	0.071
Educational Attainment						
Secondary & Higher ®						
No Education	1.203	0.074	0.855	0.111	0.852	0.163
Primary	0.874	0.247	0.941	0.588	0.922	0.507
Religion of Women						
Muslim®						
Hindu	0.901	0.349	1.185	0.122	1.198	0.169
Household Standard of Living index						
High®						
Low	@	@	0.914	0.552	0.954	0.726
Medium	@	@	1.037	0.799	0.821	0.093
Social Group of Women						
Other®						
SC	1.014	0.896	0.910	0.387	1.041	0.777
ST	0.679	0.003	1.177	0.219	1.109	0.550
OBC	@	@	1.033	0.733	0.757	0.020
Place of Residence						
Urban ®						
Rural	1.253	0.028	0.954	0.647	0.926	0.524
Regions						
South®						
North	1.822	0.000	1.210	0.234	0.568	0.002

(*Contd...*)

Central	2.055	0	1.445	0.000	0.686	0.006
East	1.334	0.004	1.802	0.000	0.840	0.180
Northeast	1.002	0.994	1.913	0.005	0.630	0.110
West	1.561	0.002	1.021	0.860	0.808	0.208
Constant	2.347	0.004	1.255	0.536	0.381	0.007

@ Data Not Available on SLI for NFHS-1 and also for OBC caste group.

Ante-Natal Care among Adolescent Women

Table 5.11 delineates the determinants of ante-natal care among adolescent women. Studies conducted on the subject have depicted that maternal healthcare, mainly ANC, has a major role in shaping obstetric health. Here, most of the factors considered in the model have been found significant except for religion. Early age at marriage was found to be having very poor performance on ANC, and at the time of NFHS-1, it was found that among those whose age at marriage was less than 18 years, 77 per cent (p>0.005) were less likely to use ANC services at the time of pregnancy.

But, surprisingly at the time of NFHS-2, the reverse situation was found, and the model shows that among those who get married before age 18, 60 per cent were more likely to use ANC services. Standard of living is highly significant for utilisation of ANC services, and as the standard of living increases the utilisation also increases. Similarly, at the time of NFHS-2, 15 per cent more women with better standard of living were using ANC services compared to women with lower standard of living. The same has been found on caste and place of residence parameters. At the time of NFHS-3, less women from rural areas (OR: 0.75, p>0.005) had utilised the services compared to urban ones.

Table 5.11: Determinants of ANC among Adolescent Women

Characteristics	*NFHS-1*		*NFHS-2*		*NFHS-3*	
	Exp β	*p Value*	*Exp β*	*p Value*	*Exp β*	*p Value*
Age of Women						
18 years & Above®						
<18 years	0.923	0.334	1.064	0.476	0.785	0.063
Age at Marriage						
18 years & Above®						
<18 years	0.341	0.000	1.597	0.025	0.665	0.184
Educational Attainment						
Secondary & Higher ®						
No Education	4.983	0.000	0.288	0.000	0.309	0.000
Primary	1.526	0.033	0.622	0.001	0.894	0.545

(*Contd...*)

Religion of Women						
Muslim®						
Hindu	1.036	0.748	0.845	0.175	0.912	0.602
Standard of Living index						
High®						
Low	@	@	0.481	0.000	0.367	0.000
Medium	@	@	0.632	0.009	0.491	0.000
Social Group of Women						
Other®						
SC	1.213	0.067	0.719	0.008	0.498	0.001
ST	2.059	0.000	0.428	0.000	0.577	0.017
OBC	@	@	0.667	0.000	0.376	0.146
Place of Residence						
Urban ®						
Rural	1.591	0.000	0.434	0.000	0.757	0.000
Regions						
South®						
North	8.443	0.000	0.109	0.000	0.174	0.000
Central	8.657	0.000	0.088	0.000	0.226	0.000
East	5.441	0.000	0.207	0.000	0.110	0.000
Northeast	9.826	0.000	0.286	0.000	0.077	0.000
West	2.547	0.000	0.556	0.001	0.161	0.000
Constant	0.036	0.000	131.487	0.000	702.593	0.000

@ Data Not Available on SLI for NFHS-1 and also for OBC caste group.

Place of Delivery among Adolescent Women

Information on place of delivery, i.e., institutional delivery among adolescent women at three different points of time or over the period 1992-93 to 2005-06, are provided in Table 5.12. It is clear from the table that among the factors considered for the model to depict the determinants for place of delivery, age at marriage, educational attainment, religion, standard of living, and place of residence have been found to be highly significant to significant in choosing institutional delivery among women in the age group of 15-19 years. Educational attainment and standard of living are positively linked to institutional delivery from 1992-93 to 2005-06.

Similarly, during NFHS-1 and NFHS-2, uneducated women rarely utilised institutional delivery – 0.14, ($p>0.005$) and 0.32, ($p>0.005$) respectively. However, over the period, institutional delivery has increased. However, it is interesting to mention here that at the time of NFHS-3, women with secondary level of education and above had fewer institutional deliveries compared to illiterate or primary educated women. Place of residence factor shows that although institutional delivery has increased in rural areas, the probability of use of institutions for delivery is much less there compared to urban areas. This may also be due to poor availability and accessibility of delivery facilities in rural areas of the country compared to urban areas.

Table 5.12: Determinants of Place of Delivery among Adolescent Women

Characteristics	NFHS-1		NFHS-2		NFHS-3	
	Exp β	p Value	Exp β	p Value	Exp β	p Value
Age of Women						
18 years & Above®						
<18 years	1.021	0.833	0.982	0.843	4.181	0.000
Age at Marriage						
18 years & Above®						
<18 years	1.874	0.003	1.524	0.022	0.056	0.000
Educational Attainment						
Secondary & Higher ®						
No Education	0.138	0.000	0.322	0.000	1.283	0.002
Primary	0.449	0.000	0.684	0.001	1.128	0.175
Religion of Women						
Muslim®						
Hindu	0.670	0.001	0.561	0.000	1.243	0.024
Household Standard of Living index						
High®						
Low	@	@	0.355	0.000	1.227	0.034
Medium	@	@	0.524	0.000	0.991	0.921
Social Group of Women						
Other®						
SC	0.837	0.000	0.719	0.010	1.357	0.003
ST	0.440	0.000	0.376	0.000	1.158	0.243
OBC	@	@	0.834	0.097	1.053	0.570
Place of Residence						
Urban ®						
Rural	0.232	0.000	0.303	0.000	0.904	0.272
Regions						
South®						
North	0.218	0.000	0.274	0.000	0.931	0.594
Central	0.214	0.000	0.213	0.000	1.136	0.212
East	0.383	0.000	0.404	0.000	1.134	0.202
Northeast	0.182	0.000	0.222	0.000	1.557	0.025
West	0.680	0.002	0.569	0.000	1.469	0.003
Constant	31.143	0.000	58.662	0.000	1.103	0.741

@ Data Not Available on SLI for NFHS-1 and also for OBC caste group.

Complication during Last Pregnancy among Adolescent Women

Table 5.13 explains the complications during pregnancy for NFHS-2 and NFHS-3. It shows that at the time of NFHS-2, women who were below the age of 18 years were at higher risk of pregnancy complications (OR: 1.32, $p>0.005$) compared to those above 18 years. Nevertheless, at the time of NFHS-3, women aged 18 years and above faced higher risk of pregnancy-related complications compared to women who were younger. Hindu women faced more pregnancy-related complications compared to Muslim women. Place of residence shows that women in rural areas experienced less pregnancy-related problems compared to urban women.

During NFHS-3, the odds ratio of pregnancy complication was 0.62 ($p>0.005$) among adolescent women in rural areas. Regional dynamics of pregnancy-related complications shows that except for the western region, all regions compared to the southern region had higher risk of pregnancy-related complications. On the other hand, women from the eastern region experienced four times ($p>0.005$) more complications during pregnancy compared to women from the southern region. However, at the time of NFHS-2, the women of southern region experienced a higher percentage of pregnancy-related complications compared to the other regions.

Table 5.13: Complications during Pregnancy among Adolescent Women

Characteristics	*NFHS-2*		*NFHS-3*	
	Exp β	*p Value*	*Exp β*	*p Value*
Age of Women				
18 years & Above®				
<18 years	1.320	0.002	0.843	0.114
Age at Marriage				
18 years & Above®				
<18 years	0.907	0.357	0.890	0.650
Educational Attainment				
Secondary & Higher ®				
No Education	0.981	0.847	0.711	0.002
Primary	1.087	0.452	0.900	0.412
Religion of Women				
Muslim®				
Hindu	1.343	0.010	1.220	0.150
Household Standard of Living index				
High®				
Low	1.000	0.999	1.076	0.591
Medium	1.023	0.854	0.993	0.955

(*Contd...*)

Social Group of Women				
Other®				
SC	1.018	0.880	1.112	0.471
ST	1.038	0.794	1.085	0.639
OBC	0.865	0.132	1.450	0.005
Place of Residence				
Urban ®				
Rural	0.829	0.077	0.619	0.000
Regions				
South®				
North	0.663	0.007	1.212	0.301
Central	0.561	0.000	1.676	0.000
East	0.678	0.000	4.062	0.000
Northeast	0.823	0.414	1.862	0.015
West	0.880	0.340	0.964	0.832
Constant	0.326	0.001	2.091	0.123

Conclusion

The findings of the study show that marriage of girls at young ages is declining. Secondly, girls given in marriage before 20 years of age are going down. This is because marriage of girls at young ages leads to teenage pregnancy and motherhood. Young women who become pregnant and give birth experience a number of health problems as well as social, economic and emotional problems. In addition to higher levels of pregnancy complications among young mothers because of physiological immaturity and inexperience associated with childcare practices, marriages at young ages also affect maternal and child health.

Thirdly, women educational attainment, religion, standard of living and rural-urban differentials and caste group differentials in relative risk of being pregnant have not been found significant. However, among the social groups, scheduled caste women have been found to face an 18 per cent higher risk of being pregnant. Early marriage leads to very poor performance on ANC. Educational attainment and standard of living are positively linked to institutional delivery. Place of residence shows that although over a period of time, institutional deliveries have increased in rural areas the probability of use of institutions for delivery is much less compared to urban areas. Regional dynamics of pregnancy-related complications show that except for the western region, all regions had a higher risk of pregnancy-related complications compared to the south. Also, women from the eastern region experienced four times more complications during pregnancy compared to women from the southern region.

References

1. Alam, N 2000. "Teenage motherhood and infant mortality in Bangladesh: Maternal age-dependent effect of parity one", Journal of Bio-social Science, Vol. 32, pp. 229-236.
2. Bhagat, R B 2002. Early Marriages in India: A Socio-demographic Study, Rajat Publications, New Delhi.
3. International Institute for Population Sciences (IIPS) and Macro International. 2007, National Family Health Survey (NFHS-3) 2005-06, India, Volume-1.
4. Raj, A, N Saggurti, D Balaiah, J G Silverman. 2009. "Prevalence of child marriage and its effect on fertility and fertility-control outcomes of young women in India: a cross-sectional, observational study", Lancet, Issue 373, pp. 1883-1889.
5. Raj Anita, Niranjan Saggurti, Michael Winter, Alan Labonte, Michele R Decker, Donta Balaiah, Jay G Silverman. 2010. "The effect of maternal child marriage on morbidity and mortality of children under 5 in India: cross sectional study of a nationally representative sample", http://dx.doi.org/10.1136/bmj.b4258 (Published 21 January 2010).
6. Sivaram M, J Richard, P S S Rao. 1995. "Early marriage among rural and urban females in south India", Journal of Biosocial Science. Vol. 27(3), pp. 325-331.
7. UNICEF, 2008. The State of the World's Children 2008, Child survival, www.unicef.org/sowc08/docs/sowc08.pdf.
8. Covington, D L, B J Justason and L N Wright. 2001. "Severity, manifestations, and consequences of violence among pregnant adolescents" *Journal of Adolescent Health 28*, pp. 55-61.
9. Gessner, B D, K A Perham-Hester. 1998, Experience of violence among teenage mothers in Alaska, Journal of Adolescent Health, *22*, pp. 383-388.

Chapter 6

Changing Scenario of Insurance Sector in India: An Analysis

Dr Suman Kalyan Chaudhury and
Dr Sukanta Sarkar

"The development of civilisation and industry in general has always shown itself so active in the destruction of forests that everything that has been done for their conservation and production is completely insignificant in comparison."
–Karl Marx

Introduction

Insurance is the most effective risk mitigation mechanism to reduce the vulnerability of the people from the impacts of disease, disability, untimely death, and natural catastrophes. In a developing country like India the need for such a safety net is much greater, particular at the low income levels where vulnerability to risks is much greater and social security programmes are not effective due to poor governance. Insurance is a capital-intensive industry. It is a long-gestation business. In order to mobilise high rates of household savings the industry needs huge sums of capital to continue growing at rates seen in the past five years. The law provides for participation of global insurance firms in the Indian market only through joint ventures with Indian partners. Insurance reform is a prerequisite for reforms in social security, healthcare system and financial markets (India Insurance Sector Assistance Review, 2012).

The insurance sector is very significant to every developing country. It develops the habit of savings which, in turn, generates long-term investible funds for improving infrastructural facilities. The nature of insurance business ensures constant inflow of funds and challenges such as unprecedented volatility, changing customer profiles and existing regulators. It helps create both direct and indirect employment in the economy.

Alongside regular jobs in insurance, there is always demand for a range of associated professionals such as brokers, insurance advisors, agents, underwriters, claims managers and actuaries. The increasing insurance business has increased the demand for highly skilled professionals as well as semi-skilled and unskilled people (Kartheeswari and Rajeswari, 2012).

The performance of life insurance industry primarily depends upon two important functions: one is underwriting and the other is settlement of claims. Life insurance contract is an agreement wherein the insurer agrees to pay a certain sum to the insured upon the happening of events specified in the policy and upon the nature and conditions of the policy. A claim is a demand on the insurer to fulfill it as a part of the promise and its settlement either at the time of the maturity or to the beneficiary/nominee in the case of death of the policy holder (Nagaraja, 2015). During the post-1990 period, services sector in most of the Asian economies witnessed growth fuelled by substantial changes in the financial sector of these economies. The insurance industry, in most of the Asian economies, ASEAN and SAARC economies in particular, was publicly owned and remained isolated from participation of either domestic private insurers or foreign insurers or participation of both (Sen, 2008).

Meaning of the Concept

From Investopedia, Insurance means a contract in which an individual or entity receives financial protection or reimbursement against losses from an insurance company. The company pools clients' risks to make payments more affordable for the insured. In insurance, the insurance policy is a contract between the insurer and the insured, known as the policyholder, which determines the claims which the insurer is legally required to pay. Insurance contracts are designed to meet specific needs and thus have many features not found in many other types of contracts. The insurance policy is generally an integrated contract, meaning that it includes all forms associated with the agreement between the insured and insurer (Insurance Policy, 2015).

Insurance is the backbone in managing the risk of the country. The insurance providers offer diversity of products to business, providing protection from risk thereby ensuring financial security. It helps individual and organisation to minimise the consequences of risk which impart significant cause on the growth and development of insurance industry (Bawa and Chattha, 2013). Life insurance was once sold primarily by career life agents, captive agents that represent a single insurance company and by independent agents who represent several insurers.

Now life insurance company products are sold by direct mail, telephone, and internet directly to the public. Despite its teeming one billion populations, India still has a low insurance penetration more particularly in the rural segment. Along side the tied agents for selling life insurance products, alternative channels like corporate agents, brokers and bancassurance have emerged and are playing a greater role in distribution of life insurance products and services (Krishnan, 2012).

Importance of Insurance

Insurance is the backbone of a country's risk management system. Risk is an inherent part of our lives. The insurance providers offer a variety of products to businesses and individuals in order to provide protection from risk and to ensure financial security. They are an important component in the financial intermediation chain of a country and are a source of long-term capital for infrastructure and long-term projects (Bhat, 2005). Along with the other objectives of insurance like financial security, tax benefits etc. one of the major objectives is saving and investment. Traditional life insurance policies like endowment were becoming unattractive and not meeting the aspirations of the policyholders as the policyholder found that the sum assured guaranteed on maturity had really depreciated in real value because of the depreciation in the value of money (Srivastava *et. al.*, 2012).

The insurance sector plays a critical role in a country's economic development. It acts as mobilise of savings, a financial intermediary, a promoter of investment activities, a stabiliser of financial markets and a risk manager. The life insurance sector plays an important role in providing risk cover, investment and tax planning for individuals; the non-life insurance industry provides a risk cover for assets. Health insurance and pension systems are fundamental to protecting individuals against the hazards of life, and India, as the second-most populous nation in the world, offers significant potential for that type of cover. Furthermore, fire and liability insurance are essential for corporations to safeguard infrastructure projects and investment risks. Private insurance systems complement social security systems and add value by matching risk with price (Rao and Srinivasulu, 2013).

Investment is primary requirement of common man to give fight to the uncontrollable circumstances to reduce the risk of life. Insurance is a tool which safeguards an individual with benefits. As there is increase in risk due to imbalances in nature, growth is found in all corners of world in the form of insurance (Kotgiri, 2013). It involves pooling funds from many insured entities (known as exposures) to pay for the losses that some may incur. The insured entities are protected from risk for a fee, with the fee being dependent upon the frequency and severity of the event occurring. In order to be an insurable risk, the risk insured against must meet certain characteristics. Risk which can be insured by private companies typically shares seven common characteristics:

1. Since insurance operates through pooling resources, the majority of insurance policies are provided for individual members of large classes, allowing insurers to benefit from the law of large numbers in which predicted losses are similar to the actual losses.
2. The loss takes place at a known time, in a known place, and from a known cause. The classic example is death of an insured person on a life insurance policy. Fire, automobile accidents, and worker injuries may all easily meet this criterion.
3. The event that constitutes the trigger of a claim should be fortuitous, or at least outside the control of the beneficiary of the insurance.
4. The size of the loss must be meaningful from the perspective of the insured.
5. There are two elements that must be at least estimable, if not formally calculable: the probability of loss, and the attendant cost.
6. Insurable losses are ideally independent and non-catastrophic, meaning that the losses do not happen all at once and individual losses are not severe enough to bankrupt the insurer; insurers may prefer to limit their exposure to a loss from a single event to some small portion of their capital base (Insurance, 2015).

Types of Insurance

Insurance companies may be classified into two groups: (a) Life insurance companies, which sell life insurance, annuities and pensions products; and (b) Non-life or property/casualty insurance companies, which sell other types of insurance. General insurance companies can be further divided into sub-categories: (a) Standard lines; and (b) Excess lines. In most countries, life and non-life insurers are subject to different regulatory regimes and different tax and accounting rules. In the United States, standard line insurance companies are insurers that have received a license or authorisation from a state for the purpose of writing specific kinds of insurance in that state, such as automobile insurance or homeowners' insurance. Excess line insurance companies typically insure risks not covered by the standard lines insurance market, due to a variety of reasons. They are typically referred to as non-admitted or unlicenced insurers (Insurance, 2015).

Life insurance is an insurance coverage that pays out a certain amount of money to the insured or their specified beneficiaries upon a certain event such as death of the individual who is insured. This protection is offered in a Family takaful plan, a Shariah-based approach to protecting you and your family. The coverage period for life insurance is usually more than a year. So this requires periodic premium payments, either monthly, quarterly or annually.

General insurance is basically an insurance policy that protects against losses and damages other than those covered by life insurance. For more comprehensive coverage, it is vital to know about the risks covered to ensure that individual and family are protected from unforeseen losses. The coverage period for most general insurance policies and plans is usually one year, whereby premiums are normally paid on a one-time basis (Insurance info, 2015).

Global Insurance Market

Global insurance premiums grew by 2.7 per cent in inflation-adjusted terms in 2010 to $4.3 trillion, climbing above pre-crisis levels. The return to growth and record premiums generated during the year followed two years of decline in real terms. Life insurance premiums increased by 3.2 per cent in 2010 and non-life premiums by 2.1 per cent. While industrialised countries saw an increase in premiums of around 1.4 per cent, insurance markets in emerging economies saw rapid expansion with 11 per cent growth in premium income (Insurance, 2015).

Insurance today has emerged as attractive and stable investment alternatives that offer total protection to life, health and wealth. In terms of returns, insurance product today offers competitive returns ranging from seven per cent to nine per cent. Besides, returns what really increases the appeal of insurance is the benefit of life protection from insurance products along with critical illness cover benefits. The trend in developed economies, where people no longer retire earlier, is now emerging in India, where once the fear was dying too earlier, now with longevity the fear also is of living too long and outliving one's assets (Krishnan, 2012).

In the United States, insurance is regulated by the states under the McCarran-Ferguson Act, with periodic proposals for federal intervention and a nonprofit coalition of state insurance agencies called the National Association of Insurance Commissioners works to harmonise the country's different laws and regulations. In the European Union, the Third Non-Life Directive and the Third Life Directive, both passed in 1992 and effective 1994, created a single insurance market in Europe and allowed insurance companies to offer insurance anywhere in the EU (subject to permission from authority in the head office) and allowed insurance consumers to purchase insurance from any insurer in the EU (Insurance, 2015).

Insurance Industry before Independence

In India, insurance has a deep-rooted history. Insurance in various forms has been mentioned in the writings of Manu, Yagnavalkya and Kautilya. Insurance practice (non-life insurance business), was developed further in India as can be seen in the historical records of medieval period of Emperor Akbar's regime, showing the developed system of providing cover by the State to the farmers for their loss by either natural hazards or damage by the hostilities and warlike operations taking place in the empire's territory (Radhakrishnan, 2012). Insurance in its current form has its history dating back until 1818, when Oriental Life Insurance Company was started by Anita Bhavsar in Kolkata to cater to the needs of European community. The pre-independence era in India saw discrimination between the lives of foreigners (English) and Indians with higher premiums being charged for the latter. In 1870, Bombay Mutual Life Assurance Society became the first Indian insurer (Insurance in India, 2015).

In 1818, a British company called Oriental Life Insurance setup the first insurance firm in India followed by the Bombay Assurance Company in 1823 and the Madras Equitable Life Insurance Society in 1829. Though all this companies were operating in India but insuring the life of European living in India only. Insurance business was subjected to Indian Company Act 1866, without any specific regulation. In 1905, the slogan "Be Indian-Buy Indian" declared by Swadeshi Movement gave birth to dozens of indigenous life insurance and provident fund companies. In 1937, the Government of India setup a consultative committee and finally first comprehensive 'insurance act' was passed in 1938 (Srivastava *et. al.* 2012). The first general insurance company, Triton Insurance Company Ltd., was established in 1850. It was owned and operated by the British. The first indigenous general insurance company was the Indian Mercantile Insurance Company Limited set up in Bombay in 1907 (Sinha, 2002).

Later in 1928, the Indian Insurance Companies Act was enacted to enable the government to collect statistical information about both life and non-life insurance business transacted in India by Indian and foreign insurers including provident insurance societies. In 1938, with a view to protecting the interest of insuring public, the earlier legislation was consolidated and amended by the Insurance Act 1938 with comprehensive provisions for detailed and effective control over the activities of insurers. By 1947, Indian Insurance Industry's domestic sector controlled over 50 per cent of premiums in Life as well as General Insurance sector (Radhakrishnan, 2012).

Insurance Industry after Independence

Insurance in India refers to the market for insurance in India which covers both the public and private sector organisations. It is listed in the Constitution of India in the Seventh Schedule as a Union List subject, meaning it can only be legislated by the Central Government (Insurance in India, 2014). The insurance amendment act of 1950 abolished principal agencies. There were a large number of insurance companies and the level of competition was high. There were also allegations of unfair trade practices. The Government of India decided to nationalise insurance business (Shikhare, 2015). The picture changed after the Independence. In 1956, 245 Indian and foreign life insurers and provident societies were nationalised, and a new single entity namely, Life Insurance Corporation (LIC) was established by passing the LIC Act 1956.

Similarly, in 1972, 107 general insurers were nationalised through the passing of General Insurance Business (Nationalisation) Act, 1972. The then existing 107 insurers were amalgamated and grouped into five companies, viz., National Insurance Company (NIC), New India Assurance Company (NIAC), Oriental Insurance Company (OIC), and United India Insurance Company (UIIC), and General Insurance Corporation (GIC). Thus, in 1956 and in 1972, the competitive, private insurance industry was transformed into monopolistic and oligopolistic state or public sector insurance industry in India (Chanbasha and Kumar, 2014).

After the nationalisation the life insurance business has grown substantially in very first year i.e. from Rs 200 crore upto 1956 to Rs 328 crores in 1957 and till privatisation in 2000 the business was transacting worth Rs 73436 crores. Prior to nationalisation of the General Insurance Business in 1972 by enactment of the General Insurance Business Nationalisation Act 1972 there were 55 Indian Companies and 52 non-Indian Companies carrying of the business of General Insurance in India. Before the nationalisation the total premium written by these companies was Rs 170 crores as on 1971 (Recent Trends in Insurance Sector, 2012).

United India Insurance Company is a leading Public Sector General Insurance Company wholly owned by Government of India with a targeted gross premium of about Rs 10,000 crores. It is a rapidly growing company with more than 1600 offices, highest network in the whole non-life insurance industry throughout the country. The company has just completed 75 years of commendable service and leading the non-life insurance industry with its innovative products and approach.

Life Insurance Corporation of India is an Indian state-owned insurance group and investment company headquartered in Mumbai. It is the largest insurance company in India with an estimated asset value of Rs 1560482 crore (US$250 billion). The company was founded in 1956 when the Parliament of India passed the Life Insurance of India Act that nationalised the private insurance industry in India. LIC offers a variety of insurance products to its customers such as insurance plans, pension plans, unit-linked plans, special plans and group schemes. Today, it has eight zonal offices, around 109 divisional offices, 2,048 branches and 992 satellite offices and corporate offices. LIC Golden Jubilee Foundation was established in 2006 as a charity organisation. This entity has the aim of promoting education, alleviation of poverty, and providing better living conditions for the under-privileged. LIC had 11,95,916 agents as on 31 March 2014, out of which the number of active agents were 11,32,677 (Life Insurance Corporation of India, 2015).

India's insurance sector is expected to quadruple to about $250 billion over the next decade from around $60 billion now, according to a report by the Confederation of Indian Industry (CII). Insurance sector in India along with banking services add up to a significant portion of India's Gross Domestic Product. Insurance is a big and one of the most rapidly growing sectors in India. It's the prime reasons why leading market players are attracted to the Indian insurance market for business expansion. The Confederation of Indian Industry indicates that it has recorded instant and steady growth with a record growth rate of 32 per cent to 34 per cent. India has the largest number of life insurance policies in the world which is great news for the leading insurance companies in India. India's state-owned life insurance corporation leads the life insurance sectors in India. Despite all these facts and figures, around 80 per cent of Indian population doesn't have life insurance coverage. Amongst these 80 per cent people most of them don't have any kind of life coverage, while some of them do have some sort of health insurance and other non-life insurance policies.

Indian health-care industry presently, offers immense opportunities to the leading players like New India Assurance, United India Insurance,

National Insurance, ICICI Lombard and Oriental Insurance, as the penetration in India is still extremely low. About 85 per cent of American Population carries health insurance subscription in global settings funded by Government or Insurance Companies. While a comparison of health-care spending patterns between India and developed countries speak about the immense potential, as only five per cent Indians avail the same. In Canada and UK, Healthcare is absolutely free of cost (Thakur and Kumar, 2013).

Insurance in India used to be tightly regulated and monopolised by state-run insurers. Following the move towards economic reform in the early 1990s, various plans to revamp the sector finally resulted in the passage of the Insurance Regulatory and Development Authority (IRDA) Act of 1999. Significantly, the insurance business was opened on two fronts. Firstly, domestic private-sector companies were permitted to enter both life and non-life insurance business. Secondly, foreign companies were allowed to participate, albeit with a cap on shareholding at 26 per cent. With the introduction of the 1999 IRDA Act, the insurance sector joined a set of other economic sectors on the growth march (Sinha, 2014).

By 2012, Indian Insurance is a US$72 billion industry. However, only two million people (0.2 per cent of the total population of one billion) are covered under Mediclaim, whereas in developed nations like USA about 75 per cent of the total populations are covered under some insurance scheme. With more and more private companies in the sector, this situation is expected to change (Insurance in India, 2015).

Privatisation of Insurance Industry

The liberalisation of Indian economy ushered in an era of competitive marketing leading to the radical changes in the entire gamut of products and services. In the huge service sector, insurance sector is one of the most important entities which has been growing relatively fast in India. At present there are twenty three players in the Indian life insurance industry out of which Life Insurance Corporation is one of the leading public companies, holds largest number of policies in the world to suit different financial requirement of an individual. With a greater choice and an increasing awareness, there is a continuous increase in the customer's expectations and they demand better quality service (Sandhu and Bala, 2011).

The economic reforms initiated in the early 90s paved the way for the growth and opening up of the financial sector, which led to a sustained period of economic growth. The insurance industry was opened up for private players in 2000, and has seen tremendous growth over the past decade with the entry of global insurance majors (Rao and Srinivasulu, 2013). The Congress government (1991-1996), that introduced reforms in various sectors of the economy could not bring about a change in the insurance sector and it was left to the BJP-led coalition to instate the present liberal structure, despite criticism from some of its left support groups. The argument behind opening up of the sector was consumer-centric, which claimed that opening up insurance would give better products and service to consumers; the opponents of privatisation argued that in a poor country like India insurance needs to have social objectives and newcomers will not have that commitment (Bhattacharya and Rane, 2012).

In 1993, Malhotra Committee, headed by former Finance Secretary and RBI Governor R.N. Malhotra, was formed to evaluate the Indian insurance industry and recommend its future direction. The Malhotra committee was set up with the objective of complementing the reforms initiated in the financial sector. The reforms were aimed at creating a more efficient and competitive financial system suitable for the requirements of the economy keeping in mind the structural changes then underway and recognising that insurance was an important part of the overall financial system where it was necessary to address the need for similar reforms. In 1994, the committee submitted the report and recommendations. The committee emphasised that in order to improve the customer services and increase the coverage of insurance policies, industry should be opened up to competitions. But at the same time, the committee felt the need to exercise caution as any failure on the part of new players could ruin the public confidence in the industry. It was decided to allow competition in a limited way by stipulating the minimum capital requirement of Rs 100 crores. The committee felt the need to provide greater autonomy to insurance companies in order to improve their performance and enable them to act as independent companies with economic motives. For this purpose, it had proposed setting up an independent regulatory body- The Insurance Regulatory and Development Authority (Newar, 2013).

In Oct. 2000, IRDA (Insurance Regulatory and Development Authority) issued licence paper to three companies, which are HDFC Life Standard, Sundaram Royal Alliance Insurance Company and Reliance General Insurance. At the same time "Principal approval" was given to Max New York Life, ICICI Prudential Life Insurance Company and IFFCO Tokio General Insurance Company. Today total 22 life insurance companies including one public sector are successfully operating in India (Srivastava *et. al.* 2012). The insurance sector has gone through a number of phases by allowing private companies to solicit insurance and also allowing foreign direct investment. India allowed private companies in insurance sector in 2000, setting a limit on FDI to 26 per cent, which was increased to 49 per cent in 2014.

The industry has benefited significantly from the participation of global insurance giants (e.g. AIG, Allianz, Aviva, Sun Life, Chubb, Prudential, and New York Life) in terms of product innovation, distribution channels and 'best practices' in operations and claim settlement and managing operational efficiency. The institutional framework for the industry has expanded to include new trade associations such as life and non-life councils, brokers associations; third party administrators; underwriters; non-life actuaries and corporate brokers. The insurance consumers have benefited immensely from the competition that has materialised in the last five years (India Insurance Sector Assistance Review, 2012).

Today there are 28 general insurance companies (Non-life) including the Export Credit Guarantee Corporation and Agriculture Insurance Corporation of India, 24 life insurance companies that have set up operations in the life segment postopening up of the sector 20 are in joint venture with foreign partners. Of the twenty two private insurers who have commenced operations in the non-life segments, 18 are in collaboration with foreign partners (Shikhare, 2015).

Insurance Regulatory and Development Authority of India

Insurance Regulatory and Development Authority of India is an autonomous apex statutory body which regulates and develops the insurance industry in India. It was constituted by a Parliament of India Act called Insurance Regulatory and Development Authority Act, 1999 and duly passed by the Government of India. The agency operates from its headquarters at Hyderabad, Telangana where it shifted from Delhi in 2001. IRDA batted for a hike in the foreign direct investment limit to 49 per cent in the insurance sector from the erstwhile 26 per cent. The FDI limit in insurance sector was raised to 49 per cent in July 2014. The IRDA Act, 1999 was passed as per the major recommendation of the Malhotra Committee report which recommended establishment of an independent regulatory authority for insurance sector in India (Insurance Regulatory and Development Authority of India, 2015).

Legal Structure

The Insurance Act of 1938 was the first legislation governing all forms of insurance to provide strict state control over insurance business. Life insurance in India was completely nationalised on 19 January 1956, through the Life Insurance Corporation Act. All 245 insurance companies operating then in the country were merged into one entity, the Life Insurance Corporation of India. The General Insurance Business Act of 1972 was enacted to nationalise about 100 general insurance companies then and subsequently merging them into four companies. All the companies were amalgamated into National Insurance, New India Assurance, Oriental Insurance and United India Insurance, which were headquartered in each of the four metropolitan cities. Until 1999; there were no private insurance companies in India. The government then introduced the Insurance Regulatory and Development Authority Act in 1999, thereby de-regulating the insurance sector and allowing private companies. The primary regulator for insurance in India is the Insurance Regulatory and Development Authority which was established in 1999 under the government legislation called the Insurance Regulatory and Development Authority Act, 1999 (Insurance in India, 2015).

The insurance sector went through a full circle of phases from being unregulated to fully regulate and then currently being partly deregulated. It is governed by a number of Acts, with the first one being the Insurance Act, 1938.

1. *The Insurance Act, 1938:* The Insurance Act, 1938 was the first legislation governing all forms of insurance to provide strict state control over insurance business.
2. *Life Insurance Corporation Act, 1956:* Even though the first legislation was enacted in 1938, it was only on 19th January, 1956 that life insurance in India was completely nationalised through a Government ordinance; the Life Insurance Corporation Act, 1956 which created the Life Insurance Corporation of India on 1st September, 1956. About 154 Indian insurance companies, 16 non-Indian companies and 75 provident funds (total 245 companies) were operating in India at the time of nationalisation.
3. *General Insurance Business (Nationalisation) Act, 1972:* The General Insurance Business (Nationalisation) Act, 1972 was enacted to nationalise the 100 odd general insurance companies and subsequently merging them into four companies. All the companies were amalgamated into National Insurance, New India Assurance, Oriental Insurance and United India Insurance and these were headquartered in each of the four metropolitan cities.

4. *Insurance Regulatory and Development Authority (IRDA) Act, 1999:* The Government of India introduced the Insurance Regulatory and Development Authority Act in 1999, thereby de-regulating the insurance sector and allowing private companies into the insurance. Further, Foreign Direct Investment was also allowed and capped at 26 per cent holding in the Indian insurance companies, which has now increased to 49 per cent. In recent years many private players entered in the Insurance sector of India.
5. *IRDA Regulations:* The IRDA opened up the market in August 2000 with the invitation for registration of companies. The Authority has the power to frame regulations under Section 114A of the Insurance Act, 1938 and has from 2000 onwards, framed various regulations ranging from registration of companies for carrying on insurance business to protection of policyholders interests (Newar, 2013).

Conclusion

Insurance is the backbone of a country's risk management system. Risk is an inherent part of our lives. The insurance providers offer a variety of products to businesses and individuals in order to provide protection from risk and to ensure financial security. The Insurance Act of 1938 was the first legislation governing all forms of insurance to provide strict state control over insurance business. Insurance companies may be classified into two groups: (a) Life insurance companies, which sell life insurance, annuities and pensions products; and (b) Non-life or property/casualty insurance companies, which sell other types of insurance.

IRDA is an autonomous apex statutory body which regulates and develops the insurance industry in India. It was constituted by a Parliament of India Act called Insurance Regulatory and Development Authority Act, 1999 and duly passed by the Government of India. The industry has benefited significantly from the participation of global insurance giants in terms of product innovation, distribution channels and 'best practices' in operations and claim settlement and managing operational efficiency. The FDI limit in insurance sector was raised to 49 per cent in July 2014.

References

1. Bawa, S. and Chattha, S. (2013). Financial Performance of Life Insurers in Indian Insurance Industry, Pacific Business Review International Volume 6, Issue 5, p. 44.

2. Bhat, R. (2005). Insurance Industry in India: Structure, Performance, and Future Challenges, VIKALPA, 30 (3), p. 94.
3. Bhattacharya, A. and Rane, O. (2012). Nationalisation of Insurance in India, Retrieved from http://ccs.in/internship_papers/2003/chap32.pdf
4. Chanbasha, S. and Kumar, M. (2014). Growth and performance of Life Insurance Industry India, International Journal of Arts and Science Research. 1(1), pp. 30-37.
5. India Insurance Sector Assistance Review (2012). Indian Insurance sector assistance review, Retrieved from http://pdf.usaid.gov/pdf_docs/PNADG470.pdf
6. Insurance (2015). Retrieved from http://en.wikipedia.org/wiki/Insurance
7. Insurance in India (2015). Retrieved from http://en.wikipedia.org/wiki/Insurance_in_India
8. Insurance info (2015). Retrieved from http://www.insuranceinfo.com.my/learn_the_basics/types_of_insurance.php?intPrefLangID=1
9. Insurance Policy (2015), Retrieved from http://en.wikipedia.org/wiki/Insurance_policy
10. Insurance Regulatory and Development Authority of India (2015). Retrieved from http://en.wikipedia.org/wiki/Insurance_Regulatory_and_Development_Authority_of_India
11. Kartheeswari, S. and Rajeswari, K. (2012). Macro Economy Blooms the Life Insurance Companies in India: An Overview, International Journal of Advances in Management and Economics, 1 (6), pp.133-139.
12. Kotgiri, S. (2013). Growth of life Insurance Business: Public and Private Insurance Players in India, IJRMBSS, 1 (1), p. 62.
13. Krishnan, M. (2012). Emerging Challenges and Directions in Life Insurance Sector, 1 (6), (http://theglobaljournals.com/ijsr/file.php?val=November_2012_1351878994_f0e2a_33.pdf)
14. Life Insurance Corporation of India (2015), Retrieved from http://en.wikipedia.org/wiki/Life_Insurance_Corporation_of_India
15. Nagaraja, B. (2015). Performance of Insurance Industry in India: A Critical Analysis, International Journal of Multidisciplinary and Scientific Emerging Research, Int. J. of Multidisciplinary and Scientific Emerging Research, Vol. 4, No.1 (http://www.ijmser.com/wp-content/uploads/2015/03/paper-1045-1052.pdf)
16. Newar, L. (2013). Understanding Reforms in the Life Insurance Sector of India, IJCAES, Volume III, pp.18-22.
17. Radhakrishnan, R. (2012). Indian life insurance industry and distribution strategy, Retrieved from http://shodhganga.inflibnet.ac.in/bitstream/10603/4911/14/14_chapter%204.pdf
18. Rao, M. and Srinivasulu, R. (2013). Contribution of Insurance Sector to Growth and Development of the Indian Economy, Journal of Business and Management, 7 (4), pp. 45-52.
19. Recent Trends in Insurance Sector (2012). Retrieved from http://www.nios.ac.in/media/documents/VocInsServices/m1-1f.pdf

20. Sandhu, H. and Bala, S. (2011). Customers' Perception towards Service Quality of Life Insurance Corporation of India: A Factor Analytic Approach, International Journal of Business and Social Science, 2 (18), p. 219.
21. Sen, S. (2008). An Analysis of Life Insurance Demand Determinants for Selected Asian Economies and India, http://www.mse.ac.in/pub/working%20paper% 2036.pdf
22. Shikhare, Y. (2015). Foreign direct investment in insurance sector in India, The Business and Management Review, Volume 5 Number 4, pp. 31-36.
23. Sinha, T. (2002). Privatisation of the Insurance Market in India: From the British Raj to Monopoly Raj to Swaraj, CRIS Discussion Paper Series, p. 3.
24. Sinha, T. (2014). The Indian insurance industry: challenges and prospects, p. 6.
25. Srivastava, A., Tripathi, S., and Kumar, A. (2012). Indian Life Insurance Industry: The changing trends, Researchers World: Journal of Arts, Science and Commerce, Volume III, Issue 2(3) (http://www.researchersworld.com/vol3/issue2/vol3_issue2_3/Paper_11.pdf)
26. Thakur, A. and Kumar, S. (2013). Health Insurance Penetration in India: Implications for Marketers, Special Issue: Proceedings of 2nd International Conference on Emerging Trends in Engineering and Management, International Journal of Advances in Engineering Sciences Vol. 3 (3), p.121.

Chapter 7

Online Newspaper Reading Habits and Attitude in the ICT Environment: A Study of Alagappa University, Karaikudi

G. Stephen, Dr Sudhir .K. Jena and Dr Manaswini Patra

"Almost half of the population of the world lives in rural regions and mostly in a state of poverty. Such inequalities in human development have been one of the primary reasons for unrest and, in some parts of the world, even violence."

–A. P.J.Abul Kalam

Introduction

Reading online newspaper is a good habit that can provide a great sense of educational value. It carries information about politics, economy, entertainment, sports, business, industry, trade and commerce. With this habit, it will not only enhance your knowledge about general information but it will likewise improve your English skills and vocabulary. Reading online newspaper daily is one of the best ways to keep up-to-date with the ever advancing world. All the important news and events of the world are brought to our doorstep by the newspapers. But reading newspapers have other benefits as well. Reading English daily can enrich the vocabulary of an individual. Online Newspapers can also act as a forum for the readers and writers. Thus, reading online and offline newspapers is a must for young learners. But unfortunately, many students of our country do not have easy access to online newspapers.

Why should Read Newspaper?

First and foremost all the students do not have an access to personal computers and the internet, but the newspapers reach everyone. Lots of information encompassing current affairs, politics, science and technology, education, health, medicine, sports, industry and the markets can be received anywhere at any time of the day through newspapers. Important data, timetables, advertisements, courses and career options for various categories of students appear in newspapers.

Reading newspapers automatically improves one's language skills. News items and articles are written by learned and intelligent people. They know how to use language as an efficient tool for expression and communication. Precision and meticulous use of words and expressions comes naturally to them. One can imbibe these qualities easily by paying attention to language and style while going through news items and articles in a newspaper.

One can sharpen one's communication skills, i.e. reading and writing. By reading newspapers regularly at an appointed time reading and comprehension abilities get enhanced. The more one reads, new words and expressions reveal their meaning to the reader's mind. Automatically the vocabulary gets enriched and the language becomes richer, fluent and more expressive. Newspapers are a treasure trove of information for students preparing for competitions and contests. Knowledge coupled with good expression sets the stage for success in any examination.

Review of Literature

Praveen Patel, Devendra Patel and Haresh Patel (2014) surveyed "Reading habits of newspaper in pharmacy college: An analytical study". They found in the time spent for reading newspaper among Pharmacy professional in SKPCPER. Out of 301, 50.17 per cent under graduate students, 13.62 per cent post graduate students and 6.98 per cent faculty members are spent less than 30 minutes per day to reading the newspaper. 23.59 per cent Pharmacy professionals are spent 30 minutes to one hour to read the newspaper.

Kishore Basumatary (2014) examined "Information literacy and reading habits: a Case study of Samelangso, Howraghat and Langsomepi Development blocks under Karbi Angling Autonomous Council of Assam, India". He found that the educated people read mostly newspaper, magazine, locally published journal and general books like novel and other leisure books. Newspaper is the most popular reading material among the educated people of the study area. Table 7.4 indicates that (80.5 per cent) of the respondents including male and female reads newspaper by shelf purchasing, followed by books (48 per cent) and magazine (45 per cent). This study also indicates that among males reading newspaper by self-purchasing is (56.5 per cent) followed by and Magazine (36 per cent) books (29 per cent). On the other hand, among females reading newspaper by self-purchasing is (24 per cent) followed by books (19 per cent) and magazine (9 per cent). Acquiring or accessing newspaper, magazine, and books from library and other means by both male and female are meager and not significant.

Akanda, *et.al.* (2013) surveyed about "Reading habit of students in social sciences and arts: A case study of Rajshahi University". They found The World Wide Web has grown in popularity and use in recent years. The respondents of this survey, like other young people, are regular users of the web. It is an encouraging sign that the majority of them browse the web for reading purposes. Cyber cafés have become major places for people to use the Internet. Many young people prefer cyber cafés because they are affordable and comfortable. On the other hand, a substantial number of the respondents access the Internet from home. The pattern of their Internet usage is also noteworthy, because, contrary to the popular belief, the majority of the students surveyed indicated that they use the Internet only for one hour a day.

Eamin Ali Akanda and Armanul Haque (2013) conducted a study "Newspaper Reading Habits of University Graduate Students in Bangladesh: A Case Study". They found expresses that majority 130 (11.85 per cent) number of the respondents read newspaper to obtain information while the second largest 125 (11.39 per cent) respondents read newspaper to broaden the horizon of general knowledge and 122 (11.12 per cent) respondents read for educational purpose while 120 (10.94 per cent) respondents read for the purpose of searching new jobs and to know the sports news respectively. The least number of respondents i.e., 10 (0.91 per cent) are for improving the status in the society. That hall libraries are the most common sources of paper-based newspapers of students i.e. 35.91 per cent students depend on hall Libraries while 30.39 per cent students depend on individual subscription, and 13.81 per cent students rely on university library. And the least number of students i.e. 4.97 per cent students depend on public library and 14.92 per cent students depend on other sources for getting newspapers.

Njeze, Miracle Eka (2013) did a case study on Use of Newspapers and Magazines in the Academic Pursuits of University Students of Covenant University in 2013 and his findings revealed that the most consulted newspapers by both male and female students are the Punch, the Nation, Guardian, and Complete Sports, while the most consulted magazines by both students are PC World, Popular Science, Leadership and Time magazine, but female students have more interest in fashion magazines like Ebony, Style, Allure and Life etc.

Prakash B Waghmare (2012) conducted a survey on E-newspaper usage at Bidar Public Library and the study reveals that, the number of respondents (76 per cent) who are not used to read the e-newspaper are qualifies up to undergraduate level, above the age of forty years and senior citizens. Twenty four per cent of the respondents are very interested in reading e – newspaper as they are under the below age of forty years and post graduate qualified. The respondents who are interested in reading online newspapers were very familiar with ICTs. The respondents who won't like to read in online, like to read hard copies because of they may feel difficulty in searching needed information, they may not like to sit in front of the screen.

Thanuskodi, S (2011) conducted a study "Reading habits among library and information science students in Annamalai University". In that study found for pleasure 54.39 per cent of the students read newspapers frequently. LIS students spend more time for (77.48 per cent) reading books. Around 20 per cent of the LIS students never read non-fiction, internet publications, comic books, poetry and novels. The students overall responded that work most often interfered with their reading and studying. The percentage of students reading religious publications sometimes was 32.17, 30.40 sometimes read fiction and poetry, 28.08 sometimes read magazines. Around one-third of the students read rarely novels, comic books, magazines and internet publications, religious publications.

Panda and Dilip Swan (2011) attempts to make the user community aware of e-news and e-news services offered by different e-news channels all around the world, provides a brief discussion of history and developments of e-news service, newspaper websites and latent advantages of e-news in the electronic era. Employs literature survey method to unfold the latest trends of e-news industry and finds that, through e-news service provide immense opportunity to the readers and simultaneous access at infinite points and reading at ones convenience, still a few key technical challenges like, navigational support, hyperlink and designing of e-newspapers needs to be proper taken care of and tackled with, concludes with recommendations that information professional should take steps to increase the usage or e-newspapers by their intended audience.

V.S. Sivankutty and Jinu Sudhakaran (2011) conducted a survey of use of online newspapers among librarians in India and it was found that librarians are making use of many features in the newspaper sites while offering library services.

Alagappa University

Alagappa University Reaccredited with 'A' Grade by National Assessment and Accreditation Council is located at Karaikudi in Tamil Nadu is accessible from Madurai and Tiruchirappalli Airports within two hours. The 440 acre green and lush campus houses all the academic activities. This University has emerged from the galaxy of institutions initially founded by the great philanthropist and educationist Dr RM Alagappa Chettiar. Alagappa University was brought into existence by a Special Act of the Government of Tamil Nadu in May 1985 with the objective of fostering research, development and dissemination of knowledge in various branches of learning. Alagappa University is recognised by the University Grants Commission of India. The University has 18 Departments, five Centres and two Constituent Colleges on its campus. Twenty eight Affiliated Colleges located in the districts of Sivaganga and Ramanathapuram are part of the University. The University offers education through Regular, Weekend, Distance and Collaborative modes.

The Distance Education Directorate offers variety of programmes to the student community spread across the country and in selected foreign countries. Through all modes of education, the University caters to the needs of the student community of around 1,00,000. As a member of the Association of Indian Universities (AIU), as well as the member of the Association of Common Wealth Universities (ACU), it has rewarding relations with other academic institutions, research laboratories and industrial establishments that promise a spectacular feature.

The University is having International Collaborations with Universities / Institutions of Higher Learning in countries like China, Malaysia, West Indies, U.S.A. and South Korea. New innovative programmes suitable are designed and offered at the University (for the foreign students). Many exchange programmes attract the attention of the teachers and students from abroad. The University's motto is "Excellence in Action" and the University keeps before it the vision of excellence in all spheres of its action.

The following objectives are evolved for the purpose of the present study:

1. The first language of the students and faculties.
2. The language in which mostly students read online Newspapers.
3. How much time are spent reading online newspapers.
4. Which online newspapers are read most by students and faculty?

5. Which sections of online newspapers are read most by students and faculty?
6. Purpose of reading online Newspaper.
7. Users Opinion about ICT environment is very useful to read the online newspapers at anytime and anywhere?
8. Reasons for approaching online newspaper instead of printed newspaper.

The study used a questionnaire, with 25 questions spread over the following areas General profile of the respondent, frequency of library visit, purpose of using library sources and services, student's opinions about library service among PG students and faculties of Alagappa University, Karaikudi.

The researcher has employed a well-structured questionnaire for collecting the data from the PG students and faculties of Alagappa University, Karaikudi. The questionnaire has been prepared in such a way that the respondents could easily understand the items. A total number of 180 questionnaires were distributed among the PG-75, Research Scholar-75 and 30 Faculty.

They are personally requested to fill up the questionnaire at their earliest convenience in order to help the investigator to collect the same during his next visit. The investigator has to make second, third and fourth visits to the University for collecting the filled-in-questionnaires from the PG students, research scholars and faculties. During these visits, the investigator could collect questionnaires from only 142 out of 180 students and faculty among whom the questionnaires were distributed. This constitutes 78.8 per cent (142/180) of the total response. While selecting sample, random sampling method has been adopted.

Data Analysis

Size of the sample

Table 7.1. Size of the sample

Users	*Distributed*	*Received*	*Percentage*
PG Students	75	58	32.2
Research Scholars	75	62	34.4
Faculty Members	30	22	12.2
Total	**180**	**142**	**78.8**

The Table 7.1 shows that the size of distribution and received questionnaire from the students and faculty. Total numbers of questionnaire distributed among PG students 75, Research scholars 75, and faculty members 30. Out of these the responses from the respondents are PG students 58 (32.2 per cent), Research Scholars 62 (34.4 per cent), and faculty members 22 (12.8 per cent) from the total sample.

Gender-wise respondent

Table 7.2: Gender-wise respondent

Gender	*PG Scholars*	*Research*	*Faculty (per cent)*	*Grand Total*
Male	24	22	13	59 (41.5)
Female	34	40	9	83 (58.5)
Total	**58**	**62**	**22**	**142 (100)**

Table 7.2 shows that among 142 students, 83 (58.5 per cent) were female and 59 (41.5 per cent) were female. This suggests a balance between male and female respondents. It is clear that this study got more respondents from female.

First language of respondents

7.3. First language of respondents

Language	*Frequency*	*Percentage (per cent)*
Tamil	142	100
English	-	-
Hindi	-	-
Total	**142**	**100**

The first language of respondents is Tamil. Hundred per cent respondent's first language is Tamil.

Preferred language for online reading newspaper (Multiple responses)

Table 7.4: Preferred language for reading online Newspaper

Language	*Frequency*	*Percentage*
Tamil	142	100
English	97	68.3
Hindi	-	-

The Table 7.4 shows that average 100 per cent of students and faculty members use Tamil for online newspaper reading, whereas 68.3 per cent use English, and none students faculty use Hindi.

Frequency of visit the library to read newspaper

Table 7.5: Frequency of visit the library to read online newspaper

Library visit frequency	*Respondents*	*Percentage*
Everyday	113	79.6
Once in a week	7	4.9
Twice in a week	20	14.1

Table 7.5 does not offer an encouraging finding, because nearly half of the respondents (113, 79.6 per cent) visit college Library every day. On the other hand, the number of students and faculty (7, 4.9 per cent) who visit the library once in a week and 20 (14.1 per cent) go to the library at least twice in a week.

Time spending for reading online Newspaper

Table 7.6: Time spending for reading online Newspaper

Time spent	*PG Scholars*	*Research*	*Faculty Users (per cent)*	*Averages of*
Less than 1 hour	31 (53.4)	21 (33.9)	2 (9.1)	32.1
1-2 hours	24 (41.4)	30 (48.4)	16 (72.7)	54.2
More than 2 hours	3 (5.2)	11 (17.7)	4 (18.2)	13.7
Total	**58(100)**	**62(100)**	**22(100)**	**100**

Reading the daily newspaper has come to be considered an essential activity in our cultural development, selective aspects of its approval or rejection by students and faculty at different academic levels might well be a matter of value to students of personality development (Fendrick, 1941). Table 7.6 reveals that 54.2 per cent majority respondents spent 1–2 hours per day reading newspaper followed by 32.1 per cent that less than one hour and 13.7 per cent more than two hours Read Newspaper daily.

Read online Newspaper daily (Multiple Responses)

Table 7.7: Read online Newspaper daily (Multiple Responses)

Online Newspaper	*Frequency*	*Percentage*
Dhinakaran	106	74.6
DhinaThanthi	136	95.8

(Contd...)

Dhinamalar	119	83.8
Dhinaboomi	45	31.7
Dhinamani	92	64.8
The Hindu Tamil	99	69.7
The Hindu English	86	60.6
The New Indian Express	81	57.0
The Economic Times	81	57.0
Business line	56	39.4

Table 7.7 attempts to disclose the information on the name of the newspaper that the users read daily where the majority number of respondents 136 (95.8 per cent) read the daily DhinaThanthi, while the second largest number 119 (83.8 per cent) of respondents prefer the daily Dhinamalar. Moreover, the daily Dhinakaran is being preferred by 106 (74.6 per cent), 99 (69.7 per cent) respondents read the daily The Hindu (Tamil), while 86 (60.6 per cent) respondents read the daily The Hindu english, The New Indian Express and The Economic Times both respondents rate is same. That is 57 per cent respondents choose to read other newspapers. Dhinaboomi and Business line online newspapers are very lowest rate of respondents rate is respectively 39.4 per cent and 31.7 per cent.

Which section of online Newspapers do you like most? (Multiple Responses)

Table 7.8: Which section of Newspaper do you like most?

Sections	*PG Scholars*	*Research*	*Faculty (Per cent)*	*Grand Total*
Sensational News	32	43	20	95 (66.9)
Editorial	45	51	22	118 (83.1)
Advertisement	29	39	22	90 (63.4)
Letter to Editors	13	27	22	62 (43.7)
Politics	31	49	22	102(71.8)
Sports	42	43	18	103 (72.5)
Cinema News	33	42	11	86 (60.6)

The Table 7.8 represents the information regarding the section of online newspaper that the users usually wish to read in their day-to-day newspaper reading. Different people prefer to read different sections of newspapers. Table 7.8 shows that the highest number 118 (83.1 per cent) of respondents prefer editorial section for the purpose of gathering the day-to-day editors thinking followed by 103 (72.5 per cent) sports, politics section 102 (71.8 per cent), sensational news 95 (66.9 per cent), Advertisement

90 (63.4 per cent), 86 (60.6 per cent) cinema news. The lowest portion i.e. 62 (43.7 per cent) of the respondents prefer the letter to editors section of online newspaper.

Purpose of reading online Newspaper

Table 7.9. Purpose of reading online newspapers

Purpose	*Frequency*	*Percentage*
To get the information	140	98.6
To broaden the horizon of the general knowledge	136	95.8
For educational purpose	121	85.2
For searching new jobs	99	69.7
For entertainment	101	71.1
To know the sports news	123	86.6
As usual task of the day	92	64.8
To pass the time	53	37.3
To improve the status of the society	78	54.9
To improve the health consciousness	87	61.3
To keep abreast with the present happenings of all over the world	124	87.3
Others	77	54.2

Newspapers are a vital source of information in enlightened societies; providing the most recent information to readers. Newspapers serve various purposes for different categories of users (Bankole & Babalola, 2011). Respondents were asked about the various purposes of reading newspapers and they mentioned different reasons for reading newspapers. Table 7.9. expresses that majority 140 (98.6 per cent) number of the respondents read newspaper to get the information while the second largest 136 (95.8 per cent) respondents read newspaper to broaden the horizon of general knowledge and 123 (11.12 per cent) respondents read to know the sports news while 121 (85.2 per cent) for educational purpose. The least number of respondents, i.e. 53 (37.3 per cent) for pass the time.

Users Opinion about ICT environment is very useful to read the online newspapers at anytime and anywhere?

Table 7.10.Users opinion about....

Opinion	*PG*	*Research Scholars*	*Faculty*	*Grand Total (Per cent)*
Yes	54	61	20	135 (95.1)
No	4	1	2	7 (4.9)
Total	**58**	**62**	**22**	**142 (100)**

This study found from the respondents "opinion about electronic environment is very useful to read the online newspapers at anytime and anywhere". Majority of the respondents said yes 135 (95.1 per cent) and least 7 (4.9 per cent). Through this environment is very essential tool and help to read the online newspaper anytime and anywhere.

Findings and Suggestions

This study shows that among 142 students, 83 (58.5 per cent) were male and 59 (41.5 per cent) were female. This suggests a balance between male and female respondents. It is clear that this study got more respondents from female. The first language of respondents is Tamil. Hundred per cent respon-dent's first language is Tamil. This study shows that average 100 per cent of students and faculty members use Tamil for newspaper reading, whereas 68.3 per cent use English, and none students faculty use Hindi.

This study does not offer an encouraging finding, because nearly half of the respondents (113, 79.6 per cent) visit college Library every day. On the other hand, the number of students and faculty (7, 4.9 per cent) who visit the library once in a week and 20 (14.1 per cent) go to the library at least twice in a week. This study reveals that 54.2 per cent majority respondents spent 1–2 hours per day reading newspaper followed by 32.1 per cent that less than 1 hour and 13.7 per cent more than 2 hours Read Newspaper daily. This study expresses that majority 140 (98.6 per cent) number of the respondents read newspaper to get the information while the second largest 136 (95.8 per cent) respondents read newspaper to broaden the horizon of general knowledge and 123 (11.12 per cent) respondents read to know the sports news while 121 (85.2 per cent) for educational purpose.

Newspaper reading also improves the communication skills and creative faculties and help the readers achieve an unbiased and informative worldview. Therefore, newspapers are considered essential for university students. This study reveals that, both Tamil and English newspapers are frequently read by the under and post graduate students and faculties of Alagappa University, Karaikudi and they prefer international section to the national section for the purpose of keeping abreast of the day-to-day happenings in different parts of the world. The study also indicate that, in spite of their interest in newspaper reading, students are prevented from newspaper reading because of various socio-cultural, administrative and environmental problems. Concerned authorities of the university must take proper actions to make sure that students can read newspapers without facing any problem.

Reference

1. Anthony, G.C. (1980). The Impact of Television on South African Daily Newspapers. *Journalism Quarterly*, 57(2). pp. 216-223.
2. Mulopoulos, Chryss (1985). Trends in multicultural programming. *Canadian Library Journals,* 42(1), pp. 23-25.
3. Praveen Patel, Devendra Patel and Haresh Patel (2014). "Reading habits of newspaper in pharmacy college: An analytical study". *Journal of Advances in Library and Information Science*. Vol. 3. (2), pp. 94-100.
4. Kishore Basumatary (2014). "Information literacy and reading habits: A Case study of samelangso, Howraghat and Langsomepi Development blocks under Karbi Angling Autonomous Council of Assam, India", e-Library Science Research Journal, Vol. 2(7).
5. Akanda, A. K. M. Eamin Ali; Hoq, Kazi Mostak Gausul; and Hasan, Nazmul. (2013). Reading habit of students in social sciences and arts: A case study of Rajshahi University. *Chinese Librarianship: an International Electronic Journal*, 35.
6. Eamin Ali Akanda and Armanul Haque (2013). "Newspaper Reading Habits of University Graduate Students in Bangladesh: A Case Study" IMPACT: International Journal of Research in Applied, Natural and Social Sciences (IMPACT: IJRANSS) Vol. 1, Issue 3, pp. 1-8.
7. Njeze, Miracle Eka, (2013). "Use of Newspapers and Magazines in the Academic Pursuits of University Students: Case Study of Covenant University", Library Philosophy and Practice (e-journal). Paper 845.
8. Prakash B Waghmare (2012). E – Newspaper Usage: A Survey, International Conference on Knowledge Management and Organisation in the Digital Era, SIT Tumkur.
9. Thanuskodi (2011). "Reading habits of among library and information science students of Annamalai University: A study". *International journal of education science*, 3(2): pp. 79-83.
10. Panda, Dilip Swan (2011). "E-Newpaper and e-news service in electronic age: an Appraisal. *Annals of Library information science, Vol. 58, pp. 55-62.*
11. V.S. Sivankutty, Jinu Sudhakaran, (2011). "The use of online newspapers among librarians in India", Library Hi Tech News, Vol. 28 Iss: 1, pp. 10-12.
12. http://alagappauniversity.ac.in/about_au.php.

Chapter 8

Urbanisation in India: Trends and Problems

Dr Archana Sethi

"The backbone of any improvement of governance, its development as well as its protection from any form of wastage or excessiveness, is a mechanism to place laws under the microscope of revision and modernisation until they resonate in tune with the methodological development and new administrative technologies." **–Khalifa bin Zayed Al Nahyan**

Introduction

Urbanisation means an increase in the proportion of people living in urban areas compared to rural areas. An urban area is a built-up area such as a town or city. A rural area is an area of countryside. As a country industrialises, the number of people living in urban areas are trends to increase. People migrated from rural areas to urban areas. Where there was employment in the new factories. The area of cities known as the inner city developed during this time as rows of terraced housing were built for workers.

Urbanisation is the process of increasing population growth in cities and suburbs; it also includes the increase of industrialisation. There is more involvement in government, industry and trade in urban areas. The word urbanisation derives from "urb," which is the Latin word for city. The United States and Europe had the majority of urbanisation occur during the Industrial Revolution in the nineteenth century. There is no universal standard of how urbanised areas are classified. In America, an urbanised area has a population of at least 50,000.

Table 8.1: Rural Urban Population in India (2011)

Sl. No.	*Area*	*Person*	*Per cent*
1.	Rural	833,087,662	68.84
2.	Urban	377,105,760	31.16
	Total	**1,210,193,422**	**100**

Table 8.1 shows that in census 2011, 31.16 per cent people are lived in urban area and 68.84 per cent people are lived in rural area. Urbanisation is inevitable due to technological advances and an increasing population. Industrialisation allows people to make a living in methods other than farming; this has led to many people abandoning the rural lifestyle. It is a process that is occurring in nearly every part of the world inhabited by humans. It has led to a greater quality of life for many, but it also has its challenges.

Urbanisation in India was mainly caused after independence, due to adoption of mixed system of economy by the country which gave rise to the development of private sector. Urbanisation is taking place at a faster rate in India. Population residing in urban areas in India, according to 1901 census, was 11.4 per cent. This count increased to 28.53 per cent according to 2001 census, and crossing 30 per cent as per 2011 census, standing at 31.16 per cent. According to a survey by UN State of the World Population report in 2007, by 2030, 40.76 per cent of country's population is expected to reside in urban areas. As per World Bank, India, along with China, Indonesia, Nigeria and the United States, will lead the world's urban population surge by 2050.[1]

After independence, India faced poverty, unemployment and economic backwardness. The first Prime Minister of India, Pandit Jawaharlal Nehru, focused on the domain of science and technology, for economic development. The mixed economy system was adopted, resulting in the growth of the Public Sector in India. The contribution of the agricultural sector to the GDP of India started to decline and the percentage contribution from secondary sector increased. The period after 1941, witnessed rapid growth of four metropolitan cities in India, which were Kolkata, Delhi, Mumbai, and Chennai. The nation's economy saw a rise due to industrial revolution and the invention of new technologies increased the standard of living of people living in urban areas. The growth of public sector resulted in development of public transport, roads, water supply, electricity, and hence the infrastructure of urban areas.[2]

Maharashtra was the most urbanised state in India till 1991, stood behind Tamil Nadu in 2001 and third after it in 2011, with Kerala being first, with the urban-total state population ratio. However, Maharashtra's urban population of 41 million, far exceeds that of Tamil Nadu which is at 27 million, as per the 2001 census.[3]

Table 8.2: Urbanisation in India

Sl. No.	*Year (per cent)*	*Urban Population*
1.	1901	10.9
2.	1911	10.6
3.	1921	11.4
4.	1931	12.1
5.	1941	13.9
6.	1051	17.3
7.	1961	18.0
8.	1971	19.9
9.	1981	23.73
10.	1991	25.72
11.	2001	27.78
12.	2011	31.16

Source: census 2011.

It is clear from the table 2 that urban population increases continuously. In 1901, urban population was 10.9 per cent and it is 31.16 per cent in 2011.

Urban Areas

Urban Units (or Town)

1. All places with a municipality, corporation, cantonment board or notified town area committee, etc. (known's Statutory town).
2. All other places which satisfied the following criteria (Known as Census Town): (a) A minimum population of 5000; (b) Atleast 75 per cent of the male main workers engaged in non-agricultural pursuits; and (c) A density of population of at least 400 per sq km.

Demographic Aspects of Urbanisation

1. Increment in the population of urban area.
2. Migration of rural population to urban area.

Table 8.3: Urbanisation Trends in India

Sl. No.	*Year*	*Percentage Increase*
1.	1951-61	26.4
2.	1961-71	38.3
3.	1971-81	46.2
4.	1981-91	30.7
5.	1991-2001	31.2
6.	2001-2011	32.2

It is clear from the Table 8.3 that urban population is increases maximum 46.2 per cent in 1971-81 due to industrialisation. There is 32.2 per cent increase in urban population in the year 2001-11.

Causes

Living in a rural area provides less job opportunities. Farming is one of the major forms of income in rural areas. The unpredictable nature of environmental factors, such as rain and drought, leads to a fluctuating income. The standard of living is difficult to improve; therefore, families opt to move to urban areas. There is a greater variety of jobs in cities. Lack of space in rural areas due to a growing population also leads to urbanisation.

Causes of Urbanisation in India

The main causes of urbanisation in India are:

1. Expansion in government services, as a result of the Second World War.
2. Migration of people during the partition of India.
3. The Industrial Revolution.
4. Eleventh five year plan that aimed at urbanisation for the economic development of India.
5. Economic opportunities are just one reason people move into cities.
6. Infrastructure facilities in the urban areas.
7. Growth of private sector after 1990.[4]

Methods of Measuring Urbanisation

1. Ratio of urban population to total population.
2. Urban-rural growth differential.
3. General growth rate.

Table 7.4: Trends in Distribution of Urban Population

Year	*Urban population (lac)*	*Urban Per cent of total population*	*No. of towns*	*Urban/ Rural ratio*
1901	256	10.8	1827	1:8.1
1951	624	17.3	2843	1:4.7
2001	2850	27.8	5161	1:2.6
2011	3771	31.2	7933	1:2.2

It is clear from the Table 8.4 that in the year 1901 there are 1827 number of city exists which increases 2843 in 1951.5161 in 2001 and 7933 in 2011. In the year 1901, the ratio of urban rural population was 1:8.1 that means there was 8.1 rural individual and 1 urban individual. There is 2.2 rural individual and 1 urban individual in the year 2011.

Advantages of Urbanisation

After the industrial revolution urban population all over the world is increasing. There is a rapid migration of rural people to urban areas for jobs and better living. As a result, the population in the towns and cities are increasing and rural population is dwindling. The rapid in rush of people to the urban areas is pressuring gits limited space and cause all type of health and environmental hazards.

1. *Growth in industrial production:* The production in various industrial sectors like cement, iron and steel, textile, fertilizers etc. are helping in the economic growth of country. Export increase and this foreign reserve increase.
2. *Growth in trade and commerce:* Urbanisation helps the nation's business sector. Rural people came to the urban places with their goods.
3. *Development in tourism industries:* People from foreign countries are attracted to good cities and town having better transport facilities. Tourism is a good of foreign currency for a country.
4. *Improvement in science, culture*: Urban places are the meeting point of all good cultures of various localities, education, science and technology developments takes place in urban places improving the society as a whole.

The convenience of goods and services is one of the benefits of urbanisation. There is access to more educational and medical services, which allows increased literacy and better health. There is also less use of personal vehicles and more availability of public transportation. There is more social integration in urbanised areas. People of different religions, ethnic backgrounds, social classes and races reside in the same area. This leads to more understanding and acceptance of differences. Another benefit of urbanisation is the possibility of greater earning potential because of the availability of more jobs.

Challenges

The rapidity of growth in urbanised areas is a challenge. Although there are more opportunities, the constantly increasing population leads to more competition. This leads to large amounts of people that are out of work and extremely poor. Pollution is an issue that plagues many urbanised areas. Factories and vehicles emit fumes into the air, which may lead to respiratory issues. The development of more area to build houses and businesses negatively affects the environment. The destruction of habitats displaces many animals. It may also be difficult to finance the increase of an urbanised area due to its rapid growth.

More than 50 per cent of people worldwide live in cities, and the World Health Organisation predicts that this proportion will continue to increase. People migrate to cities for many reasons, including family ties and job opportunities. Urbanisation changes the economic, social and political setup of a country or region and has several major negative impacts. The rapid inflows of rural population to urban places give rise to housing problem and thus slum are developed in these places.

1. **Lack of Jobs:** Urbanisation leads to a deficit in jobs. Businesses and governments cannot produce enough jobs to meet the demand of a fast-growing population. Unemployment rates soar as a result, causing people to apply for government-funded programmes and benefits. The government loses money, reducing the amount of energy, healthcare, education, public transportation, waste management and physical security offered. Poverty spreads and stunts economic growth.
2. **Air Pollution:** Suspended particulates in the air come from motor vehicle fuel combustion. Soot, dust, lead and smoke make up the particulates. They pose a serious threat to health. Lead alone can cause brain damage, learning disabilities and premature death in children. The World Health Organisation stated suspended particulate concentration should add up to less than 90 micrograms per cubic meter. The suspended particulate concentration soars over that measurement in cities with a population of eight million or more. The increase in population in urban places pressurises water and sanitation facilities. It results in environmental pollution, health hazards.
3. **Biodiversity Threatened:** City growth destroys natural areas flowing with new and endangered animal and plant life. No matter how small, each species plays an important role in how the Earth works. Without this variation in life, humans suffer. Biodiversity protects water and soil from contamination, stores and recycles nutrients, breaks down and absorbs pollutants and

helps areas to recover faster from disasters. Biodiversity also provides people with medicine, food and air. Urbanisation limits our access to these resources.

4. **Disease:** Urbanisation has led to reduced physical activity and unhealthy nutrition. The World Health Organisation predicts that by 2020, noncommunicable diseases such as heart disease will account for 69 per cent of all deaths in developing countries. Another urbanisation-related threat is infectious diseases. Air travel carries bacteria and viruses from one country to the next. In addition, people relocating from rural areas are not immune to the same diseases as long-time city residents, which put them at a greater risk of contracting a disease.
5. **Crime:** Rapid urbanisation affects crime rates. Residents of different beliefs and behaviours thrown together suddenly do not have time to adjust or adapt to different viewpoints, leading to violence. The government's inability to prevent widespread poverty causes an increase in theft and other crimes. Frustration and alienation linked to a lower status, limited access to education, money and other resources push young people to join organised crime. The unemployment increases in urban areas. Due to the various criminal activities, corruption etc. increase affecting the law and order system.

How to Stop Rapid Urbanisation

1. No single individual can prevent urbanisation. Government should make law and do some activities for that.
2. Make school and college in rural areas. So that rural children don't have to come to cities for education.
3. Everyday usable materials should be sold at cheap rates in rural areas.
4. Daily wages in rural areas should be equal or as per city. There are the few things which can prevent urbanisation to same extent.

References

1. Singh, Kamaldeo Narain (1978). Urban Development in India. Abhinav Publications. ISBN 978-81-7017-080-8. Retrieved 13 June 2012.
2. Sivaramakrishnan, K.C., Dasgupta, Biplab and Buch, Mahesh (1993). Urbanisation in India: Basic Services and People's Participation. Concept Publishing Company. p. 2. ISBN 978-81-7022-480-8.
3. Singh, Sunil Kumar, Pathak, Ganesh Kumar'(2003). 'Trends in Urban population' Yozna, July

4. Shivhare, J.P. and Yadev, R.N. 'Trends in Urban population in Chhattisgarh' (2006) Research Link, March-May, pp. 65-66.
5. "Rural-Urban distribution of population" Census of India Press Release. Retrieved 19 November 2013.
6. "The Indian Industrial Revolution". Srcindore.org. Retrieved 15 June 2012
7. "Role of private sector in India's growth ~ Business News This Week". Businessnewsthisweek.com. 8 February 2009. Retrieved 21 June 2012
8. Business Standard (15 June 2012). "Victims of urbanisation: India, Indonesia and China". Rediff.com. Retrieved 15 June 2012.
9. Census 2011.

Chapter 9

Economic Development in India: An Overview

Dr Rakesh Joshi and Dr Sukanta Sarkar

"Some might complain that nuclear disarmament is little more than a dream. But that ignores the very tangible benefits disarmament would bring for all humankind. Its success would strengthen international peace and security. It would free up vast and much-needed resources for social and economic development. It would advance the rule of law." **–Ban Ki-moon**

Introduction

Economic development originated in the post-war period of reconstruction initiated by the US. In 1949, during his inaugural speech, President Harry Truman identified the development of undeveloped areas as a priority for the west. Economic development is the sustained, concerted actions of policy makers and communities that promote the standard of living and economic health of a specific area. Economic development can also be referred to as the quantitative and qualitative changes in the economy. The scope of economic development includes the process and policies by which a nation improves the economic, political, and social well-being of its people. In the United States, Project Socrates outlined competitiveness as the driving factor for successful economic development in government and industry. Economic development typically involves improvements in a variety of indicators such as literacy rates, life expectancy, and poverty rates.[1]

Regional development is the provision of aid and other assistance to regions which are less economically developed. Regional development may be domestic or international in nature. Business development comprises a number of tasks and processes generally aiming at developing and implementing growth opportunities within and between organisations. Business development had its origins in the Industrial Revolution.

Career Development is the lifelong process of managing learning, work, leisure, and transitions in order to move toward a personally determined and evolving preferred future. Corporate development refers to the planning and execution of a wide range of strategies to meet specific organisational objectives. The process of corporate development can also be applied to the task of growing the company through mergers and acquisitions.[2]

Importance of Development

Training and career development are very vital in any company or organisation that aims at progressing. Training simply refers to the process of acquiring the essential skills required for a certain job. A properly trained employee becomes more informed about procedures for various tasks. The worker confidence is also boosted by training and development. A well organised training and development programme gives the workers constant knowledge and experience. Employees gain standard methods to use in their tasks. The moment they gain the necessary skills and knowledge, employees will become more confident.[3]

Organisational development is the use of organisational resources to improve efficiency and expand productivity. It can be used to solve problems within the organisation or as a way to analyse a process and find a more efficient way of doing it. The process of organisational development identifies areas of company operations where change is needed. An organisational development analysis brings together sales projections and consumer demand to help determine the rate of company growth. When a company is involved in organisational development, it analyses work processes for efficiency and accuracy.[4]

Countries are divided into two major categories by the United Nations, which are developed countries and developing countries. The classification of countries as a Developed and Developing country is based on economic status like GDP, GNP, per capita income, industrialisation, standard of living, etc. Developed Countries is a country which provides free, healthy and secured atmosphere to live but the countries which lacks the same is known as Developing Countries.[5]

Developed Economy

A developed country, industrialised country is a sovereign state that has a highly developed economy and advanced technological infrastructure relative to other less industrialised nations. Developed countries have post-industrial economies, meaning the service sector provides more wealth than the industrial sector. While GDP per capita is often used to measure how developed a country is, it includes components that do not contribute to a citizen's standard of living. In 2015, the ten largest advanced economies by nominal GDP were the United States, Japan, Germany, France, the United Kingdom, Italy, Canada, South Korea, Australia and Spain.[6]

Income per capita, economic growth, unemployment, and population growth rate is partly an indicator to measure the success of development. Grouping the countries into developed and developing countries is generally based on economic and technological sectors.[7] The important features of developed economies are: (a) Industrial and service sectors dominated the economy; (b) The work to be performed is divided and subdivided into small pieces and individuals or group is required to perform only a part of the work; (c) Capital plays a dominant role in the economy; (d) Commodities are produced and manufactured on very large scale, mechanisation is adopted in the industrial production.[8]

The Human Development Index is a composite statistic used to rank countries according to their development levels from "very high" to "low." Countries are placed based on life expectancy, education, standard of living, child welfare, healthcare, economic welfare, and population happiness. Formulas are used to factor all the variables and determine the scores of countries.[9] The first economic category is developed nations, which can generally be categorised as countries that are more industrialised and have higher per capita income levels. To be considered a developed nation, a country generally has a per capita income around or above $12,000. In addition to having high per capita income and stable population growth rates, developed nations are also characterised by their use of resources.[10]

Developing Economy

A developing country is a nation with an underdeveloped industrial base, and a low Human Development Index relative to other countries. According to authors such as Walt Whitman Rostow, developing countries are in transition from traditional lifestyles towards the modern lifestyle which began in the Industrial Revolution in the eighteenth and nineteenth centuries. Kofi Annan, former Secretary General of the United Nations, defined a developed country as "one that allows all its citizens to enjoy a free and healthy life in a safe environment." Developing countries are, in general, countries that have not achieved a significant degree of industrialisation relative to their populations, and have, in most cases, a medium to low standard of living. There is a strong association between low income and high population growth. There are many factors hinder the development, like as (a) Illness/Disease; (b) Malnutrition/ Underdevelopment of the body and brain; (c) Knowledge gap; (d) Political Instability.[11]

The underdeveloped or the developing countries, as these are popularly known, inspite of their diverse structure, have some common characteristics. In developing nations general levels of living tend to be low for the vast majority of people. Throughout the developing world, levels of labour productivity are extremely low compared with those in developed countries. Low productivity is due to low level of technology. The sharp differences in productivity between developed and underdeveloped nations can be traced to the level of technology in these countries. One of the principal manifestations of and factors contributing to the low level of living in developing nations is their relatively inadequate and inefficient utilisation of labour. The vast majorities of people in Third World Nations live and work in rural area. Almost 80 per cent are rurally based compared with less than 35 per cent in economically developed countries.[12]

Economic Development during British Period

The economy of India under the British Raj describes the economy of India during the years of the British Raj from the 1850s to 1947. British investors built a modern railway system in the late 19th century—it was the fourth largest in the world and was renowned for quality of construction and service. Two new railway companies, Great Indian Peninsular Railway (GIPR) and East Indian Railway (EIR) began in 1853–54 to construct and operate lines near Bombay and Calcutta. The Indian economy grew at about one per cent per year from 1880 to 1920, and the population also grew at one per cent. The entrepreneur Jamsetji Tata (1839–1904) began his industrial career in 1877 with the Central India Spinning, Weaving, and Manufacturing Company in Bombay.[13]

The growth of a new land system in India affected tremendously India's economic and social life. In 1793, Lord Cornwallis introduced permanent settlement in Bengal and neighbouring areas. Under this system, each peasant holding a plot of land was recognised as the landlord and made directly responsible to the state for the annual payment of land revenue. Apart from exploitative policy in agricultural system, British ruined Indian economy through its industrial and commercial policies which favoured the Britishers at the cost of Indian economy. Tata wanted to set up an iron and steel plant in Central Provinces in 1880s but the government did not grant permission, preventing India to develop iron and steel industry. Dadabhai Naoroji emphasised that the drain of wealth and capital from the country was responsible for absence of development of India. According to him, "The drain consist of two elements – first, that arising from the remittances by European officials of their savings, and for their expenditure in England for their various wants both there and in India: from pensions and salaries paid in England, and second that arising from remittance by non-official Europeans."[14]

The Industrial revolution has helped the English merchants accumulate a lot of capital from the countries of Asia, Africa and America. They now wanted to invest this wealth in setting up industries and trade with India. They were interested in having more raw materials from India as well as sending their finished goods back. Earlier, Indian handloom had a big market in Europe. The British succeeded in selling their goods at a cheap price as foreign goods were given free entry in India without paying any duty. On the other hand, Indian handicrafts were taxed heavily when they were sent out of the country. The main aim of the British was to transform India into a consumer of British goods. As a result, textile, metal work, glass and paper industries were soon out of work.

Another major economic impact of the British policies in India was the introduction of a large number of commercial crops such as tea, coffee, indigo, opium, cotton, jute, sugarcane and oilseed. Commercialisation of agriculture further enhanced the speed of transfer of ownership of land thereby increasing the number of landless labourers. It brought in a large number of merchants, traders and middlemen who further exploited the situation. Time bound and excessive demand of revenue by the British government forced the peasants to take loans from the moneylenders. These moneylenders often exploited the peasants by charging high interest rates. When the British came to India, they brought new ideas such as liberty, equality, freedom and human rights from the Renaissance, the Reformation Movement and the various revolutions that took place in Europe. These ideas appealed to some sections of our society and led to several reform movements in different parts of the country.[15]

The main changes which the British made in Indian society were at the top. They replaced the wasteful warlord aristocracy by a bureaucratic-military establishment, carefully designed by utilitarian technocrats, which was very efficient in maintaining law and order. The British educational effort was very limited. There were no major changes in village society, in the caste system, the position of untouchables, the joint family system, or in production techniques in agriculture. From the 1820s to the 1850s the British demonstrated a strong urge to change Indian social institutions, and to Westernise India. They stamped out infanticide and ritual burning of widows (sati). They abolished slavery and eliminated dacoits (religious thugs) from the highways. One of the most significant things the British did to Westernise India was to introduce a modified version of English education. Macaulay's 1835 Minute on Education had a decisive impact on British educational policy and is a classic example of a Western rationalist approach to Indian civilisation. Education could have played a major role in encouraging social mobility, eliminating religious superstition, increasing productivity, and uplifting the status of women.[16]

The introduction of the railways, telegraph and postal system linked different parts of India and promoted an exchange of ideas among the people, especially among her leaders. The first telegraph line from Calcutta to Agra was opened in 1853. The improvement in communications eventually helped to foster a sense of unity among Indians. The concept of the country as a whole now took precedence over regional and provincial isolationism. Books, journals and newspapers circulated widely and were now easily available to educated Indians all over the country.[17]

Economic Development after Independence

Pandit Jawaharlal Nehru laid the foundations of modern India. His vision and determination have left a lasting impression on every facet of national endeavour since Independence. It is due to his initiative that India now has a strong and diversified industrial base and is a major industrial nation of the world. The goals and objectives set out for the nation by Pandit Nehru on the eve of Independence, namely, the rapid agricultural and industrial development of our country, rapid expansion of opportunities for gainful employment, progressive reduction of social and economic disparities, removal of poverty and attainment of self-reliance remain as valid today as at the time Pandit Nehru first set them out before the nation.[18]

When India achieved Independence in 1947, the national consensus was in favour of rapid industrialisation of the economy which was seen not only as the key to economic development but also to economic sovereignty. Building on the so-called "Bombay Plan" in the pre-Independence era, the first Industrial Policy Resolution announced in 1948 laid down broad contours of the strategy of industrial development. The Indian Constitution was adopted in January 1950, the Planning Commission was constituted in March 1950 and the Industrial (Department and Regulation) Act (IDR Act) was enacted in 1951 with the objective of empowering the government to take necessary steps to regulate the pattern of industrial development through licensing. The Industrial Policy Resolution - 1956 was shaped by the

Mahalanobis Model of growth, which suggested that emphasis on heavy industries would lead the economy towards a long-term higher growth path. Monopolies Inquiry Commission was set up in 1964 to review various aspects pertaining to concentration of economic power and operations of Industrial Licensing under IDR Act, 1951.[19]

Higher agricultural growth has been a feature of higher overall GDP growth achieved in the 1980s and 1990s, after the relative stagnation of the 1960s and 1970s. The drought of 1965 to 1967, and the associated difficulties of importing food at that time, gave a jolt to the Indian Government. The pre-occupation with food security and its equation with food self-sufficiency led to restrictive trade policies controlling both import and export of agricultural goods. This policy combined with that of high protection to industry resulted in a decline in terms of trade for agriculture until the early 1990s. The Central Government has announced the availability of incentive funds for states to carry out appropriate agriculture market policy reforms. This agenda of reform needs to be pushed with vigour but much greater discussion is required with the states and also among experts. Very significant changes are taking place in the agricultural sector. The green revolution and white revolution were relatively easy to achieve from the policy point of view. Wheat, rice and milk are relatively homogeneous products. The green revolution was also aided considerably by a large domestic and international research and extension effort.[20]

The economic development in India followed socialist-inspired policies for most of its independent history, including state-ownership of many sectors. In the late 2000s, India's growth reached 7.5 per cent, which will double the average income in a decade; States have large responsibilities over their economies. Planned economic development since independence, in which the state took an active role to stimulate economic growth through a more active utilisation of the human and physical resources had made perceptible differences in the economy. The industrial base had expanded and become substantially diversified. Infrastructural facilities had vastly improved though they were still inadequate in some crucial aspects.[21]

India consumes the second-largest amount of oil in the Asia-Pacific region behind China. India's labour force is growing by 2.5 per cent every year, but employment is growing only at 2.3 per cent a year. The annualised 1999–2008 growth rates for Maharashtra (9.7 per cent), Gujarat (9.6 per cent), Haryana (9.1 per cent), or Delhi (8.9 per cent) were significantly higher than for Bihar (5.1 per cent), Uttar Pradesh (4.4 per cent), or

Madhya Pradesh (6.5 per cent), Tamil Nadu (9.9). India is the seventh largest economy in the world and the third largest by purchasing power parity adjusted exchange rates (PPP). India is tenth in the world in factory output.[22]

The major weaknesses of the Indian economy, which have emerged during the latter half of the eighties, are the growing pressure on balance of payments, steadily mounting foreign debt, structural imbalance in the pattern of industrial growth, persistent fiscal imbalance, stagnation in the overall savings rate, continuing pressure on the price level and vulnerability of the economy to external shocks like the Gulf crisis. In mid-eighties, the country's credit worthiness was rated very highly by international agencies and this facilitated large scale external commercial borrowing to finance the country's growing trade deficit.[23]

With the development process, significance of primary sector declines while that of secondary and tertiary sectors increases. After independence, Indian economy has also experienced such changes. The share of primary sector in GDP at factor cost (at 1999-2000 prices) which was 56.5 per cent in 1950-51 declined to 34.6 per cent in 1990-91 and then to 19.7 per cent in 2007-08. The secondary sector's share in GDP was 13.6 per cent in 1950-51 increased to 23.2 per cent in 1990-91 and further to 24.7 per cent in 2007-08. Tertiary sector's share in GDP increased from 29.9 per cent in 1950-51 to 55.6 per cent in 2007-08, and in 2009-10 it was over seven per cent. Since independence, significant progressive changes have taken place in the banking and financial structure of India.[24]

A remarkable feature of the Indian macroeconomic story since independence has been the continuous rise in household savings over the decades. As might be expected, this rise has been characterised by continuing increases in financial savings as a proportion of GDP. The spread of the financial sector, of bank branches in particular, post office savings and the like, helped in mobilising household financial savings. Their financial liabilities did not grow correspondingly since there were few financial products available for household credit. While gross financial savings of the household sector have continued their upward trajectory in the recent few years, households' financial liabilities have also been increasing rapidly, albeit from a low base. In view of the key role played by investment in the growth process, it is important to have reliable and timely estimates of domestic savings and investment. Improvement in public finances and public sector savings has contributed significantly to the step-up in domestic savings and investment rates since 2002-03 onwards. Higher savings and investment rates, in turn, have led to a higher growth trajectory of the Indian economy.[25]

The reform process in India was initiated with the aim of accelerating the pace of economic growth and eradication of poverty. The process of economic liberalisation in India can be traced back to the late 1970s. The reforms of the last decade and a half have gone a long way in freeing the domestic economy from the control regime. An important feature of India's reform programme is that it has emphasised gradualism and evolutionary transition rather than rapid restructuring or "shock therapy". The economic reforms initiated in 1991 introduced far-reaching measures, which changed the working and machinery of the economy. Industrial policy was restructured to a great extent and most of the central government industrial controls were dismantled. Massive deregulation of the industrial sector was done in order to bring in the element of competition and increase efficiency. Import licencing was abolished relatively early for capital goods and intermediates which became freely importable in 1993, simultaneously with the switch to a flexible exchange rate regime. Financial sector reforms have long been regarded as an integral part of the overall policy reforms in India. India has recognised that these reforms are imperative for increasing the efficiency of resource mobilisation and allocation in the real economy and for the overall macroeconomic stability.[26]

The centre of economic reforms has been liberalisation, privatisation and globalisation. Liberalisation means to unshackle the economy from bureaucratic cobweb to make it more competitive. Privatisation means such an economic process through which some public sector undertaking is brought either partially or completely under private ownership. Globalisation means integrating the economy with the rest of the world. Following are its chief features: (a) free flow of goods and services in all the countries; (b) free flow of capital in all the countries; (c) free flow of information and technology in all the countries; and (d) Free movement of people in all the countries.[27]

Prime Minister Narasimha Rao converted the prevailing economic crisis into an opportunity to launch massive economic reforms. First, he introduced an economist (rather than a politician) into the Cabinet as Finance Minister and gave the new Minister his full support, allowing him to evolve and implement path-breaking economic reforms. The Rao government recognised in 1991 that the time had come to reshape India's economic policies by drawing appropriate lessons from the 'East Asian Miracle' based on more export-oriented and more globally connected strategies of development, as successfully practiced earlier by Japan and South Korea and also by the South East Asian tigers Malaysia, Singapore, Indonesia and Thailand. The Rao government, after launching the relatively aggressive (by past Indian standards) reforms, was soon confronted with the political constraints of 'competitive populism' during elections held at the state level in 1993.

Macro-economic management reforms have focused on controlling the politically difficult problems of reducing the fiscal and (even more so) revenue deficits. Faced with the necessity of reducing the fiscal deficit in the crisis year of 1991-92, Finance Minister Singh attempted to reduce fertilizer and food subsidies in 1991-92 and to some extent in 1992-93. Since 1991, several efforts have been made through the annual budget process to achieve tax reforms. Consistent with the spirit of the market-oriented and private sector-led economic reforms launched since 1991, the government has reoriented the role of planning in India. It has been recognised that market forces and the state should be given roles that play to their comparative advantages and that they should work together as partners in the economic development of the nation.[28]

The economic liberalisation in India refers to the ongoing economic liberalisation, initiated in 1991, of the country's economic policies, with the goal of making the economy more market-oriented and expanding the role of private and foreign investment. Attempts were made to liberalise the economy in 1966 and 1985. The first attempt was reversed in 1967. In the 80s, the government led by Rajiv Gandhi started light reforms. The fruits of liberalisation reached their peak in 2006, when India recorded its highest GDP growth rate of 9.6 per cent. An Organisation for Economic Co-operation and Development report states that the average growth rates 7.5 per cent will double the average income in a decade and more reforms would speed up the pace. In response, Prime Minister Narasimha Rao, along with his finance minister Manmohan Singh, initiated the economic liberalisation of 1991. The reforms did away with the Licence Raj, reduced tariffs and interest rates and ended many public monopolies, allowing automatic approval of foreign direct investment in many sectors.[29]

The main objectives of the new fiscal policy are to establish economic structural adjustment at the first stage and then to establish market economy by removing all controls and restrictions on it. The new fiscal policy has introduced three significant things Deregulation, Privatisation and Exit Policy. Excepting 15 important industries all other industries have been made free from licence system. The Economic liberalisation has helped

India to grow at faster pace. India is now considered one of the major economies of Asia. India has emerged as a leading exporter of services, software and information-technology products. Many companies such as Wipro, TCS, HCL Technologies, Tech Mahindra have got worldwide fame.[30]

India's economic performance in the post-reforms period has many positive features. The average growth rate in the ten year period from 1992-93 to 2001-02 was around 6.0 per cent. Opinions on the causes of the growth deceleration vary. World economic growth was slower in the second half of the 1990s and that would have had some dampening effect, but India's dependence on the world economy is not large enough for this to account for the slowdown. Critics of liberalisation have blamed the slowdown on the effect of trade policy reforms on domestic industry. Fiscal profligacy was seen to have caused the balance of payments crisis in 1991 and a reduction in the fiscal deficit was therefore an urgent priority at the start of the reforms.

The central government's effort must be directed primarily towards improving revenues, because performance in this area has deteriorated significantly in the post-reform period. There is also room to reduce central government subsidies, which are known to be highly distortionary and poorly targeted (e.g. subsidies on food and fertilizers), and to introduce rational user charges for services such as passenger traffic on the railways, the postal system and university education. State governments also need to take corrective steps. Sales tax systems need to be modernised in most states. Liberalising foreign direct investment was another important part of India's reforms, driven by the belief that this would increase the total volume of investment in the economy, improve production technology, and increase access to world markets. The policy now allows 100 per cent foreign ownership in a large number of industries and majority ownership in all except banks, insurance companies, telecommunications and airlines.[31]

Conclusion

When India achieved Independence in 1947, the national consensus was in favour of rapid industrialisation of the economy which was seen not only as the key to economic development but to economic sovereignty. The Central Government has announced the availability of incentive funds for states to carry out appropriate agriculture market policy reforms. With the development process, significance of primary sector declines while that of secondary and tertiary sectors increases. A remarkable feature of the Indian macroeconomic story since independence has been the continuous rise in household savings over the decades. The reform process in India was initiated with the aim of accelerating the pace of economic growth and eradication of poverty. The centre of economic reforms has been liberalisation, privatisation and globalisation. Liberalisation means to unshackle the economy from bureaucratic cobweb to make it more competitive.

References

1. Economic development (2015). Retrieved from https://en.wikipedia.org/wiki/Economic_development
2. Wikipedia.
3. Importance of training and development, Available at http://www.artof-thestart.com/importance-of-training/
4. The Importance of Organisational Development, Retrieved from http://smallbusiness.chron.com/importance-organisational-development-11904.html
5. Difference between Developed Countries and Developing Countries, Available at http://keydifferences.com/difference-between-developed-countries-and-developing-countries.html
6. Developed country, Available at https://en.wikipedia.org/wiki/Developed_country
7. The characteristics of developed and developing countries, Available at http://dailytape.com/2011/09/01/the-characteristics-of-developed-and-developing-countries.html
8. What are the important features of Developed economies?, See http://www.preservearticles.com/2012011620887/what-are-the-important-features-of-developed-economies.html
9. http://listverse.com/2012/02/13/top-10-highly-developed-countries/
10. Economic Inequality: Differences in Developed and Developing Nations, Available at http://study.com/academy/lesson/economic-inequality-differences-in-developed-and-developing-nations.html
11. Developing country, Available at https://en.wikipedia.org/wiki/Developing_country
12. What are the Common Characteristics of Underdeveloped Countries?, http://www.preservearticles.com/2011103116271/what-are-the-common-characte-ristics-of-underdeveloped-countries.html
13. Economy of India under the British Raj, Available at https://en.wikipedia.-org/wiki/Economy_of_India_under_the_British_Raj
14. Bhimasen Hanta, Indian Economy during British Rule, Available at http://www.yourarticlelibrary.com/economics/indian-economy-during-british-rule/39741/
15. Impact of British rules in India: Economic, Social and Cultural (1757-1857), http://www.nios.ac.in/media/documents/secsocscicour/english/lesson-05.pdf

16. The Economic and Social Impact of Colonial Rule in India, http://www.ggdc.net/MADDISON/articles/moghul_3.pdf
17. Mamta Aggarwal, Social and Economic Impact of British Rule in India, http://www.historydiscussion.net/british-india/social-and-economic-impact-of-british-rule-in-india/1595
18. http://dipp.nic.in/English/Policies/Industrial_policy_statement.pdf
19. http://www.drnarendrajadhav.info/drnjadhav_web_files/Published% 20papers/Indian%20Industrial%20Policy%20Since%201956.pdf
20. Rakesh Mohan, A Decade After 1991: New Challenges Facing the Indian Economy, http://www.rakeshmohan.com/docs/RBIBulletinNov2002.pdf
21. http://shodhganga.inflibnet.ac.in/bitstream/10603/604/10/10_chapter4.pdf
22. Economic development in India, https://en.wikipedia.org/wiki Economic_development_in_India
23. Bakul H Dholakia, India's Economic Crisis: Nature and Remedies, http://www.vikalpa.com/pdf/articles/1991/1991_july_sep_47_53.pdf4
24. Significant Structural Changes in India's Economic Structure since Independence, http://www.yourarticlelibrary.com/economics/4-significant-structural-changes-in-indias-economic-structure-since-independence/2754/
25. Rakesh Mohan, The Growth Record of the Indian Economy, 1950-2008: A Story of Sustained Savings and Investment, http://aboutcorporateindia.com/devOld/files/growth_record_indian_economy.pdf
26. http://indiainbusiness.nic.in/newdesign/index.php?param=economy_ landing/217/2
27. What are the Economic Reforms in India since 1991?, http://www.yourarticle-library.com/economics/what-are-the-economic-reforms-in-india-since-1991/897/
28. Charan D. Wadhva, India trying to liberalise: Economic reforms since 1991, http://apcss.org/Publications/Edited%20Volumes/RegionalFinal% 20chapters/Chapter16Wadhva.pdf
29. Economic liberalisation in India, Available at https://en.wikipedia.org/wiki/Economic_liberalisation_in_India
30. http://www.importantindia.com/1859/economic-reforms-in-india-since-1991/
31. Montek S. Ahluwalia. Economic Reforms in India since 1991: Has Gradualism Worked?, http://planningcommission.nic.in/aboutus/speech/spemsa/msa008.pdf

Chapter 10

Correlation between Individual Governance Mechanism and Indian Companies Performance

Dr Ch. Sudipta Kishore Nanda

"The human face is the organic seat of beauty. It is the register of value in development, a record of Experience, whose legitimate office is to perfect the life, a legible language to those who will study it, of the majestic mistress, the soul."
–Eliza Farnham

Introduction

Corporate Governance is the set of processes, customs, policies, laws and institutions affecting the way a corporation is directed or controlled. Corporate Governance includes the relationships among the many participants involved and goal for which the corporation is governed. In this regard, corporate governance has succeeded in attracting a good deal of public interest because of its importance for the economic health of corporations and society in general. However, the concept of corporate governance has been considerable interest in the corporate governance practices of modern corporations, particularly the high profile collapses of firms such as Satyam, Enron Corporation etc.

The question of corporate governance in India has come mainly in the wake of economic liberalisation, deregulation of industry and business as also the demand for a new corporate ethos and stricter compliance with the legislation. The new economic policies adopted by the Government of India since 1991 has necessitated the demand for introduction and implementation of a proper corporate governance policy in management of companies not only in the interests of their stakeholders but also for the overall development of the country.

There has been considerable research in the domain of corporate governance in recent years in India. In the light of the growing importance of India in the world economy as a source of intellectual capital and outsourcing possibilities, there is an urgent need to understand the governance structures in India. India's cultural values are different from other countries values, are shaped by history and institutions and form the backdrop of businesses in a country. The dynamism of these influences in India has resulted in a complex blend of ownership forms that include family governance, professional and foreign-owned firms. The corporate governance also has to take into account the legal, regulatory, institutional and ethical environment of the community. Corporate success and sustainable economic growth rest with good governance. A firm which has good governance system has better image and greater value, higher profits and higher sales growth than those with poor governance system (Paul *et. al.*, 2003).

Furthermore, it will promote enterprise and ensure accountability. Different countries follow different models of corporate governance depending upon their environment, cultural background etc. The importance of corporate governance had not been felt and practice in the past until the economic crisis hit many parts of the Western and Asian countries. The current wave of reform of Corporate Governance commenced with the Cadbury code of practice published by the London Stock of Exchange in 1992. It has now become the subject of intense debate in the background of the recent scam involving the world's leading firms that include Enron, WorldCom, Xerox and others and has become a mainstream issue and subject of discussion for boardroom, academics circles, government and regulators. These incidents highlighted the importance and status of corporate governance the world over.

In effectual, poor corporate structure increase the risk of fraud, corporate failure or both. Further, with the wave of globalisation, mergers and acquisition, there is an increasing competition where only the strong survive, brought the corporation towards better governance system. Corporate governance concerns the exercise of power in corporate entities and has wider implications and is critical to economic and social well-being, firstly, in providing the incentives and performance measures to achieve business success, and secondly, in providing the accountability and transparency to ensure the equitable distribution of the resulting wealth. Thus, the quantity, quality and frequency of financial disclosure, accountability, transparency in corporate functioning for maximising shareholders wealth are the progressive elements and indeed the underlying spirit of corporate governance. Failure in corporate governance is a real threat to the future of every corporation and to the economy, therefore the weakness of corporate should be tackle and assess for healthy future.

Literature Review

Brown, Robinson, Caylor (2004), study the linkages between Corporate Governance to Firm Performance using 2,327 firms based on 51 corporate governance provision provided by Institutional Investors Services (ISS) and using Pearson and Spearman correlation analysis finds that firms with poor governance are relatively less profitable and less valuable. Further they find that executive and director compensation are highly associated with good performance while governance category, charter/by laws, is least associated with good performance.

Johnson, Boone, Breach, Friedman (2000) study whether the weakness of legal institutions for corporate governance had an important affect on the extent of depreciation and stock market declines in the context of Asian countries during the crisis. Taking a sample of 25 firms of emerging markets and using regression co-efficient analysis finds that managerial agency problems can make countries with weak legal system vulnerable to loss of investor confidence that results in fall in asset value and decline in exchange rate. They find that corporate governance variables affect more variation in exchange rate and stock market performance than macroeconomic variables.

Todd Milton (2004), in his study on corporate governance and dividend policy in emerging market, with a sample of 365 firms from 19 countries found that firms with stronger corporate governance have higher dividend payout and also there is an increase negative relationship between dividend payout and growth opportunities. Moreover, firms with stronger governance show higher profits. The study also reveals that countries with stronger investor protection have a limitation of dividend payout. Further, country level investor protection and firm level corporate governance are complementary to each other. (Shareholder prefers higher dividend paid when the firm has weak legal protection and vice versa. CG rating developed by credit Lyonnais Securities Asia, CLSA-2001 is used.)

Bernard Black (2001), in his study on the relationship between CG behaviour and market value of Russian firm took a sample of 21 Russians firms. The study reveals that CG behaviour has a strong impact/effect on the market value in a country where legal and cultural constraint on corporate behaviour is weak. According to the reports of World Bank, Public corporations in East Asia typically have low levels of transparency and disclosure quality. Some commentators and policy advisors believe that a closer adherence to international disclosure rules and the adoption of international accounting standards are essential for improving corporate transparency in the region (World Bank, 1998, *East Asia)*.

Jayanth R. Varma (2002) studies and documents the accounting scandals and corporate frauds that came to light during 2001 and 2002 of Enron and other companies in the United States and elsewhere. It then describes the failure of governance and supervision as well as the failure of market discipline that took place and go on to analyze the lessons that can be drawn from these episodes. He concluded that while the Enron and related scandals represent a massive regulatory failure those failures are inherent in the regulatory process. Regulators are poor at detecting fraud, and therefore suggest that market discipline should be strengthened. Further the study also suggest four important measures: encouraging hostile take-over, allowing free short selling, permitting and facilitating class action lawsuits, and promoting competition in the securities industry.

Joh, (2003) study the affect of poor corporate governance system on firm profitability in the context of Korean firms before the crisis and also investigate whether other factor also contribute to poor performance. Using a data of 5829 Korean firms for the period 1993-1997 in which firm profitability was measure through its performance by using accounting profitability and regression analysis while controlling industry fixed effect. He concluded that poor corporate governance and weak legal environments prevails even before the crisis that contribute for poor firm performance besides this lower controlling by family ownership and financial investment in affiliated firm also effects firm profitability. Firms with higher control-ownership disparity showed lower profitability.

Back, Kang and Park (2004) study the effect of corporate governance on firm performance during Korean crisis (1997), using a sample of 644 non-financial listed on the Korean Stock Exchange between November 1997-December 1998 and using a statistical regression analysis, they concluded that firms with larger equity ownership by foreign investors experience a smaller reduction in their share value. Firms that have higher disclosure quality and alternative sources of external financing also suffer less and affiliated firms also exhibits larger drop in equity value. Firms that have higher cash flow than the voting rights and those that borrow more from the bank has lower returns and similar effects on diversified firms, those with high leverage and those that are small and risky.

They also find that agency problem between controlling shareholders and minority shareholders is much serious during the crisis and concentrated ownership has strong incentives to maximise either their own utility or overall size rather than individual firms.

Klapper and Love (2004) investigate the determinants of firm-level governance, their relationship with the country legal environments and the correlations between governance and performance taking data from 495 firms in 25 countries. Using Tobin's Q (as a market valuation of the firm) and Return on Assets (ROA) as a measure of operating performance finds that governance is higher in countries with stronger legal protection (using three legal efficacy measures - judicial efficiency, antidirectors rights and legality), however there is no systematic relationship between variation in firm level ranking and country legal-efficiency.

Drobetz et.al., (2004) tried to find evidence for a possible relationship between corporate governance and firm performance within a single jurisdiction. Rather than looking at the regulatory environment or ownership structure that effects all firms within a country they focus on the relationship between a large set of governance proxies and firm performance in German public listed firms. To measure the relationship, they use corporate governance rating as a proxy for firm level governance quality and found that CG is highly correlated with better operating performance, higher stock return and higher valuation. For investigating expected stock return, Historical return and dividend yields (d/p2) of 50 months is used and for CG and firm valuation Tobin's Q and Market-to-book-ratio is used and find that expected stock return are negatively correlated with firm level.

Fama and Jensen (1983) suggest that the board has no important function of alleviating agency costs that arise from the separation of ownership and decision control in corporations. Short *et. el.* (1999) also take this view and argue that the board of directors is the central corporate governance control mechanism responsible for monitoring the activities of managers. Jensen (1993) describes the board of directors as the apex of the internal control system in an organisation. Therefore, the board of directors exists to protect the interests of shareholders from where it receives its authority for internal control from the stakeholders (Jensen, 1993).

Prior study explains that board size is an important aspect of effective corporate governance (Pearce and Zahra, 1992; Jensen, 1993; Yermack, 1996) and is related to firm performance (Haniffa and Hudaib, 2006). A larger board is more likely to have a greater range of expertise to monitor the actions of management effectively, which is required not only for enhancing the monitoring activities of managers (Monks and Minow, 1995). On the contrary others (Lipton and Lorsch, 1992; Yermack, 1996) argue that a small board is more effective. They argue that large boards may be less cohesive and slow in making decisions (Lipton and Milliken, 1999). Jensen 1993 argues that large boards are less likely to function effectively and are easier for the CEO to control.

Empirically, the evidence on the importance of board size on firm performance is mixed. Holthausen and Larcker (1993) consider board size among other variables that are more likely to influence firm performance. They fail to detect consistent evidence of a relationship between board size and firm performance.Yermark (1986); Haniffa and Hudaib (2006) in their study by using Tobin's Q as a measure of firm performance find in inverse relationship, suggesting that small boards of directors are more effective. In their research study, they argue that whilst the market may percieve large boards as ineffective, they are beneficially to the company as they provide the diversity of knowledge that is necessary for directing the operations of the company.

The degree of board independence, as represented by the presence of non-executive directors on the board, is argued to improve monitoring, thereby ensuring that managers pursue shareholders interests. Fama (1980); Fama and Jensen (1983), in their study they argue that the variability of the board of directors as an internal control mechanism is enhanced by the inclusions of NEDs. NEDs are percieved to be independent of executive directors (Cadbury Committee, 1992) and therefore have incentives to carry out their monitoring role effectively.

Fama and Jensen (1983); Shivdasani (1993) also suggest that NEDs are more unlikely to collude with executive directors to expropriate share-holder wealth. In addition, NEDs have incentives to develop reputations as experts in decision control and are concerned about maintaining their reputation because the external labour market prices them according to their performance as NEDs.

Moreover, Haniffa and Hudaib (2006) say that, the presence of NEDs on board ensures that executive directors are not the sole evaluators of their performance and thus improving transparency. This literature suggests that a higher proportion on non-executive directors on the board improves the ability of the board to monitor managerial performance. However, other literature Demb and Neubauer, 1992; Patto and Baker, 1987 argues that a higher proportion of NEDs may also be detrimental. They may stifle strategic actions, lead to excessive monitoring of managers, lack business knowledge to make them effective and lack real independence to influence the CEO.

Lins (1996) shows that companies with a higher proportion of NEDs are more likely to participate in major restructuring events such as mergers, takeovers and tender offers. Weisbach (1998) documents that board with higher proportion of NEDs are more likely to remove poor performing CEOs. Rosenstein and Wyatt (1990) reveal an increase in shareholder wealth following the addition of NEDs to the board.

Size and independence of the board cannot in themselves lead to its effectiveness in the monitoring role unless it is diligent or active. Board diligence is important characteristics for its effectiveness (Kalbers and Fogarty, 1993) suggest that the frequency of meetings can be a proxy of diligence. Vafeas (1999) study suggests that the frequency of board meetings is a proxy for the time directors spend monitoring managerial performance. Lipton and Lorsch (1992) suggest that board meeting time is an important resource in stirring the company to better performance. Thus, boards that meet more frequently allow directors more time to confer, set strategy and to execute their monitoring role more effectively (Vafeas, 1999). Abbott *et. el.* (2003) suggest, when boards hold regular meetings they are more likely to remain informed and knowledgeable about relevant performance of the company leading them to take or influence and direct the appropriate action to address the issue.

The proceeding discussion suggest that board that meet more frequently are more likely to perform better their roles of monitoring performance in accordance with shareholder's interests. Empirically, the evidence is inconclusive. Vafeas (1999) find that firms with boards that meet more frequently are valued less by the market as reflected in lower Tobin's Q ratio and suggest that the market may perceive more board meetings as expensive in terms of managerial time, travelling expenses and director's meeting fees. However, Vafeas (1999) also find that boards meet more frequently after crises and thus improving the company's performance.

Objectives of the Study

The relations between governance and performance of firms have been looked into with the help of the following objectives: (a) Examining the association between governance practices at firm level with their respective performance; and (b) Identifying the cause and effect relationship between individual governance mechanism (Board process and structure, Ownership structure, Audit committee, Remuneration committee and grievance committee) and the firm performance.

For carrying out the above objectives, the corporate governance information relating to Board of Directors, ownership structure, Audit committee, Remuneration committee and grievance committee and their financial statements are collected through secondary source. Different performance measures spread across three categories: operating performance, market value added and shareholder payout are used in the study. Operating performance would be measured through return on equity, profit margin and sales growth. To represent the market value added, the study used P/B ratio that are collected from the website of Bombay Stock Exchange. P/B is in fact the single MVA measure considered by economics, finance and law researchers. Further the performance measures like EBITDA margin, ROE, Sales growth are collected from the PROWESS (CMIE) data base.

Dividend payout ratio is also considered in the study. Several theories have been put forward to explain the information that dividend pay-out might convey, most prominently the cash flow signalling and the free cash flow hypotheses. The free cash flow hypothesis asserts that the value of the firm should increase if over-investing managers pay out more of the cash flows as dividends. Positive abnormal returns in case of dividend increases and negative abnormal returns in case of dividend reductions are also expected according to the cash flow signalling hypothesis, however. Hence, dividend pay-out ratio is used as a proxy for future expected performance of firms. The information on dividend payout ratios for different companies is gathered from the PROWESS data base.

BSE 200 companies representing different size across industries are to be considered for the study as more than that would have been difficult to manage for a clinical exploration. The companies chosen are listed in BSE irrespective of their boundaries confined to India or abroad. The study made an attempt to focus on five years data from 2006-2010 but due to non-availability of data of five years for all the companies finally the study could include only 163 companies from the BSE 200 list.

Analysis and Interpretation

To investigate the relationship between facets of corporate governance and six different performance variables and to draw reliable conclusion, a multivariate regression framework is used. Table 10.1 through Table 10.5 reports our examination of the main effects of the explanatory variable (i.e. facets of corporate governance) on six different dependent variables (i.e. firms' performance measures).

Table 10.1: Impact of Individual Governance Components on P/B Ratio

Dependent Variable: PB				
Method: Panel Least Squares				
Sample: 2006 2010				
Cross-sections included: 163				
Total panel (balanced) observations: 815				
Variable	*Co-efficient*	*Std. Error*	*t-Statistic*	*Prob.*
C	9.380825	4.047772	2.317528	0.0207**
BO	-0.76126	0.251743	-3.02395	0.0026*
OW	0.404607	0.136967	2.954039	0.0032*
AC	0.286133	0.257648	1.110558	0.2671
RC	0.121282	0.084634	1.433007	0.1522
CG	-0.21153	0.067649	-3.12695	0.0018*
R-squared	0.022646	Mean dependent var	5.443399	
Adjusted R-squared	0.016606	S.D. dependent var	9.370876	
S.E. of regression	9.292744	Akaike info criterion	7.30368	
Sum squared resid	69861.28	Schwarz criterion	7.338304	
Log likelihood	-2970.25	Hannan-Quinn criter.	7.316969	
F-statistic	3.749073	Durbin-Watson stat	1.055416	
Prob (F-statistic)	0.002315			

* and ** indicate significance at one per cent and five per cent level of confidence.

Table 10.1 reports the analysis of the impact of the five different constituents of corporate governance on Price to Book value ratio. It can be observed that the relationship between Price to Book and Board, Ownership and Governance committee are significant showing significant predictive power at five per cent and one per cent level of significance. A negative correlation between firm value and the size of a firm's board of directors supporting the previous studies by Yermack's (1996) who studied of Fortune 500 industrial firms, partly confirmed by Bhagat and Black (1996).

However, the model lacks predictive power with adjusted R-squares is 2.2 per cent.

Table 10.2: Impact of Individual Governance Components on EBITA Margin

Dependent Variable: EM				
Method: Panel Least Squares				
Sample: 2006 2010				
Cross-sections included: 163				
Total panel (balanced) observations: 815				
Variable	*Co-efficient*	*Std. Error*	*t-Statistic*	*Prob.*
C	43.93216	12.20286	3.600154	0.0003*
BO	1.807627	0.758933	2.381801	0.0175*
OW	-0.21683	0.412916	-0.52513	0.5996
AC	-2.21756	0.776735	-2.85497	0.0044*
RC	0.2993	0.255148	1.173043	0.2411
CG	0.056285	0.203941	0.275985	0.7826
R-squared	0.019163	Mean dependent var	37.59837	
Adjusted R-squared	0.013101	S.D. dependent var	28.20026	
S.E. of regression	28.01493	Akaike info criterion	9.510687	
Sum squared resid	634932.5	Schwarz criterion	9.545311	
Log likelihood	-3869.61	Hannan-Quinn criter.	9.523976	
F-statistic	3.161089	Durbin-Watson stat	0.057225	
Prob (F-statistic)	0.007813			

* and ** indicate significance at one per cent and five per cent level of confidence.

Table 10.2 presents analysis of the impact of five governance variables on firms' EBITA margin. Board and Remuneration Committee share a positive and significant predictive relationship with firms' EBITA margin. But audit committee negatively related to EBITA margin implying that more the number of audit activities, the EBITA margin will decline and vice-versa. Nevertheless, the model here again lacks predictive power as it has R-square value of 1.9 per cent.

Table 10.3: Impact of Individual Governance Components on ROE

Dependent Variable: ROE
Method: Panel Least Squares
Sample: 2006 2010

(*Contd...*)

Cross-sections included: 163				
Total panel (balanced) observations: 815				
Variable	*Co-efficient*	*Std. Error*	*t-Statistic*	*Prob.*
C	11.87639	8.934828	1.329224	0.1841
BO	-0.82281	0.555684	-1.48072	0.1391
OW	0.979504	0.302334	3.239809	0.0012*
AC	1.372106	0.568719	2.412627	0.0161*
RC	0.305323	0.186817	1.634343	0.1026
CG	-0.26118	0.149324	-1.74911	0.0807
R-squared	0.024402 Mean dependent var		25.18676	
Adjusted R-squared	0.018372 S.D. dependent var		20.70335	
S.E. of regression	20.51229 Akaike info criterion		8.88726	
Sum squared resid	340390.1 Schwarz criterion		8.921885	
Log likelihood	-3615.56 Hannan-Quinn criter.		8.90055	
F-statistic	4.046955 Durbin-Watson stat		0.47984	
Prob (F-statistic)	0.001237			

* and ** indicate significance at one per cent and five per cent level of confidence.

Table 10.3 reports explanatory power of the corporate governance variables of the Return on Equity. Both Audit committee and Ownership structure share a positive relationship with ROE at one per cent level of significance. As both the variables are part of the monitoring mechanism of the agency theory of governance, the significance of the coefficients indicates that stronger monitoring will improve the return on equity and slack monitoring will result in lesser return on equity. But the model in explaining such relationship lacks predictive power as it has an R-squared value of 2.4 per cent.

Table 10.4: Impact of Individual Governance Components on Sales Growth

Dependent Variable: SG
Method: Panel Least Squares
Sample: 2006 2010
Cross-sections included: 163
Total panel (balanced) observations: 815

(*Contd...*)

Variable	*Co-efficient*	*Std. Error*	*t-Statistic*	*Prob.*
C	74.63557	19.92573	3.745688	0.0002*
BO	-3.77717	1.239242	-3.04797	0.0024*
OW	-0.15533	0.674241	-0.23038	0.8179
AC	-0.51935	1.268311	-0.40948	0.6823
RC	0.253054	0.416625	0.607392	0.5438
CG	-0.05825	0.33301	-0.17492	0.8612
R-squared	0.013265 Mean dependent var		26.53041	
Adjusted R-squared	0.007167 S.D. dependent var		45.90966	
S.E. of regression	45.74486 Akaike info criterion		10.49137	
Sum squared resid	1692907 Schwarz criterion		10.526	
Log likelihood	-4269.23 Hannan-Quinn criter.		10.50466	
F-statistic	2.17514 Durbin-Watson stat		1.649108	
Prob (F-statistic)	0.055			

* and ** indicate significance at one per cent and five per cent level of confidence.

In Table 10.4, none other except Board as governance variable shares a significant predictive relationship with Sales growth as a measure of performance of the firms. Though the relationship is negative it is significant. It indicates that sales will decline due to bigger size of the Board, the reason being decision making process gets delayed larger board. Again here also the predictive power of the model is not significant as indicated by the smaller R-square value of 1.3 per cent.

The Table 10.5 reports the impact of governance explanatory variables on Dividend Payout. Only Audit committee explains the dividend payout.

Table 10.5: Impact of Individual Governance Components on Dividend Payout Ratio

Dependent Variable: DP
Method: Panel Least Squares
Sample: 2006 2010
Cross-sections included: 163
Total panel (balanced) observations: 815

(*Contd...*)

Variable	*Co-efficient*	*Std. Error*	*t-Statistic*	*Prob.*
C	16.48814	8.561643	1.925815	0.0545*
BO	-0.77222	0.532475	-1.45025	0.1474
OW	0.022154	0.289706	0.076471	0.9391
AC	1.44101	0.544965	2.644226	0.0083*
RC	-0.12779	0.179014	-0.71385	0.4755
CG	-0.09942	0.143087	-0.69482	0.4874
R-squared	0.010415	Mean dependent var	24.93432	
Adjusted R-squared	0.004299	S.D. dependent var	19.69793	
S.E. of regression	19.65555	Akaike info criterion	8.801931	
Sum squared resid	312549.5	Schwarz criterion	8.836556	
Log likelihood	-3580.79	Hannan-Quinn criter.	8.81522	
F-statistic	1.702859	Durbin-Watson stat	0.743529	
Prob(F-statistic)	0.131432			

* and ** indicate significance at one per cent and five per cent level of confidence.

That means frequent audit activities result in more dividend payout. But again the model lacks explanatory power with an R-squared value of one per cent. We can conclude that the Ordinary Least Square model in the aforementioned multivariate regression analysis fails to carry significant predictive power. Further, it assumes that all the firm are homogenous even through the presence of heterogeneity is in cross-sectional series.

Thus, for appropriate model to be applied for the multivariate analysis, we have applied Hausman Test with the null hypothesis that the random effect is applicable and alternative hypothesis is application of fixed effect model. The results are reported in the Table 10.6 are per which we cannot reject the null hypothesis of the application of random effect model for our study of the impact of the different facets of governance on performance variables of the firm.

Table 10.6: Hausman Test Result

	Hausman Test			
Dependent Variable	***Chi-Sq. Statistic***	***D F.***	***Prob.***	***Model***
P/B Ratio	1.140132	5	0.9505	Random Effect
EBITDA Margin	5.669088	5	0.3398	Random Effect

(Contd...)

ROE	7.02094	5	0.2191	Random Effect
Sales Growth	0.612991	5	0.9874	Random Effect
Payout Ratio	2.326241	5	0.8024	Random Effect

The results of Panel data analysis are reported in Table 10.7 through Table 10.11.

Table 10.7: Impact of Individual Governance components on P/B Ratio – Panel Data Analysis

Dependent Variable: PB				
Method: Panel EGLS (Cross-section random effects)				
Sample: 2006 2010				
Cross-sections included: 163				
Total panel (balanced) observations: 815				
Swamy and Arora estimator of component variances				
Variable	*Co-efficient*	*Std. Error*	*t-Statistic*	*Prob.*
C	9.515971	5.593683	1.701199	0.0893***
BO	-0.63848	0.303149	-2.10616	0.0355**
OW	0.374095	0.217301	1.721555	0.0855**
AC	0.185547	0.359085	0.516722	0.6055
RC	0.096045	0.127218	0.754963	0.4505
CG	-0.18945	0.104378	-1.81503	0.0699***
		Effects Specification		
			S.D.	Rho
Cross-section random			5.923521	0.4005
Idiosyncratic random			7.247871	0.5995
		Weighted Statistics		
R-squared	0.009479	Mean dependent var		2.613002
Adjusted R-squared	0.003357	S.D. dependent var		7.242726
S.E. of regression	7.23056	Sum squared resid		42295.32
F-statistic	1.548307	Durbin-Watson stat		1.739815
Prob (F-statistic)	0.172418			
		Unweighted Statistics		
R-squared	0.022135	Mean dependent var		5.443399
Sum squared resid	69897.84	Durbin-Watson stat		1.052765

*, ** and *** indicate significance at one per cent, five per cent and 10 per cent level of confidence.

Table 10.7 reports impact of five corporate governance variables on Price to Book ratio. Board impacts negatively to Price to Book ratio which is significant at five per cent level of confidence. On the other hand, ownership and governance committee impacts positively to PB ratio which is significant at 10 per cent confidence level. Further, PB is not explained by other governance factors like audit committee and remuneration committee.

Table 10.8: Impact of Individual Governance components on EBITDA Margin – Panel Data Analysis

Dependent Variable: EM				
Method: Panel EGLS (Cross-section random effects)				
Sample: 2006 2010				
Cross-sections included: 163				
Total panel (balanced) observations: 815				
Swamy and Arora estimator of component variances				
Variable	*Co-efficient*	*Std. Error*	*t-Statistic*	*Prob.*
C	29.9745	8.156984	3.674704	0.0003*
BO	0.302232	0.32218	0.938083	0.3485
OW	-0.34848	0.654025	-0.53282	0.5943
AC	0.068707	0.495183	0.138751	0.8897
RC	0.278271	0.2259	1.231832	0.2184
CG	0.188402	0.237972	0.791697	0.4288
		Effects Specification		
			S.D.	Rho
Cross-section random			27.74943	0.9561
Idiosyncratic random			5.947734	0.0439
		Weighted Statistics		
R-squared	0.004341	Mean dependent var		3.587529
Adjusted R-squared	-0.00181	S.D. dependent var		5.944809
S.E. of regression	5.950194	Sum squared resid		28642.49
F-statistic	0.705472	Durbin-Watson stat		1.195139

(*Contd...*)

Prob (F-statistic)	0.619426		
		Unweighted Statistics	
R-squared	0.002868	Mean dependent var	37.59837
Sum squared resid	645480.7	Durbin-Watson stat	0.053033

*, ** and *** indicate significance at one per cent, five per cent and 10 per cent level of confidence.

As reported in Table 10.8, governance does not contribute EBITA margin of the firms. The reported results are not statistically significant.

Table 10.9: Impact of Individual Governance components on ROE – Panel Data Analysis

Dependent Variable: ROE				
Method: Panel EGLS (Cross-section random effects)				
Sample: 2006 2010				
Cross-sections included: 163				
Total panel (balanced) observations: 815				
Swamy and Arora estimator of component variances				
Variable	*Co-efficient*	*Std. Error*	*t-Statistic*	*Prob.*
C	37.31131	12.24875	3.046132	0.0024*
BO	-1.78081	0.609441	-2.92203	0.0036*
OW	0.897127	0.535073	1.676645	0.094***
AC	0.291251	0.787011	0.370072	0.7114
RC	0.317166	0.295789	1.07227	0.2839
CG	-0.25855	0.251119	-1.0296	0.3035
		Effects Specification		
S.D.	Rho			
Cross-section random	16.07927	0.6061		
Idiosyncratic random	12.96307	0.3939		
		Weighted Statistics		
R-squared	0.015116	Mean dependent var		8.542624
Adjusted R-squared	0.009029	S.D. dependent var		13.03824
S.E. of regression	12.97925	Sum squared resid		136284.8

(*Contd...*)

F-statistic	2.483278	Durbin-Watson stat	1.191908
Prob (F-statistic)	0.030356		
	Unweighted Statistics		
R-squared	0.013967	Mean dependent var	25.18676
Sum squared resid	344030.8	Durbin-Watson stat	0.472164

*, ** and *** indicate significance at one per cent, five per cent and 10 per cent level of confidence.

Table 10.9 shows that Return on Equity is negatively affected by the Board which is statistically significant at one per cent confidence level and positively impacted by the ownership structure of the firms. But since the R-squared value is only 1.5 per cent, the model lacks explanatory power.

Table 10.10: Impact of Individual Governance components on Sales Growth – Panel Data Analysis

Dependent Variable: SG				
Method: Panel EGLS (Cross-section random effects)				
Sample: 2006 2010				
Cross-sections included: 163				
Total panel (balanced) observations: 815				
Swamy and Arora estimator of component variances				
Variable	*Co-efficient*	*Std. Error*	*t-Statistic*	*Prob.*
C	77.28332	23.44246	3.296724	0.001*
BO	-3.99422	1.402494	-2.84794	0.0045*
OW	-0.14213	0.821294	-0.17305	0.8627
AC	-0.52116	1.496861	-0.34817	0.7278
RC	0.248959	0.501364	0.496564	0.6196
CG	-0.07836	0.402637	-0.19462	0.8457
		Effects Specification		
			S.D.	Rho
Cross-section random			16.0254	0.1217
Idiosyncratic random			43.04946	0.8783
		Weighted Statistics		
R-squared	0.011339	Mean dependent var		20.3907
Adjusted R-squared	0.005229	S.D. dependent var		43.04526
S.E. of regression	42.93258	Sum squared resid		1491154
F-statistic	1.855685	Durbin-Watson stat		1.872138

(Contd...)

Prob (F-statistic)	0.099767		
	Unweighted Statistics		
R-squared	0.013224	Mean dependent var	26.53041
Sum squared resid	1692978	Durbin-Watson stat	1.648955

*, ** and *** indicate significance at one per cent, five per cent and 10 per cent level of confidence.

None other governance factors except Board impacts sales growth of the firms as per the results reported in Table 10.10. The size of the Board is negatively related with sales growth that means when size of the Board increases, growth in sales declines and vice-versa.

Table 10.11: Impact of Individual Governance components on Payout Ratio – Panel Data Analysis

Dependent Variable: DP

Method: Panel EGLS (Cross-section random effects)

Sample: 2006 2010

Cross-sections included: 163

Total panel (balanced) observations: 815

Swamy and Arora estimator of component variances

Variable	*Co-efficient*	*Std. Error*	*t-Statistic*	*Prob.*
C	10.93466	11.93802	0.915953	0.36
BO	-1.07671	0.612882	-1.75679	0.0793***
OW	0.086318	0.49749	0.173507	0.8623
AC	2.039589	0.767168	2.658596	0.008*
RC	-0.01038	0.281771	-0.03683	0.9706
CG	-0.15183	0.235721	-0.6441	0.5197
		Effects Specification		
			S.D.	Rho
Cross-section random			14.49112	0.5345
Idiosyncratic random			13.52399	0.4655
		Weighted Statistics		
R-squared	0.011054	Mean dependent var		9.603846
Adjusted R-squared	0.004942	S.D. dependent var		13.53511
S.E. of regression	13.50162	Sum squared resid		147475.7
F-statistic	1.808473	Durbin-Watson stat		1.57482
Prob (F-statistic)	0.108712			
		Unweighted Statistics		
R-squared	0.008338	Mean dependent var		24.93432
Sum squared resid	313205.4	Durbin-Watson stat		0.741519

*, ** and *** indicate significance at one per cent, five per cent and 10 per cent level of confidence.

In Table 10.11, it is observed that Dividend payout ratio is negatively related to size of the Board and positively related with the audit committee at statistical significance level of 10 per cent, one per cent and five per cent respectively. More the activities of the audit committee, one can expect a better dividend payout ratio. However, increase in Board size results in lesser dividend payout ratio. Nevertheless, the model lack significant explanatory power as indicated by the R-squared value of 1.1 per cent.

Impact of Individual Governance Components on Firm Performance

The study investigates the relationship between various facets of corporate governance and six different performance variables independently. In order to draw a reliable conclusion, a multivariate regression framework is used. The analysis of the impact of the five different constituents of corporate governance (Board Process and Structure, Ownership Structure, Audit Committee, Remuneration Committee and Grievance Committee) on Price to Book value ratio exhibits that the Price to Book ratio is impacted by three governance facets like Board process and Structure, Ownership and Governance committee. A negative correlation between firm value and the size of a firm's board of directors supports the findings of many of the previous studies.

A subsequent analysis of the impact of five governance variables on firms' EBITA margin reveals that both Board structure and process and Remuneration Committee share a positive and significant predictive relationship with firms' EBITA margin while the audit committee negatively related to EBITA margin implying that more the number of audit activities, the EBITA margin will decline and vice-versa. Similarly an analysis of the impact of corporate governance variables of the Return on Equity highlights that both Audit committee and Ownership structure share an influencing relationship with ROE. As both the variables are part of the monitoring mechanism of the agency theory of governance, the significance of the coefficients indicates that stronger monitoring will improve the return on equity and slack monitoring will result in lesser return on equity.

A cursory look at the impact of individual governance facets portrays that none other than Board Process and Structure shares a significant predictive relationship with Sales growth as a measure of performance of the firms. Though the relationship is negative it is significant. It indicates that a higher growth in sales is hampered due to bigger size of the Board, more and more meetings etc. The possible reason may be the delay in decision-making process that is prevalent in a larger board. In case of

Dividend Payout ratio, it's only the Audit committee that explains the dividend payout signifying that a stringent audit activities result in more dividend payout.

The above results obtained through Ordinary Least Square model in the aforementioned multivariate regression analysis may have some limitation as the model assumes that the entire firm are homogenous even through the presence of heterogeneity is in cross-sectional series. Thus, a further verification through a panel data analysis is thought to be appropriate for the multivariate analysis. In order to specify the panel regression model, we have applied Hausman Test with the null hypothesis that the random effect is applicable and alternative hypothesis is application of fixed effect model. The result of Hausman Test favoured the application of random effect model for the study.

The panel result reports the impact of three out of five corporate governance variables on Price to Book ratio. While the Board Process and Structure impacts Price to Book ratio negatively, ownership structure and governance committee impacts the ratio positively. PB ratio is not explained by other governance factors like audit committee and remuneration committee. Interestingly none of the governance facets has a significant influence on the EBITA margin of the firms. Another measure of performance, Return on Equity is found to be negatively affected by the Board Process and Structure and positively impacted by the ownership structure of the firms.

Consistent with the OLS result, the sales growths of the firms are not influenced by any governance variable other than Board Process and Structure. The size of the Board is negatively related with sales growth. The panel data analysis also reveals that Dividend payout ratio is negatively influenced by the Board Process and Structure and positively related with the audit committee. More the activities of the audit committee, one can expect a better dividend payout ratio. However, increase in Board size results in lesser dividend payout ratio.

Conclusion

Summarising the results of the analysis of individual impact of governance facets on performance variables under a random effect model, no facets of governance impacts the EBITDA margin. Further, Board structure impacts negatively to the performance in terms of P/B ratio, Return on Equity, Sales growth and Dividend payout ratio. It shows that though it is good to have more number of board meetings and attendance, but presence of independent directors and CEO duality impacts the performance negatively and significantly. However, positive performance in terms of P/B ratio, ROE, and dividend payout ratio contributed by ownership, grievance committee and audit committee.

References

1. Jensen and Meckling (1976). Theory of a managerial Behaviour, Agency Costs and Ownership Structure, Journal of Financial Economics, 3(1), pp. 305-360.
2. Johnson, Boone, Breach, Friedman (2000). Corporate Governance in an ASIAN Financial Crisis, Journal of Financial Economics, 58, pp. 141-186.
3. Yermack, 1996. Higher Market Valuation of companies with a small board of Directors, Journal of Financial Economics, 40, pp. 185-211.
4. Brown, Robinson, Caylor (2004), Corporate Governance and firm Performance. www.issproxy.com
5. Back, Kang & Park (2004). Corporate Governance and firm value: Evidence from the Korean Financial crisis, Journal of Financial Economics, Vol. 71, pp. 265 - 313.
6. Drobetz *et.al.,* (2004). Corporate Governance and Expected Stock Returns: Evidence from germany, European Financial Management, Vol. 10, No. 2, pp. 267-293.
7. Short *et.al.,* (1999). Managerial Ownership and performance of firms : Evidence from U K, Journal of Corporate Finance, Vol. 05, pp. 79-101.
8. Lipton and Lorsch, 1992. A modest proposal for improved corporate governance, Business Lawyer, 48, pp. 59-77.
9. Rosenstein and Wyatt (1990). Outside Directors, Board independence and shareholder Wealth, Journal of Financial Economics, 26, pp. 175-191.
10. Ananya Mukherjee Reed (2002), *"Corporate Governance Reforms in India"* Journal of Business Ethics 37 : pp. 249-268.
11. Lipton and Lorsch (1992). A modest proposal for improved corporate governance, Business lawer, 48, pp. 59-77.
12. Bernard S. Black and Vikramaditya S. Khanna. *"Can Corporate Governance Reforms Increase Firm's Market Values : Event Study Evidence from India"* pp. 01–34.
13. Kamala Gollakoti and Vipin Gupta. *"History, ownership forms and corporate governance in India"* Journal of Management History Vol. 12, No. 2, 2006, pp. 185-198.
14. Stijn Claessens and Joseph P H Fan. *"Corporate Governance in Asia : A Survey"* International Review of Finance 3:2, 2002, pp. 73-103.
15. Kamala Gollakota, Vipin Gupta. *"History, Ownership forms and Corporate Governance in India"* Journal of Management History Vol. 12 No. 2, 2006 pp. 185-198.
16. Ajay Kumar Garg. *"Influence of Board Size and Independence on firm performance : A study of Indian firms"* VIKALPA, Vol. 32 , No. 3, July-September 2007, pp. 39-60.

17. Balatbat, C, A Naira, Taylor. L Stephen, Walter S Terry (2004). "Corporate Governance, Insider Ownership and Operating Performance of Australian IPO", Accounting and Finance. Vol. 44, pp. 299-328.

18. Barnhart, S. W. and Rosenstein, S., 1998. Board composition, managerial ownership, and firm performance: an empirical analysis. The Financial Review, Vol. 33, pp. 1-16.

19. Bauer, R., Gunster, N. and Otten, R., 2003. Empirical evidence on corporate governance in Europe. Journal of Asset Management, forthcoming.

20. Bernard Black. "*The CG behavior and market value of Russian firms*". Emerging market review, 2 (2001), pp. 89-108.

21. Bhagat S and Black B (2002), "Board Independence and Long term performance", Journal of Corporation Law, 27, pp. 1-12.

22. Bhagat, S. and Black, B., 2002. The non-correlation between board independence and long-term firm performance. Journal of Corporation Law, Vol. 27, No. 2, pp. 231-273.

23. Black, B., Jang, H. and Kim, W., 2002. Does corporate governance affect firm value? Evidence from Korea. Working paper, Stanford Law School, Korea University Business School, and KDI School of Public Policy and Management.

Chapter 11

Growth and Progress of Indian Agriculture and Industrial Sector

Dr D. Pulla Rao and Dr Sukanta Sarkar

> *"A successful economic development strategy must focus on improving the skills of the area's workforce, reducing the cost of doing business and making available the resources business needs to compete and thrive in today's global economy."*
> **–Rod Blagojevich**

Introduction

Agriculture was the key development in the rise of sedentary human civilisation, whereby farming of domesticated species created food surpluses that nurtured the development of civilisation. The study of agriculture is known as agricultural science. Until the Industrial Revolution, the vast majority of the human population laboured in agriculture. In the past century agriculture has been characterised by increased productivity, the substitution of synthetic fertilisers and pesticides for labour, water pollution, and farm subsidies. Cropping systems vary among farms depending on the available resources and constraints; geography and climate of the farm; government policy; economic, social and political pressures; and the philosophy and culture of the farmer.[1]

Industry is the production of goods or services within an economy. The major source of revenue of a group or company is the indicator of its relevant industry. Following the Industrial Revolution, perhaps a third of the world's economic output is derived from manufacturing industries. Industries can be classified in a variety of ways. At the top level, industry is often classified according to the three-sector theory into sectors: primary or extractive, secondary or manufacturing, and tertiary or services. The industrial revolution led to the development of factories for large-scale production, with consequent changes in society. In an industrial society, industry employs a major part of the population. This occurs typically in the manufacturing sector.[2]

Primary Sector

The primary sector of the economy is the sector of an economy making direct use of natural resources. This includes agriculture, forestry, fishing and mining. The secondary sector produces manufactured goods, and the tertiary sector produces services. Primary industry is a larger sector in developing countries; for instance, animal husbandry is more common in Africa than in Japan. In developed countries primary industry has become more technologically advanced, for instance the mechanisation of farming as opposed to hand picking and planting.[3]

Secondary Sector

The secondary sector of the economy includes those economic sectors that produce a finished, usable product: production and construction. This sector is often divided into light industry and heavy industry. Many of these industries consume large quantities of energy and require factories and machinery to convert the raw materials into goods and products. This sector generally takes the output of the primary sector and manufactures finished goods or where they are suitable for use by other businesses, for export, or sale to domestic consumers.[4]

Growth of Agriculture in India

The history of agriculture in India dates back to the Rigveda. The economic contribution of agriculture to India's GDP is steadily declining with the country's broad-based economic growth. As per the 2010 FAO world agriculture statistics, India is the world's largest producer of many fresh fruits and vegetables, milk, major spices, select fibrous crops such as jute, several staples such as millets and castor oil seed. India is the second largest producer of wheat and rice, the world's major food staples. India ranked within the world's five largest producers of over 80 per cent of agricultural produce items, including many cash crops such as coffee and cotton, in 2010. India exported $39 billion worth of agricultural products in 2013, making it the seventh largest agricultural exporter worldwide, and the sixth largest net exporter. It has become one of the world's largest suppliers of rice, cotton, sugar and wheat. India exported around two million metric tonnes of wheat and 2.1 million metric tonnes of rice in 2011 to Africa, Nepal, Bangladesh and other regions around the world. In the years since its independence, India has made immense progress towards food security.[5]

Agriculture, with its allied sectors, is unquestionably the largest livelihood provider in India, more so in the vast rural areas. It also contributes a significant figure to the Gross Domestic Product (GDP). This section provides the information on agriculture produces; machineries, research etc.[6] The Department of Agriculture and Cooperation under the Ministry of Agriculture is responsible for the development of the agriculture sector in India. It manages several other bodies, such as the National Dairy Development Board (NDDB), to develop other allied agricultural sectors.

Several players have invested in the agricultural sector in India, mainly driven by the government's initiatives and schemes. The central government recognises the importance of microirrigation, watershed development and 'Pradhan Mantri Krishi Sinchai Yojana'; thus, it allocated a sum of Rs 5,300 crore (US$ 830 million) for it. The Department of Agriculture and Cooperation under the Ministry of Agriculture has inked MOUs/ agreements with 52 countries including the US. The agriculture sector in India is expected to generate better momentum in the next few years due to increased investments in agricultural infrastructure such as irrigation facilities, warehousing and cold storage.[7]

The government got a boost with advance estimates of foodgrain production pegged at an all-time high of 257.44 million tonnes (MT) for the 2011-12 crop year, higher by 5 MT than the April projections. The boost in agriculture has come partly from eastern India where the second Green Revolution plan of UPA has paid substantial dividends. As against the 2010-11 rice produce of 95.8 MT, the new estimates put the 2011-12 produce at 104.32 MT. Wheat production is pegged at 93.90 MT, against 86.87 MT in the previous crop year. The worrying bit came from lower than expected oilseed production. Gujarat, Haryana and Punjab have been the worst hit so far from the failing monsoon but the well-established irrigation system in the two northern states is likely to compensate to some extent.

Table 11.1: Agricultural Production-Foodgrains

(Million tonnes)

Year	*Cereals*				*Pulses (2)*	*Total Food - grains (1+2)*
	Rice	*Wheat Cereals*	*Coarse*	*Total (1)*		
1953-54	28.21	8.02	22.97	59.20	10.62	69.82
1960-61	34.58	11.00	23.74	69.32	12.70	82.02
1970-71	42.22	23.83	30.55	96.60	11.82	108.42

(Contd...)

1980-81	53.63	36.31	29.02	118.96	10.63	129.59
1990-91	74.29	55.14	32.70	162.13	14.26	176.39
2000-01	84.98	69.68	31.08	185.74	11.07	196.81
2001-02	93.34	72.77	33.37	199.48	13.37	212.85
2002-03	71.82	65.76	26.07	163.65	11.13	174.78
2003-04	88.53	72.15	37.60	198.28	14.91	213.19
2004-05	83.13	68.64	33.46	185.23	13.13	198.36
2005-06	91.79	69.35	34.06	195.20	13.39	208.59
2006-07	93.35	75.81	33.92	203.08	14.20	217.28
2007-08	96.69	78.57	40.76	216.02	14.76	230.78
2008-09	99.18	80.68	40.03	219.90	14.57	234.47
2009-10	89.09	80.80	33.55	203.45	14.66	218.11
2010-11	95.32	85.93	43.68	226.53	18.24	244.78
2011-12	104.32	93.90	42.01	240.23	17.21	257.44

Note: Data for 2011-12 are based on Advance Estimates.

Source: Ministry of Agriculture, Government of India.

The above table shows that production of foodgrains is increasing continuously but production of pulses are increasing very slowly compare to other foodgrains.

Table 11.2: State-wise Production of Foodgrains

(*Thousand tonnes*)

State/ Union Territory	*Year*	*Rice*	*Wheat*	*Coarse Cereals*	*Pulses*	*Foodgrains*
Andhra Pradesh	2011-12	8792.2	7.6	2119.1	739.0	11657.9
Arunachal Pradesh	2008-09	163.9	5.2	77.7	9.0	255.8
Assam	2011-12	009.0	59.0	16.0	108.0	4192.0
Bihar	2011-12	7201.0	4787.3	1557.0	509.3	14054.6
Chhattisgarh	2011-12	6028.4	128.6	188.3	496.5	6841.8
Gujarat	2011-12	1764.0	4100.0	2419.0	783.0	9066.0
Haryana	2011-12	3759.0	12684.4	1387.0	127.0	17957.4
Himachal Pradesh	2011-12	131.6	595.8	752.0	35.6	1515.0
Jammu & Kashmir	2011-12	544.7	406.3	529.9	14.0	1494.9
Jharkhand	2011-12	3418.1	335.3	417.5	492.3	4663.1
Karnataka	2011-12	4038.0	194.0	6907.0	1061.0	12200.0
Kerala	2011-12	555.4	-	0.6	3.6	559.5
Madhya Pradesh	2011-12	1838.2	10580.2	2467.1	4160.1	19045.6
Maharashtra	2011-12	2806.0	1313.0	5982.0	2215.0	12316.0
Odisha	2011-12	5815.2	2.7	258.2	357.2	6433.3
Punjab	2011-12	0542.0	17206.7	550.0	53.3	28352.0

(*Contd...*)

Rajasthan	2011-12	253.4	9319.7	7030.2	2360.0	18963.3
Tamil Nadu	2011-12	6893.9	-	2347.3	399.5	9640.6
Uttar Pradesh	2011-12	14025.0	30293.0	3549.0	2426.0	50293.0
Uttarakhand	2011-12	599.0	874.0	331.0	49.0	1853.0
West Bengal	2011-12	14853.0	884.0	364.9	187.8	16289.7
All States	**2010-11**	**93109.9**	**85819.0**	**41929.1**	**17988.5**	**239146.6**
All India	**2011-12**	**104322.0**	**93903.6**	**42008.5**	**17207.9**	**257441.9**

Source: Agricultural Statistics at a Glance, Ministry of Agriculture, Government of India.

The above table shows that contribution of Uttar Pradesh in global production is higher than other states.

Wheat production is expected to be a record 90.23 million tonnes against 84.27 million tonnes, while rice output is likely to be 103.41 million tons compared to 94.11 million tonnes in 2010-11. Cotton production at 35.2 million bales (of 170 kg each) will be higher than 33.9 million bales. A committee of eminent industrialists like Mukesh Ambani, Jamshyd Godrej and M S Banga had given 15 recommendations including liberalising agri-procurement, streamlining norms for private investment in agriculture supply chain and revisiting Minimum Support Price (MSP) norms. The committee of industrialists had also suggested linking agri-credit with crop insurance, increasing competition in rural banking, promoting R&D investments in high-yielding hybrids, promoting sustainable agricultural practices, leveraging and promoting technical innovations, conducting land reforms in a phased manner and setting up of agricultural parks.

Table 11.3: Agricultural Production-Major Commercial Crops

(Million tonnes)

Year	*Oilseeds*	*Coffee*	*Cotton*	*Jute*	*Sugarcane*	*Tea*	*Tobacco*
1955-56	5.73		4.18	5.39	60.54		0.30
1960-61	6.98		5.60	5.26	110.00		**0.31**
1970-71	9.63	110.23	4.76	6.19	126.37	419.00	0.36
1980-81	9.37	118.65	7.01	8.16	154.25	569.60	0.48
1990-91	18.61	169.73	9.84	9.23	241.05	720.34	0.56
2000-01	18.44	301.20	9.52	10.56	295.96	848.43	0.34
2001-02	20.66	300.60	10.00	11.68	297.21	851.41	0.55
2002-03	14.84	275.30	8.62	11.28	287.38	845.97	0.49
2003-04	25.19	270.50	13.73	11.17	233.86	878.65	0.55
2004-05	24.35	275.50	16.43	10.27	237.09	906.84	0.55
2005-06	27.98	274.00	18.50	10.84	281.17	948.94	0.55
2006-07	24.29	288.00	22.63	11.27	355.52	973.07	0.52
2007-08	29.76	262.00	25.88	11.21	348.19	987.02	0.49

(Contd...)

2008-09	27.72	262.30	22.28	10.37	285.03	972.77	0.62
2009-10	24.88	289.60	24.23	11.82	292.30	991.18	0.69
2010-11	32.48	302.00	33.43	10.62	342.38	966.73	-
2011-12	30.01	314.00	35.20	11.57	357.67	978.96	-

Note:

1. Data for 2011-12 are based on Advance Estimates.
2. Data for 1953-54 to 1969-70 relate to total five major oilseeds viz., groundnut, castorseed, sesamum, rapeseed and mustard, and linseed.
3. Oilseed data comprises total for nine oilseeds out of the eleven in all.
4. Coffee and Tea data measured in million kg.
5. Cotton data measured in million bales of 170 kg each.
6. Raw jute and the Mesta data measured in million bales of 180 kg each.

Source: Ministry of Agriculture, Government of India.

The above table shows that production of various commercial crops is increasing continuously. Production of tea, sugarcane and coffee are more ahead than other.

Table 11.4: State-wise Production of Commercial Crops

(*Thousand tonnes*)

State/ Union Territory	*Year*	*Oilseeds*	*Cotton*	*Sugarcane*	*Raw Jute and Masta*
Andhra Pradesh	2011-12	2312.7	1147.3	12163.2	491.4
Assam	2011-12	148.0		965.0	637.0
Bihar	2011-12	139.1	-	12071.9	1894.0
Chhattisgarh	2011-12	170.9	-	24.4	3.0
Gujarat	2011-12	4931.0	12000.0	14176.6	
Haryana	2011-12	885.2	2650.0	6959.0	
Himachal Pradesh	2011-12	8.6	-	28.3	-
Jammu & Kashmir	2011-12	47.0	-	-	-
Jharkhand	2011-12	174.5	-	457.3	
Karnataka	2011-12	946.4	1200.0	38808.0	1.0
Kerala	2011-12	2.2	-	156.1	-
Madhya Pradesh	2011-12	7716.3	2000.0	2677.0	2.1
Maharashtra	2011-12	4544.0	7200.0	81859.1	30.8
Odisha	2011-12	159.4	325.0	884.7	101.5
Punjab	2011-12	67.5	2300.0	4670.0	
Rajasthan	2011-12	5734.8	1335.0	429.1	-
Tamil Nadu	2011-12	1139.5	450.0	39283.7	3.0
Uttar Pradesh	2011-12	937.0	-	128819.0	-

(*Contd...*)

Uttarakhand	2011-12	31.0	-	6596.0	-
West Bengal	2011-12	745.5	-	1175.0	8623.0
Union Territories	**2011-12**	**149.7**	**25.0**	**435.3**	**64.5**
All India	**2011-12**	**30012.2**	**35200.0**	**357667.1**	**11569.1**

1. Oilseeds data comprises total for nine oilseeds out of eleven in all.
2. Cotton data measured in thousand bales of 170 kg each.
3. Jute and Mesta data measured in thousand bales of 180 kg each.
4. All India data are inclusive of Union Territories.
5. The States of Chhattisgarh, Jharkhand and Uttarakhand were carved out of Madhya Pradesh, Bihar and Uttar Pradesh, respectively during 2000-01.The production figures of Madhya Pradesh, Bihar and Uttar Pradesh for the period 1980-81 to 1999-2000 refer to those of the undivided States.

Source: Agricultural Statistics at a Glance, Ministry of Agriculture, Government of India.

The above table shows that highest quantity of oilseeds are produced in Madhya Pradesh, cotton in Maharashtra, sugarcane in Uttar Pradesh and jute in West Bengal.

Table 11.5: Area under Cultivation – Foodgrains

(Million hectares)

Year	*Cereals*				*Pulses*	*Total Foodgrains*
	Rise	*Wheat*	*Coarse Cereals*	*Total*		
1954-55	30.77	11.26	43.92	85.95	21.91	107.86
1960-61	34.13	12.93	44.96	92.02	23.56	115.58
1970-71	37.59	18.24	45.95	101.78	22.54	124.32
1980-81	40.15	22.28	41.78	104.21	22.46	126.67
1990-91	42.69	24.17	36.32	103.18	24.66	127.84
2000-01	44.71	25.73	30.26	100.70	20.35	121.05
2001-02	44.90	26.34	29.52	100.76	22.01	122.77
2002-03	41.18	25.20	26.99	93.37	20.50	113.87
2003-04	42.59	26.60	30.80	99.99	23.46	123.45
2004-05	41.91	26.38	29.03	97.32	22.76	120.08
2005-06	43.66	26.48	29.04	99.18	22.39	121.60
2006-07	43.81	27.99	28.71	100.51	23.19	123.70
2007-08	43.91	28.04	28.48	100.43	23.63	124.06
2008-09	45.54	27.75	27.45	100.74	22.09	122.83
2009-10	41.87	28.34	27.52	97.73	23.39	121.12
2010-11	42.56	29.25	27.64	99.45	26.28	125.73

Note: Data for 2011-12 are based on Advance Estimates.

Source: Ministry of Agriculture, Government of India.

The above table shows that area under cultivation of foodgrains (i.e. rice, wheat, pulses) is increased since independence but areas of coarse cereal is decreased.

Table 11.6: Area under Cultivation: Commercial Crops

(Million hectares)

Year	*Oilseeds*	*Sugarcane*	*Tea*	*Coffee*	*Cotton and Mesta*	*Raw Jute*	*Tobacco*
1955-56	12.09	1.85	-	-	8.09	0.94	0.41
1960-61	13.77	2.42	-	-	7.61	0.90	0.40
1970-71	16.64	2.62	0.35	0.14	7.61	1.08	0.45
1980-81	17.60	2.67	0.38	0.19	7.82	1.30	0.45
1990-91	24.15	3.69	0.42	0.22	7.44	1.02	0.41
2000-01	22.77	4.32	0.50	0.31	8.53	1.02	0.26
2001-02	22.64	4.41	0.51	0.32	9.13	1.05	0.35
2002-03	21.49	4.52	0.52	0.33	7.67	1.04	0.33
2003-04	21.49	4.52	0.52	0.33	7.67	1.04	0.33
2004-05	27.52	3.66	0.52	0.33	8.79	0.92	0.37
2005-06	27.86	4.20	0.56	0.38	8.68	0.90	0.37
2006-07	26.51	5.15	0.57	0.38	9.14	0.94	0.37
2007-08	26.69	5.06	0.58	0.39	9.41	0.96	0.35
2008-09	27.56	4.42	0.58	0.39	9.41	0.90	0.39
2009-10	26.22	4.18	0.58	0.40	10.28	0.91	0.44
2010-11	26.82	4.94	0.58	0.40	11.14	0.86	-
2011-12	26.48	5.10	-	0.41	12.18	0.91	-

Note:

1. Data for 2011-12 are based on Advance Estimates.
2. Data for 1953-54 to 1969-70 relate to total of five major oilseeds, viz., groundnut, castor seed, sesamum, rapeseed and mustard, and linseed.
3. Oilseed data comprises total for nine oilseeds out of the eleven in all.

Source: Ministry of Agriculture, Government of India.

The above table shows that areas under oilseeds, sugarcane, and coffee are increased in significant rate since independence i.e. doubles or more than this. Area under cultivation of jute decreased but area of tobacco, cotton and tea increased in negligible rate.

Small Scale Industries

Small-scale industries (SSIs) have been playing an important role in the overall economic development of a country like India, where millions of people are unemployed or underemployed. Poverty has become the most important problem for our country today. According to Micro, Small and Medium Enterprises Development (MSMED) Act 2006, the micro, small and medium enterprises (MSMEs) are classified into two classes, namely, manufacturing enterprises that are engaged in the manufacture or production of goods pertaining to any industry specified in the first schedule to the Industries (Development and Regulation) Act, 1951 and service enterprises.

The SSI sector now faces problems such as fierce competition and natural threat to indigenous technology. The process of liberalisation, privatisation and globalisation (LPG) posed several threats and challenges for SSIs in India.[8]

The SSIs in India are broadly classified into two types: Traditional industries and Modern industries. Both the types of SSIs are prevalent in India. Under traditional industries basically Khadi village industries, handlooms, Sericulture etc. are included while modern SSI industries include small scale, export oriented ancillaries and small scale service and business enterprise. Small enterprises assume special position in India because of their role as creators of large scale employment opportunities apart from contributing significantly to industrial production, exports and regional dispersal. The SSIs have to face a large number of problems, including lack of finance (Funds), technological lag, and managerial inefficiency etc.[9]

The small-scale industries contribute a lot to the progress of the Indian economy. They have also a great potential for the future development of the economy. The small-scale industries provide large scope for employment on a massive scale. In 2001, the employment generated in this sector was 19.2 million. This is of great significance for a country like India which is a labour-surplus economy, and where labour-force is increasing at a very rapid rate. The small-scale industries also contribute a sizeable amount to the industrial output of the country. Out of the total output of the manufacturing sector, as much as 40 per cent comes from these industries. Many products of the small-scale industries like handloom cotton fabrics, silk fabrics, handicrafts, carpets, jewellery, etc. are exported to foreign countries. The small-scale industries used resources which are available locally which would otherwise have remained unused. These resources are the hoarded wealth, family-labour, artisan's skills, native entrepreneurship, etc.[10]

Small scale industries play a vital role in the development of economy, mainly in developing countries. If population of India is taken into consideration it can be said that this sector has a wide scope in India. If small scale industrial sector is developed other economy-related problems can be dissolved automatically.[11] The Small Scale Industries in India has today become a growth engine for the economy, contributing substantially to increase in the GDP, employment and exports. This sector has continued to increase its contribution in India's economic development. It is estimated that in terms of value, the SSI sector alone constitutes 40 per cent share of the value added in manufacturing sector and one-third of national exports. The definition of Small Scale Industries varies from one country to another. In most of the countries of the world, the criterion for defining a small enterprise is related to the size of employment. For instance, in the USA, small business is one which has employment of less than 500 people. In the U.K., it is less than 20 skilled workers, in Sweden and Italy less than 50 and 500 people respectively. In some countries both employment and investment are taken into account.[12]

The basic objectives underlying the development of small-scale are the increase in the supply of manufactured goods, promotion of capital information the development of indigenous entrepreneurial talents and skills and the creation of broader employment opportunities. This sector provides a wider scope for the potential entrepreneur to develop his or her own industry. By establishing a link between agriculture and allied industries, the rural entrepreneur can exploit opportunities in areas of farming, agricultural processing and marketing. Small-scale business provides good scope for the growth of entrepreneurial activities. An entrepreneur has good opportunity and vast scope in selling service rather than manufacturing a product. The entrepreneur can achieve better results if the size of the business is small.[13]

Major problems faced by the small scale industries are: (1) finance, (2) raw Material, (3) idle Capacity, (4) technology, (5) marketing, (6) infrastructure, (7) under utilisation of capacity and (8) project planning. Finance is one of the most important problem confronting small scale industries. Small scale industries normally tap local sources for meeting raw material requirements. These units have to face numerous problems like availability of inadequate quantity, poor quality and even supply of raw material is not on regular basis. There is under-utilisation of installed capacity to the extent of 40 to 50 per cent in case of small scale industries. Small scale entrepreneurs are not fully exposed to the latest technology. These small scale units are also exposed to marketing problems. Infrastructure aspects adversely affect the functioning of small scale units. There is inadequate availability of transportation, communication, power and other facilities in the backward areas. Most of the small-scale units are working below full potentials or there is gross underutilisation of capacities. Another important problem faced by small scale entrepreneurs is poor project planning.[14]

The success of a small enterprise revolves around the entrepreneur and its employees, provided the employees are skilled and efficient.

Small-scale units find it very difficult to compete with the product of large-scale units and imported articles which are comparatively very cheap and of better quality than small unit's product. Absence of adequate infrastructure adversely affects the quality, quantity and production schedule of the enterprises which ultimately results in under-utilisation of capacity. Most of the small units employ outdated and traditional technology and equipment. Lack of appropriate technology and equipment create a major stumbling block for the growth of small-scale industries.[15]

Small scale and cottage industries in India occupy a vital position in the planned industrial development in the country. Not only they provide immediate large scale employment but also offer a method of ensuring a more equitable distribution of the national income. Moreover they facilitate an effective mobilisation of capital.[16] The development of small-scale industries is hampered by a diversity of problems. There are certain problems common to all types of cottage and small scale industrial units. The non-availability of adequate finance, paucity of raw materials, absence of technical and managerial guidance, and non-availability of industrial accommodation and marketing facilities are the other major problems facing the small-scale sector. The problems of small-scale industries may be classified as external and internal. External problems are those, which are beyond the control of the industrialists, such as the availability of power, and other infrastructural facilities required for running the units. Contrarily, the internal problems are those which are not influenced by external forces like problems involved in organisation, structure, and production process, channel of distribution, technology, know-how, training, industrial relations and inadequacy of management.[17]

The Central Government constantly assesses and monitors the impact of liberalisation/globalisation and changing economic scenario on the growth and development of economy, including that of small scale industries in the country. Government has put in place several measures to help small enterprises. These include schemes of assistance for technology upgradation, infrastructure development, cluster development, adoption of modern management practices, marketing, etc. Further, steps have been taken to enhance credit flow to the SSI units, sensitise them to matters relating to global trade liberalisation and facilitate information dissemination through the use of information technology.[18]

The small scale industrial units should be given adequate degree of priority in the allocation pattern of essential, but scarce raw materials, imported components and equipment. Marketing of their products at remunerative prices is the major problem of small-scale industrial units. Market research, intelligence and information systems should be strengthened and the results made available to those units. The small scale industrial units should be encouraged to replace their outmoded equipment with that incorporating an up-to-date technology, and facilities and incentives should be provided wherever required.[19]

Small-scale industries are occupying a very important place in the industrial structure of Indian economy. Appropriate steps should be taken to remove all those problems the industries suffer for their survival and growth. The environment in which the industry operates must be conducive for the development of industries. The government should conduct detailed surveys of the existing small industries and draws up productive programmes for them. The government should make necessary arrangement for imparting proper education and training to workers engaged in small-scale units.[20]

The government should provide the credit to small and cottage industries at lower rate of interest. Further, commercial banks are also providing loan to develop the industries. The government imports the raw material for the cottage industries from abroad and provides them at lower price to encourage them. The government also purchases finished products from them and sells it at showroom. Government display centres inside and out-side the country are creating the demand. The government has set up various institutions like industrial, vocational, commercial and polytechnic institutions to provide the qualified workers to the cottage and small scale industries. For the training of weavers the small corporation have set up carpet training development centres. These are working very usefully.[21]

Heavy Industries

It is industry that involves one or more characteristics such as large and heavy products; large and heavy equipment and facilities (such as heavy equipment, large machine tools, and huge buildings); or complex or numerous processes. From the late nineteenth century through the mid-twentieth, as the chemical industry and electrical industry developed, they involved components of both heavy industry and light industry, which was soon also true for the automotive industry and the aircraft industry. Modern shipbuilding (since steel replaced wood) is considered heavy industry.[22] Heavy industries has been beautifying the built world for over ten years. As an architectural design and custom construction company, Heavy Industries has manufactured and installed some of Canada's best known public artworks and most complex architectural projects. Through technology, experience, and expertise, Heavy Industries has become a single source for designing, fabricating, and installing custom features for artists, architects, and design professionals.[23]

Heavy Industry in India comprises of the heavy engineering industry, machine tool industry, heavy electrical industry, industrial machinery and auto-industry. These industries provide goods and services for almost all sectors of the economy, including power, rail and road transport. Heavy Electrical Industry is an important manufacturing sector, catering to the need of energy sector and other industrial sectors. Major equipments like boilers, turbo generators, turbines, transformers, condensers, switch gears and relays and related accessories are manufactured by Heavy Electrical Equipment manufacturers. The performance of this Industry is closely linked to the power programme of the country.

The Indian textile machinery industry is a significant component of the capital goods industry. This industry comprises of over 1446 machinery and components manufacturing units with over 600 units producing complete machinery, and the remaining parts and accessories. Cement plants based on raw mill grinding, pyro-processing and cement grinding process technology, for capacities upto 10,000 TPD, are being manufactured in collaboration with foreign technology providers. The petroleum industry in India is undergoing a major change. With the ongoing process of liberalisation, the industry has been thrown open for private sector in all major areas of exploration, production, refining and marketing, and this has resulted in increased demand for the oil field and related equipments.[24]

Special Economic Zone

The term special economic zone (SEZ) is commonly used as a generic term to refer to any modern economic zone. In these zones business and trades laws differ from the rest of the country. To encourage businesses to set up in the zone, financially libertarian policies are introduced. These policies typically regard investing, taxation, trading, quotas, customs and labour regulations. Additionally, companies may be offered tax holidays. India was one of the first countries in Asia to recognise the effectiveness of the Export Processing Zone model in promoting exports, with Asia's first EPZ set up in Kandla in 1965. The Special Economic Zones Act was passed by the Government of India in May 2005, it received Presidential assent on the 23rd of June, 2005. While introducing the act, then Prime Minister of India, Manmohan Singh, said: "SEZs are here to stay. The objectives of SEZs can be explained as: Generation of additional economic activity;

Promotion of exports of goods and services; Promotion of investment from domestic and foreign sources; Creation of employment opportunities; and Development of infrastructure facilities.[25]

Special Economic Zone is defined as "a specifically delineated duty free enclave and shall be deemed to be foreign territory for the purposes of trade operations and duties and tariffs". The Government has converted eight Export Processing Zones located at Kandla and Surat (Gujarat), Cochin (Kerala), Santa Cruz (Mumbai-Maharashtra), Falta (West Bengal), Madras (Tamil Nadu), Visakhapatnam (Andhra Pradesh) and Noida (Uttar Pradesh) into Special Economic Zones and all are functional now. In addition, three new Special Economic Zones approved for establishment at Indore (Madhya Pradesh), Manikanchan - Salt Lake (Kolkata) and Jaipur have since commended operations. The functioning of the SEZs is governed by a three-tier administrative set up. The Board of Approval is the apex body and is headed by the Secretary, Department of Commerce. The Approval Committee at the Zone level deals with approval of units in the SEZs and other related issue.[26]

Special Economic Zones in India were established in an attempt to accelerate foreign investment and endorse exports from India and recognising the need of a global platform to expose the domestic firms and producers to the competitive world market. SEZs are controlled by a three-tier Organisational Set-up described as under: (a) Supreme controlling body in the Department is known as The Board of Approval; (b) At district level, The Unit Approval Committee tackles with SEZs development and other associated issues; (c) Every district is led by a Development Commissioner, who also controls the Unit Approval Committee.[27]

Conclusion

Agriculture, with its allied sectors, is unquestionably the largest livelihood provider in India, more so in the vast rural areas. It also contributes a significant figure to the Gross Domestic Product. Small scale industries play a vital role in the development of economy, mainly in developing countries. The basic objectives underlying the development of small-scale are the increase in the supply of manufactured goods, promotion of capital information the development of indigenous entrepreneurial talents and skills and the creation of broader employment opportunities. Major problems faced by the small scale industries are: finance, raw material, idle capacity, technology, marketing, infrastructure, under-utilisation of capacity, and project planning.

References

1. Agriculture, https://en.wikipedia.org/wiki/Agriculture
2. Industry, https://en.wikipedia.org/wiki/Industry
3. Primary sector of the economy, https://en.wikipedia.org/wiki/Primary_sector_of_the_economy
4. Secondary sector of the economy, https://en.wikipedia.org/wiki/Secondary_sector_of_the_economy
5. Agriculture in India, https://en.wikipedia.org/wiki/Agriculture_in_India
6. http://india.gov.in/topics/agriculture
7. Indian Agriculture Industry: an overview, http://www.ibef.org/industry/agriculture-india.aspx
8. Susmitha Mohan M. Growth and performance of small scale industries in India with special reference to Kerala, Available at http://www.lfymag.com/admin/issuepdf/15-18_Small%20Scale%20Industries_FFYApril-14.pdf
9. Dr Reetu Sharma, Problems and prospects of small scale industrial units, Asia Pacific Journal of Marketing & Management Review, Vol.1 No. 2, October 2012, http://indianresearchjournals.com/pdf/APJMMR/2012/October/15.pdf
10. Role of small scale and cottage industries, Available at http://www.trcollege.net/study-material/24-economics/48-role-of-small-scale-and-cottage-industries
11. Sangita G.Patil and Dr P.T. Chaudhari, Problems of Small Scale Industries in India, International Journal of Engineering and Management Research, Volume-4, Issue-2, April-2014, pp. 19-21.
12. Dr Ramavat Vaijayanti, Problems faced by small scale sector- an analysis, http://www.abhinavjournal.com/images/Commerce_&_Management/Jan13/13.pdf
13. Scope for entrepreneurship in small business sector, Available at http://www.thirawiyan.in/2012/07/scope-for-entrepreneurship-in-small.html
14. Smriti Chand, Major Problems faced by the Small Scale Industries of India, http://www.yourarticlelibrary.com/industries/10-major-problems-faced-by-the-small-scale-industries-of-india/23457/
15. What are the problems faced by Small Scale Industries in India?, http://www.preservearticles.com/201101153374/problems-faced-by-small-scale-industries-in-india.html
16. Problems Faced by Small Scale Industries in India, http://www.important-india.com/7726/problems-faced-by-small-scale-industries-in-india/
17. Problems faced by small scale industries, Chapter V, http://shodhganga.inflibnet.ac.in/bitstream/10603/4912/11/11_chapter%205.pdf
18. Ministry of Small Scale Industries: OUTCOME BUDGET 2007-08, Available at http://msme.gov.in/Outcome_Budget-2007-08-SSI.pdf
19. Smriti Chand, Measures to Remove Difficulties faced by Small-Scale Industries in India, Available at http://www.yourarticlelibrary.com/industries/6-measures-to-remove-difficulties-faced-by-small-scale-industries-in-india/23463/
20. What are the measures to be taken for survival and growth of Small Scale Industries? http://www.preservearticles.com/201101153375/measures-to-be-taken-for-survival-and-growth-of-small-scale-industries.html

21. http://studypoints.blogspot.in/2011/07/discuss-various-measures-to-solve_7365.htm
22. Heavy industries, https://en.wikipedia.org/wiki/Heavy_industry
23. http://heavyindustries.ca/
24. http://indiainbusiness.nic.in/newdesign/index.php?param=industry-services_landing/341/1
25. Special economic zone, https://en.wikipedia.org/wiki/Special_economic_ zone
26. http://indiainbusiness.nic.in/newdesign/index.php?param=industry-services_landing/369/2
27. http://business.mapsofindia.com/sez/india/

Chapter 12

Constitutional Rights and Other Law Provision for Child

Dr Jaydevi G. Rajyaguru and Dr Parmeshwari Rajyaguru

"We need to revise our economic thinking to give full value to our natural resources. This revised economics will stabilize both the theory and the practice of free-market capitalism. It will provide business and public policy with a powerful new tool for economic development, profitability, and the promotion of the public good." **–Paul Hawken**

Introduction

The Universal declaration of Human Rights started with the golden line: "All Human beings are born free and equal in dignity and rights." Human Rights are seen as 'inherent, inalienable and universal rights' basic to a human being for the reason of his/her being born as a human being. The concept of family to child fulfils physical need of human beings by providing security and shelter from factors, hostile to life. Viewed from a psychological perspective, it Psychological need by providing a sense of personal space and privacy viewed from a sociological perspective it fulfils. Social needs are by providing a gathering area and communal space for the human family i.e., the relationship of blood consanguinity and marriage, the basic unit of society. Viewed from an economic perspective, it also fulfils. Economics needs by functions as a centre for commercial production. This system of living in a group under the set standards, Endures the civil, political, social, economic and cultural rights of human being. The society or the community grows the basic cell i.e. the family and its support structures.

The children are greatest gift of humanity and a very important segment of human society. But unfortunately child has been exploited and discrimination in every society. They can be found working in homes doing household chores, factories, fields, hotels, restaurants etc. children are generally made to work under unhygienic condition for long hours and wages paid to them are generally very low. Sometimes children are exploited by their own guardians and parents. Both boys and girls are being exploited sexually, physically as well as emotionally. The children who are illegitimate or orphans or children of people who have stigma attached to their reputation such as prostitution and under trials are further exploited and looked down by the strangers with perverted mentality children are the easiest victim of sexual abuse.

Children are abused for organ and flesh trade. According to study the child abuse in India, as in other developing societies is a phenomenon which is widespread and cuts across ethnic. The study revealed that 69 per cent suffered physical abuse in one or more situations. Children faced highest level of physical abuse within family.[1] Pandit Jawaharlal Nehru asked 65 years ago "who lives if India dies? Who dies if India lives? If India is to live children are to live well. So the future well-being of a nation depends upon as to how the children grow and develop. The children need special legislation measures to protect them from exploitation and abuse and to save them from certain liabilities and to develop their personality in view of their weak position.

Declaration of the Right of the Child[1]

This declaration adopted in 1924 by the League of Nations, which the lays down that mankind 'owes to the child the best it has to give, The 1959 United Nation Declaration of the Rights of Child emphasise that child by reason of this physical and mental immaturity need special safeguards and care including appropriate legal protection, before as well as after birth, and the mankind owes to child the best it has to give. The declaration mentions interlaid that the opportunities and facilities by law and other means, to enable him to develop physically, mentally, spiritually and socially, in a healthy and normal manner and in conditions of freedom and dignity. The child is entitled to free and compulsory education at least in the elementary stages. That the child shall be protected against all forms of neglect, cruelty and exploitation and shall not be subject of trafficking in any form and that he shall not be admitted to employment before an appropriate minimum age.

The Universal Declaration of Human Rights 1948, the international covenant on Rights and the international covenant on ESC rights, 1966 are some other international instruments that convey the rights of the child. Through a resolution in 1976, the United Nations declared the year 1979 to be the international year of child. On 20th November, 1989

General Assembly of the United Nations adopted the convention on the rights of the child, wherein a set of standards to be adhered to by all state parties in securing the best interest of the child has been prescribed.

United Nations Conventions on Child Rights, 1989

The convention emphasises social reintegration of child victims to the every possible extent, without resorting to judicial proceedings. The child rights convention incorporates the whole spectrum of human rights and sets up the specific ways, which should be made available to boys and girls; it applies to all children and young people under the age of 18. The best interest of the child is the major building block in the philosophy of the convention. India has also acceded to the convention on the rights of the child on 11th 12. 1992. Child rights convention has established various committees to look into the progress made by the signatory countries in the direction of enacting laws and other policies and other development to save the child rights.

National Legal Framework

In India at the domestic level a good effort has been made for uplifting the position of the child. The consciousness relating to child rights and welfare is also reflected in some of the provision of Indian constitution.

- **Article 15(3)** enables the state to make special provisions for the children. It reads: "Nothing in this article shall prevent the state from making any special provision for women and children".
- **Article 21-A** provides fundamental rights to free and compulsory education for children of 6-14 years of age. It reads: [2] "The state shall provide free and compulsory education to all children of the age of six to fourteen years in such manner as the state may by law determine".
- **Article 23** prohibits trafficking in human beings and forced labour, it reads as: "Traffic in human beings, beggar and other similar forms of forced labour are prohibited and any contravention of the provisions shall be an offence."
- **Article 24** provides that, "no child below the age of fourteen years shall be employed to work in any factory or mine or engaged in any other hazardous employment."
- **Article 39(e)** provides that the state shall direct its policy towards securing that the tender age of the children are not abused and the citizens are not forced by way of economic necessity to avocation unsuited to their age or strength.

- **Article 39(f)** casts a duty on state to declare that children are given opportunities and facilities to develop in a healthy manner and in conditions of freedom and dignity and that childhood and in conditions of freedom and dignity and that childhood and youth are protected against exploitation and against moral and material abandonment.
- **Article 47** cast and duty upon the state to raise the level of Nutrition and the standard of living and to improve public health.
- **Article 51-A(k)**[3] cast a duty upon a parent or guardian to provide opportunities for education to his child or as the case may be, ward between the age of six and fourteen years.

The Child Labour (Prohibition and Regulation) Act 1986, have been enacted with a view to prohibit the engagement of children in certain employments and to regulate the conditions of work of children in certain other employments[4] employment of Children who have not completed 14 years of age is an offence under the Child Labour Prohibition and Regulation Act, 1986 and its punishable for one or fine of Rs 20,000 or both. Repetition of such offence is punishable with Imprisonment of two years. In addition as per the directions of the Hon'ble Supreme Court of India Rs 20,000 is payable by the guilty employers for rehabilisation of the child.[5]

Apart from this the Indian Penal Code, 1860 deplores child exploitation and considers exposing a child below 12 years of age to physical risk or deserting it with the care of child.[6] Kidnapping or maiming a child for begging or for prostitution is an offence.[7] Section125 of the Criminal Procedure Code deals with responsibility of parents to maintain, (b) their child, who having sufficient means neglect or refuses to maintain his legitimate or illegitimate. Minor child's, where married or not unable to maintain itself, (c) his legitimate or illegitimate minor child (not being a married daughter) who has attained majority where such child it by reason of any physical or mental abnormality or injury unable to maintain itself.

Juvenile Justice Act: This act is an important piece of legislation relating to child welfare. This law provides for the care, protection, treatment, development and rehabilitation of delinquent and neglected juveniles.[8] The Government of India having ratified the Convention has found it expedient to re-enact the existing law relating to Juveniles Act bearing in mind the Standard Minimum Rules for the Administration of Juvenile Justice 1985 (the Beijing Rules), the United Nation Rules for the international instruments. To achieve these objective the JUVENILE

JUSTICE (CARE AND PROTECTION OF CHILDREN) Act, 2000 has been passed by both the houses of parliament and received the assent of the President on 30th December, 2000.

Conclusion

To conclude, it may be pointed out that despite numerous laws enacted both at center and state level for children. The effective implementation of these laws is missing. In fact to-date in our country there is no single legislation for dealing exclusively with all type of problem of child exploitation and child abuse. In existing statutes most of the legal provisions are merely idealised postulates and for from reality, due to peculiar socio-economic structure of our country. It is only a dream to provide necessary facilities and protection to the children. In fact, a large number to children of tender age are exposed to labour and are abused by their own parents, who want their children to seek employment to augment the income of their families and to expose them to the work which is not suitable to their age.

References

1. Study on child abuse in India 2007 (ministry of women and child welfare along with prayas NGO).
2. Added by 86th Constitutional Amendment Act, 2002.
3. Added by 86th Constitutional Amendment Act, 2002.
4. In August 2006, the ministry of Labour added certain occupations in the list of hazardous occupations.
5. M.C. Mehta v/s U.O.I. 1996. (6) Scc-756.
6. Section 318 IPC, 1860 Concealment of birth by secret disposal of dead body.
7. Section 361 IPC, 1860 kidnapping from lawful guardianship.
8. The Juvenile Justice Act, 2000.

Chapter 13

Managerial and Operational Efficiency: A Study of Indian Cement Industry

Dr Biswajit Prasad Chhatoi

"With the development of industrial capitalism, a new and unanticipated system of injustice, it is libertarian socialism that has preserved and extended the radical humanist message of the Enlightenment and the classical liberal ideals that were perverted into an ideology to sustain the emerging social order."

–Noam Chomsky

Introduction

Ratio is the quantitative relationship expressed in mathematical term between two individual and group of figures connected with each other in some logical manner. Further, quantitative relationship between two or more accounting figures that appear in the profit loss and accounts or balance sheet is called financial/accounting ratio. It is one of the common and widely accepted means of communicating processed financial information to different groups of stake holders of a firm. The financial ratio analysis is based on the principle that 'a single accounting figure by itself may not communicate any meaningful information but when expressed as a relative to some other figure, it gives some significant information'. Ratio analysis is relevant in better assessing the performance of an organisation. In this respect ratio analysis helps in disclosing details about financial position, liquidity position, overall solvency, operating efficiency and overall profitability.

Profit maximisation and wealth maximisation are two main objectives of every organisation. These two objectives may be achieved through a better management of recourses. The recourses for any organisation are nothing other than "seven Ms," which stands for man, machine, material, method, minute, management and money. Managerial efficiency aims at right combination of people, process, and technology for enhanced productivity and value of any organisation through proper management of 'seven Ms.'

Investment made in different assets to earn profit through sales. The managers are responsible for efficient management of different assets. The level of efficiency in managing assets directly affects the sale and profitability of the organisation. A number of ratios are available to measure the performance/efficiency of current and fixed assets. These ratios in group are known as Activity Ratios/ Turnover Ratios/Performance Ratios. Through this ratio the managerial efficiencies can be easily measured. Performance Ratios is a measure of 'movement' and indicates frequency/speed an account has moved/turned over during a period. It shows how efficiently and effectively the assets of the firm are being utilised. The Activity Ratios therefore, measure the effectiveness with which the firm uses its resources.

The profitability or the operational efficiency of the firm is measured through Profitability Ratios (P Ratios). Different groups of stakeholders through this ratio analysis, measure the operational efficiency of the firm for different reasons. Management is interested in the overall profitability and operational efficiency of the firm, whereas, the equity shareholders are interested in the ultimate returns available to them. Creditors, as stake-holders, can measure the profitability of the firm in terms of the P Ratios. Sales revenue is one of the determinants of profit. That means, when a firm makes sale it is supposed to earn profit. Profit itself an unclear and ambiguous term as it could mean several things - profit before tax or after tax, or short or long-term profit, total profit or profit per share, total operating profit or profit accruing to share holder, profit from the point of total fund employed or share holder profit only.

Literature Review

Deloof (2003) conducted a research on working capital management and profitability in which he investigated the relationship between gross operating income and receivables, inventories and accounts payables of Belgian companies. A negative relation is found between gross profitability and number of days under average collection period, inventory holding period. He has suggested the wealth maximisation is possible only through reduction in number of days of average collection period, inventory holding period.

Collier *et.al.* (2004), in their article 'An example of the use of financial ratio analysis: the case of Motorola' exhibit how the financial data for a actual company converted into financial ratio when the data is not homogenous. They concluded that computation of financial ratio is complicated for companies that do not readily fall into a single industry because of the integration of different industry characteristics makes the computation process more complicated.

In their study "The Relationship between working capital management and profitability of listed companies in the Athens stock exchange" Lazaridis and Tryfonidis (2006), examine the relationship between gross profit and accounts receivables, accounts payables, inventory. The sample is consisting of 131 firms listed on the Athens Stock Exchange. The period of study is four years i.e. from 2001 to 2004. By using correlation and regression tool for research they indentified statistically significant relationship between profitability and accounts receivables, accounts payables, inventory.

Paradogonas (2007), in his research article "Financial performance of large and small firms: evidence from Greece" attempted to specify different factors that determine a firm's profitability. This study conducted in Greek on 3035 manufacturing firms, collecting data over five years from 1995-1999. Regression model is used to arrive at any conclusion. The dependant variable of the regression model is profitability and the independent variables are size, managerial efficiency, debt structure, investment in fixed assets and sales. They concluded that investment in fixed assets significantly affects profitability of the firm.

According to Ibam (2008), the fixed assets acquired for the purpose of generating sales revenue. Fixed assets turnover ratio establishes relationship between fixed assets and sales to measure the efficiency and productivity of fixes assets management. From an investor's point of view higher the ratio is better indication of asset management. White (2008), conducted research on "Accounts Receivable: Analysing the Turnover Ratio". He referred that receivables which appear in asset side of balance sheet is due to credit sale of the organisation. The life of these receivables is less than one accounting period. The efficiency in managing this current asset can easily accessed from accounts receivable turnover ratio.

Zain (2008), in his articles on the use and computation of profitable ratio discussed return on Return on Assets ratio. This ratio establishes relationship between Net Profit and Total Assets. This ratio indicates company's ability to generate income/profit using its assets. A high ratio indicates better utilisation of assets whereas low ratio indicates difficulties in utilisation of assets to generate income. Further, describing profit margin ratio he concluded that it is a relationship between sales and profits through which the operating efficiency of a firm can easily assessed. Jo (2009), in his articles "Inventory Analysis: A Guide to Analysing Inventory for Small Business Owners" discussed on measurement of financial performance through inventory turnover ratio analysis. Inventory includes inventory: Raw Materials, Work-in-Progress and Finished Goods whereas inventory turnover ratio includes inventory turnover and average inventory holding period. This ratio is applicable to all these three inventory is a yardstick to know about effective inventory management which discloses company's financial performance analysis.

Gopinathan (2009), in his articles "Financial Ratio Analysis for Performance Check: Financial Statement Analysis with Ratios can Reveal Problem Areas" discussed about the Financial Ratio Analysis for Performance evaluation. He concluded that the financial statement of a company contain substantial amount of financial information. The ratio of these information helps in evaluating the overall performance of a company which guide the investors in their investment decision. James (2009), in his work on financial statement analysis to know the profitability concluded that income statement and balance sheet are the two major source of information for any type of financial analysis. The operating/profit performance can be measured through ratios of Income Statement and Balance Sheet. The profit ratios are the indicator of company's performance in terms of profits compared to revenue generated from sales. Further in his research on asset turnover ratio, he concluded that balance sheet is the showcase of net worth of the company. The performance of the assets in terms of generating revenue can be measured by comparing it with sale figure appears in income statement.

Mtetwa (2010) pointed out that the fixed assets are the productive assets which have life more than one account period and being used in production of goods or services. The fixed assets appear in the balance sheet are tangible or intangible in nature. The performance of these assets can be easily estimated fixed asset turnover. Dong and Su (2010) examined the relationship between component of working capital and profitability of Vietnamese firms over three years from 2006 to 2008. They observed a significantly negative relationship between gross operating profit and inventory days, and receivable days. They concluded that the profitability of the firm decreases due to increase in number of days in inventory and receivable days under cash conversion cycle. Gill *et. al.* (2010) established relationship between working capital management and profitability in their article "The Relationship between Working Capital Management and Profitability: Evidence from the United States". The period of study is three years i.e. from 2005 to 2007 on 88 US listed firms. The sample is drawn from the New York Stock Exchange. The authors do find statistically significant relationship between average inventory days and profitability of a firm whereas negative relation between accounts receivable and profitability. They concluded that profitability of the firms can be increased by reducing the number of days in account receivables.

Karaduman *et. al.* (2010), investigated the impact of working capital management practices on the profitability. He considered return on assets as the yardstick to measure the profitability and receivable and inventory days as component of working capital.140 companies from the Istanbul Stock Exchange selected randomly for the study, from 2005-2008. They indentified a statistically significant negative association between return on assets and accounts receivable, inventory days. Jamali and Asadi (2012), investigated the relationship between the management efficiency and profitability of a firm on Indian automobile industry. Thirteen automobile companies in Pune are selected for the study over a period 2006 to 2010. Pearson Coefficient correlation is applied on two variables Gross Profit Ratio and Assets Turnover Ratio to prove the hypothesis. They concluded that profitability and management efficiency are highly correlated to each other.

Okwo *et.al.,* (2012), in their article "Investment in Fixed Assets and Firm Profitability: Evidence from the Nigerian Brewery Industry" measure the impact of level of investment in fixed assets on operating profit. This study based on a sample of four Nigerian brewery companies over eleven years from 1999 to 2009. Regression technique and correlation statistical tool is used to ascertain the impact of level of fixed asset on profitability of the firm. They concluded that the relationship between these two variables is positive. Further, they suggested that investment in fixed asset does not have any strong and statistical impact on the profitability of firm.

Dhillon and Vachhrajani (2013), attempted to measure impact of operational efficiency on overall profitability. He conducted his research on Gujarat Industries Power Company Limited over a period of six years i.e. from 2005-06 to 2010-11. Activity ratio is considered as the source of operational efficiency whereas Earning Power is considered as the indicator of profitability. Using Karl Pearson's coefficient correlation tool on the secondary data he indentified that insignificant positive correlation between operational efficiency.

Variables of the Study

This section explains the description and estimation of variables related to managerial efficiency and operational/ profitability.

Inventory Turnover Ratio: It establishes relationship between the cost of goods sold and the average inventory held during a period by the firm.

- Inventory Turnover Ratio = Cost of goods sold /Average Inventory
- Average inventory = (Opening Inventory + Closing Inventory)/2
- Cost of goods sold = Opening Stock + Purchase - Closing Stock or Net Sales - Gross profit.

In manufacturing firm, the inventories consist of Raw Materials, Work-in-Progress and Finished Goods. Activity ratio is calculated for each of individual component as follows:

- R/M Turnover Ratio: Annual Material Consumed/ Average Raw Material Inventory.
- W/P Turnover Ratio: Annual Cost of Production Average work-in-progress.
- FG Turnover Ratio: Annual Cost of Production/ Average Finished Goods.

No ideal standard is set to evaluate this ratio. The ratio of one firm compared with the past ratio of same firm or ratio of other firms to come at a conclusion. Normal, higher the ratio, the better it is. But this is true only up to a point. The negative correlation between value of average inventory and the ratio compels the firm to take seriously a low level of stock due to high I/T Ratio which may result in frequent stock outs. The concept of I/T Ratio can be extended to find out the number of Days of Inventory Holding.

- Inventory Holding Period = Days in a Year/ Inventory Turnover Ratio

Receivables Turnover Ratio (R/T Ratio): The speed of converting receivables in to cash affects the liquidity position of the firm. The liquidity of debtors is judged through Receivables Turnover and Average collection period. The R/T Ratio attempts to throw light on the collection and credit policies of the firm. The velocity of receivables collection by matching the annual credit sales to the average receivables is Receivables Turnover Ratio.

- Receivable Turnover Ratio = Annual Net Credit Sales/ Average Receivables
- Average collection period = 365/ Receivable Turnover Ratio

A high R/T Ratio means a low average collection period depicts highly liquid receivables and a very restrictive credit policy. A very restrictive credit policy could limit the profits by denying the credit to potential customers who may then go elsewhere. To draw a perfect policy, the R/T Ratio and the average collection period of the firm should be compared with the industry's acceptable standard and be viewed in terms of the credit policy of the firm.

Turnover Ratio on Solvency of the Firm: Inventory and Receivable Turnover Ratio calculated with reference to the current assets and pays attention on the liquidity position of the firm. However, some other Activity Ratios may also be calculated as follows:

- Fixed Asset Turnover Ratio = Net Sales/ Average Fixed Assets
  - o Fixed Asset means written down value of fixed assets
- Asset Turnover Ratio = Net Sales/ Average Assets
  - o Average Assets means average of tangible assets
- Total Asset Turnover Ratio = Net Sales/ Average Tangible Assets
  - o Total Asset means Tangible and Intangible assets of the firm
- Investment Turnover Ratio = Net Sales/ Average Investment

All the above ratios measure per rupee sales generated by per rupee of assets being maintained by the firm. Fixed Asset Turnover Ratio considered only the written down value of all the fixed assets. Asset turnover ratio considered all tangible assets whereas total asset turnover ratio considered tangible as well as intangible asset as a whole. Higher the ratio, the greater is the sales made per rupee of asset employed in the firm and hence higher is the profit. An increase in these ratios over a period discloses that more sales have been generated per rupee of assets.

The Profit Margin refers to the profit contributed by per rupee sales revenue and therefore, the Profit Margin ratios measure the relationship between profit and the sales. Different Profit Margin ratios have been suggested as follows:

Gross Profit Ratio (GP Ratio): The gross profit is the difference between the sales revenue and the cost of production including direct expenses. The GP Ratio is also called the average mark up ratio.

- Gross Profit Ratio= (Gross Profit/ Net Sales) × 100

This Ratio reflects the efficiency with which the firm produces/ purchases the goods. At a constant efficiency change in GP Ratio is because of change in selling price or cost price or raw material consumption per unit. The GP Ratio should be analysed and studied as a time series by comparing the result with other firm or with industry.

Operating Profit Ratio (OP Ratio): The operating profit refers to the profit generated by the operation of the firm. The operating profit is also known as the Earnings before Interest and Taxes (EBIT). The OP Ratio is percentage of pure profit earned on every rupee of sales made.

- Operating Profit Ratio = (Operating Profit/ Net Sales) × 100

This Ratio measures the efficiency with which the firm not only manufactures/purchases the goods but also sells the goods. The OP Ratio in conjunction with the GP Ratio can depict whether changes in the profitability of the firm are caused by change in manufacturing efficiency or administrative efficiency. It can help to identify the corrective measures to improve the profitability.

Net Profit Ratio (NP Ratio): The NP Ratio measures the efficiency of the management in generating additional revenue over and above the cost of manufacturing, administrative, selling and distributing the product. The NP Ratio is the relationship between the net profit (after tax) and the net sales.

- Net Profit Ratio = (Net Profit/ Net Sales) × 100

This ratio also indicates the net contributions made by every one rupee of sales. It simply discloses the proportion of sales revenue available to the owners and the extent to which the sales revenue can decrease or the cost can increase without inflicting a loss on the owners.

The difference between net profit and operating profit is due to financial charges and tax. An analysis of the GP Ratio, OP Ratio and the NP ratio over long period helps to identify the reasons for variations in the profitability.

Overall Profitability

The operating efficiency of an organisation in terms of the efficient utilisation of the resources is reflected in different profit ratios. Out of three profit ratios consider in this research work net profit margin is best one to reflect efficient utilisation of the resources. A high profitability is an indicator of better performance but a low margin does not necessarily imply a lower rate of return on investments/assets turnover. So the overall operating efficiency of an organisation can be accessed through earning power/ return on assets (ROA) ratio. Earning power is the combination of Net Profit

Margin and Assets Turnover. The earning power is the overall profitability of an organisation. This ratio has two elements profitability on sales as reflected in the net profit margin, and in assets turnover.

Earning Power = Net Profit Margin x Assets Turnover

Statement of the Problem

Managerial efficiency simply refers to efficient management of sales of an organisation. This can be easily estimated from the turnover ratios. The turnover ratios on inventory and receivable disclose efficient management of current assets whereas turnover ratios on fixed assets indicate the efficiency of management in managing same. Operating efficiency of a firm may measure through the profitable ratios. In both the ratio denominator is sale or related item. In this context, it is right time to answer the questions; do the fluctuations in efficiency ratio affects the profitability of an organisation? Do these ratios of companies belongs to one industry is similar.

Objectives and Methodology

Objectives of the study

On the basis of the research gap, the present study outlined following objectives-

- To examine the managerial efficiency of sample companies.
- To examine the operational efficiency of sample companies.
- To analyse the impact of managerial efficiency on operational efficiency over the period of study.

Methodology

The current study is analytical in nature. Critical evaluations of the secondary data (basically panel type data) were made to draw any conclusion on research area. The data covered the annual different financial ratios (explained in variables of the study).

Sampling

For the purpose of the study, Cement Industry in India was considered as its universe. The companies satisfied certain criteria have been identified and taken as sample frame. Purposively two criteria were considered for sieving out the companies.

- The company should be a listed company in any one of the stock exchanges.
- Chronological availability of the data for the period of 10 years i.e., 2003 to 2012.

Based on the above conditions seven companies from Cement Industry was selected. Each selected company was treated as a sample unit of research. The total sample unit was approximated to seven companies.

Sample Size

The companies selected from Cement Industry were Ambuja Cement, ACC, OCL, Indian Cements, Madras Cement, Birla Cement and Prism Cement.

Period of the Study

Period of the study for the above research work was covered ten financial years i.e., from 2003 to 2012.

Data

The cross sectional indicators like; Inventory Turnover Ratio, Receivables Turnover Ratio, Fixed Asset Turnover Ratio, Asset Turnover Ratio, Total Asset Turnover Ratio, Investment Turnover Ratio for managerial efficiency and Gross Profit Ratio, Operating Profit Ratio, Net Profit Ratio, Overall Profitability Ratio for Operational Efficiency are collected over a period from 2003 to 2012 which, constitute the panel data matrix for the study.

Sources of Data

The data for the study collected from secondary sources. The sources for the study were Annual reports and website of selected companies, website of BSE and NSE, and money control.com.

Techniques used

Descriptive as well as inferential statistical tools were used to arrive at any conclusion. The first and second hypothesis for the study is tested with 90 per cent of significance level whereas a third hypothesis for the study is tested with 95 per cent.

Hypotheses

In order to conduct the study and examine the objectives, the researchers formed following hypotheses for testing.

$H_0$1: Managerial efficiency among selected sample is uniform

$H_0$2: Operational efficiency among selected sample is uniform

$H_0$3: There is no impact of Managerial efficiency on Operational efficiency

Limitation of the Study

The study depends more on empirical procedures rather than theoretical proof on Managerial and Operational efficiency. The researcher has drawn conclusion by way of analysing the financial ratios and not used any actual figure or theoretical modelling. The period of study is restricted to the financial years covering 2003-2012. The sample size for the study is seven companies those are only from Cement Industry therefore any generalisation of the findings of the study may be subjected to certain cautions. Several other qualitative factors, which have an influence on Managerial and Operational efficiency and such factors, are not taken into consideration in this study.

Analysis and Interpretations

Table 12.1: Details of Inventory Turnover Ratio

Year/ Companies	*Ambuja*	*ACC*	*OCL*	*Indian*	*Madras*	*Birla*	*Prism*
2003	7.97	8.93	4.13	5.59	9.01	9.31	7.79
2004	7.96	7.27	3.93	6.42	13.27	10.26	8.44
2005	8.28	5.37	4.86	5.83	5.68	11.11	7.22
2006	15.41	9.33	5.19	7.24	10.04	11.6	9.28
2007	9.96	24.85	5.81	9.09	12.33	11.13	9.04
2008	7.54	27.51	9.83	27.47	37.03	20.17	31.66
2009	11.36	25.22	12.44	26.36	23	26.19	26.28
2010	9.19	19.04	12.55	25.93	23.84	18.37	14.81
2011	10.38	18.59	10.39	23.24	18.18	15.87	12.95
2012	11.17	11.15	6.39	8.98	16.82	19.77	13.9
N	10	10	10	10	10	10	10
Range	7.87	22.14	8.62	21.88	31.35	16.88	24.44
Minimum	7.54	5.37	3.93	5.59	5.68	9.31	7.22
Maximum	15.41	27.51	12.55	27.47	37.03	26.19	31.66
Mean	9.92	15.73	7.55	14.62	16.92	15.38	14.14
Std. Deviation	2.37	8.29	3.40	9.71	9.20	5.60	8.34
Skewness	1.43	.23	.53	.47	1.13	.73	1.47
Kurtosis	2.47	-1.78	-1.58	-2.12	1.45	-.44	1.16

Source: Compiled & Computed Data.

Table 12.1 contents the inventory turnover ratio of the selected Cement Companies. The average value of inventory turnover ratio reveals transforming inventory into receivables through sales in a year. In other words, it gives average inventory holdings. Highest average value of average inventory turnover recorded for Madras Cements whereas the lowest value recorded for OCL. To judge whether each company's inventory turnover is good or not, it was compared with the average inventory turnover of the industry. The average industry inventory turnover is 13.47. Companies like Ambuja and OCL is below the industry average.

Table 12.2: Details of Debtors Turnover Ratio

Year/ Companies	*Ambuja*	*ACC*	*OCL*	*Indian*	*Madras*	*Birla*	*Prism*
2003	40.83	18.02	4.49	4.69	11.93	27.14	11.63
2004	44.27	20.91	5.01	7.54	14.06	32.12	16.71
2005	58.66	16.34	5.8	7.07	16.68	26.43	27.84
2006	91.7	27.75	6.77	7.27	21.23	30.96	41.75
2007	48.14	27.4	9.38	9.01	27.33	63.03	84.76
2008	33.39	24.12	8.65	10.66	31.59	58.53	252.69
2009	37.6	31.22	10.71	10.1	33.41	69.73	372.31
2010	52.58	40.04	12.46	8.79	22.89	102.72	13.43
2011	45.92	42.62	12.46	9.23	15.5	64.65	14.14
2012	42.84	40.29	11.65	18.11	16.63	56.18	14.74
N	10	10	10	10	10	10	10
Range	58.31	26.28	7.97	13.42	21.48	76.29	360.68
Minimum	33.39	16.34	4.49	4.69	11.93	26.43	11.63
Maximum	91.70	42.62	12.46	18.11	33.41	102.72	372.31
Mean	49.59	28.87	8.74	9.25	21.13	53.15	85.00
Std. Deviation	16.45	9.51	3.07	3.56	7.51	24.32	125.14
Skewness	2.13	.26	-.12	1.80	.58	.70	1.87
Kurtosis	5.33	-1.37	-1.69	4.73	-1.07	.37	2.55

Source: Compiled & Computed Data.

The Average debtors' turnover of cement industry is 36.53 times. In other word, the industry as whole is able to turnover its debtors 36.53 times. In a year the book debts remain outstanding for: 365/36.53 = 9.99 or 10 days. Among sample companies average debtors' turnover is maximum for Prism Cement whereas minimum for OCL. Companies like; Abuja, Birla and Prism have performed better than industry performance as because the average debtors' turnover is higher than industry average.

Table 12.3: Details of Investments Turnover Ratio

Year/ Companies	*Ambuja*	*ACC*	*OCL*	*Indian*	*Madras*	*Birla*	*Prism*
2003	9.03	19.41	6.81	13.78	19.14	17.17	24.44
2004	9.07	17.69	5.93	15.85	28.3	17.38	22.94
2005	9.55	12.29	8.35	14.97	19.95	21.01	20.31
2006	17.19	22.4	9.43	24.76	25.75	26.83	25.27
2007	11.13	24.85	9.92	29.09	47.1	23.53	23.93
2008	7.54	27.51	9.83	27.47	37.03	20.17	31.66
2009	11.36	25.22	12.44	26.36	23	26.19	26.28
2010	9.19	19.04	12.55	25.93	23.84	18.37	14.81
2011	10.38	18.59	10.39	23.24	18.18	15.87	12.95
2012	11.17	11.15	6.39	8.98	16.82	19.77	13.9
N	10	10	10	10	10	10	10
Range	9.65	16.36	6.62	20.11	30.28	10.96	18.71
Minimum	7.54	11.15	5.93	8.98	16.82	15.87	12.95
Maximum	17.19	27.51	12.55	29.09	47.10	26.83	31.66
Mean	10.56	19.82	9.20	21.04	25.91	20.63	21.65
Std. Deviation	2.62	5.36	2.34	6.98	9.52	3.79	6.09
Skewness	1.96	-.30	.02	-.57	1.47	.61	-.16
Kurtosis	5.03	-.67	-1.06	-1.26	1.80	-.84	-.80

Source: Compiled & Computed Data.

In investment turnover ratio, in examine individual result, it is observed OCL has lowest value of investment turnover ratio is 5.39 in year 2004 whereas Madras Cement has the highest value in 2007. The industry average in investment turnover ratio is 18.4. The average score of Ambuja Cement and ACC is below industry average. The average score of Madras Cement and OCL respectively high and low in the industry.

Table 12.4: Details of Fixed Assets Turnover Ratio

Year/ Companies	*Ambuja*	*ACC*	*OCL*	*Indian*	*Madras*	*Birla*	*Prism*
2003	0.86	1.33	1.66	0.61	0.63	2.9	0.76
2004	0.87	1.45	1.68	0.75	0.73	3.23	0.95
2005	1.07	1.05	1.59	0.88	0.76	3.12	1.15

(Contd...)

2006	2.28	1.72	1.44	1.21	1.01	2.6	1.56
2007	1.68	1.26	1.54	1.32	1.39	2.95	2.14
2008	1.1	1.25	1.21	0.7	0.74	1.47	1.25
2009	1.15	1.19	0.93	0.68	0.65	1.33	0.86
2010	0.85	0.96	0.93	0.69	0.58	1.51	1.61
2011	0.88	0.97	0.9	0.62	0.5	1.23	1.22
2012	0.96	1.12	0.79	0.69	0.58	1.04	1.55
N	10	10	10	10	10	10	10
Range	1.43	.76	.89	.71	.89	2.19	1.38
Minimum	.85	.96	.79	.61	.50	1.04	.76
Maximum	2.28	1.72	1.68	1.32	1.39	3.23	2.14
Mean	1.17	1.23	1.27	.82	.76	2.14	1.31
Std. Deviation	.46	.23	.35	.25	.26	.89	.42
Skewness	1.93	.94	-.14	1.48	1.82	.04	.65
Kurtosis	3.41	.98	-2.03	.90	3.49	-2.23	.29

Source: Compiled & Computed Data.

The detail of fixed asset turnover ratio is presented in Table 12.4. It is clear from the table that the highest range, highest average value, highest deviation and highest individual score of this ratio belongs to Birla Cement. The industry average score in fixed asset turnover ratio is 1.24. Birla Cement and Prism Cement have performed better than industry.

Table 12.5: Details of Total Assets Turnover Ratio

Year/ Companies	*Ambuja*	*ACC*	*OCL*	*Indian*	*Madras*	*Birla*	*Prism*
2003	0.52	1.23	1.01	0.39	0.64	2.07	0.66
2004	0.6	1.3	1.11	0.41	0.77	2.46	0.85
2005	0.79	0.99	0.96	0.49	0.71	2.24	1.04
2006	1.43	1.46	0.93	0.64	1.01	2.01	1.59
2007	1.14	1.55	1.02	0.65	1.17	1.75	1.87
2008	1.05	1.35	0.73	0.75	0.77	1.41	1.44
2009	1.08	1.23	0.82	0.73	0.68	1.2	0.96
2010	1.01	1.11	0.85	0.7	0.68	0.89	1.45
2011	1.05	1.22	0.85	0.61	0.58	0.72	1.43
2012	1.11	1.53	0.97	0.71	0.8	0.68	2.08
N	10	10	10	10	10	10	10
Range	.91	.56	.38	.36	.59	1.78	1.42

(Contd...)

Minimum	.52	.99	.73	.39	.58	.68	.66
Maximum	1.43	1.55	1.11	.75	1.17	2.46	2.08
Mean	.98	1.30	.93	.61	.78	1.54	1.34
Std. Deviation	.27	.18	.11	.13	.18	.65	.45
Skewness	-.39	-.08	-.14	-.79	1.38	-.08	.11
Kurtosis	.10	-.61	-.34	-.91	1.52	-1.62	-.84

Source: Compiled & Computed Data..

The average total assets turnover ratio of the industry is 1.07. Comparing industry average with individual average it is observes that ACC, Birla Cement and Prism Cement average asset turnover ratio is higher than industry average. The minimum score of average value is indentified for Indian Cements whereas the highest value is recorded for Birla Cement.

Table 12.6: Details of Asset Turnover Ratio

Year/ Companies	*Ambuja*	*ACC*	*OCL*	*Indian*	*Madras*	*Birla*	*Prism*
2003	0.59	0.87	0.76	0.5	0.43	1.07	0.57
2004	0.54	0.96	0.87	0.35	0.48	1.15	0.66
2005	0.7	0.69	0.95	0.39	0.47	1.3	0.74
2006	1.37	1.19	0.95	0.51	0.61	1.11	0.95
2007	1.09	1.26	1.08	0.58	0.87	1.36	1.19
2008	1.1	1.25	1.21	0.7	0.74	1.47	1.25
2009	1.12	1.34	0.93	0.62	0.65	1.31	0.98
2010	1.05	1.13	0.93	0.62	0.58	1.09	2.15
2011	1.09	1.27	0.9	0.53	0.5	0.79	1.55
2012	1.15	1.5	0.9	0.65	0.75	0.72	1.97
N	10	10	10	10	10	10	10
Range	.83	.81	.45	.35	.44	.75	1.58
Minimum	.54	.69	.76	.35	.43	.72	.57
Maximum	1.37	1.50	1.21	.70	.87	1.47	2.15
Mean	.98	1.15	.95	.55	.61	1.14	1.20
Std. Deviation	.27	.24	.12	.11	.14	.24	.54
Skewness	-.65	-.65	1.00	-.54	.53	-.57	.72
Kurtosis	-.71	.05	1.99	-.48	-.72	-.33	-.58

Source: Compiled & Computed Data.

The top three average score are 1.2, 1.15 and 1.14 is indentified respectively for Prisim Cement, ACC and Birla Cement. The average assets turnover ratio of the cement industry is 0.94. Comparing industry average with individual average it is observes that Indian Cement and Madras Cement average asset turnover ratio is less than industry average.

Table 12.7: Details of Operating Profit Margin

Year/ Companies	*Ambuja*	*ACC*	*OCL*	*Indian*	*Madras*	*Birla*	*Prism*
2003	27.6	13.25	16.59	4.67	24.54	5.21	16.03
2004	27.92	17.02	16.17	11.77	23.82	6.7	20.49
2005	28.12	18.21	13.77	12.24	20.5	11.26	22.91
2006	34.71	29.17	14.28	17.3	20.75	14.72	26.52
2007	36.2	28.15	19.84	33.04	35.25	31.51	43.17
2008	28.85	24.66	26.1	35.88	37.26	33.38	38.58
2009	27.07	31.95	24.43	27.94	30.75	24.71	27.23
2010	25.18	21.42	28.33	20.54	30.88	33.31	17.78
2011	22.92	18.42	20.74	10.26	24.12	20.88	9.6
2012	25.41	19.33	14.1	21.49	29.52	18.27	6.2
N	10	10	10	10	10	10	10
Range	13.28	18.70	14.56	31.21	16.76	28.17	36.97
Minimum	22.92	13.25	13.77	4.67	20.50	5.21	6.20
Maximum	36.20	31.95	28.33	35.88	37.26	33.38	43.17
Mean	28.40	22.16	19.44	19.51	27.74	20.00	22.85
Std. Deviation	4.12	6.07	5.34	10.28	5.86	10.62	11.66
Skewness	.99	.33	.55	.33	.34	.00	.44
Kurtosis	.49	-1.04	-1.22	-.96	-1.15	-1.47	-.29

Source: Compiled & Computed Data.

Table 12.7 contents the operating profit ratio of the selected Cement Companies. The average value of operating profit ratio reveals excess of sales revenue over and above operating cost in a year. Highest average value of operating profit ratio recorded for Ambuja Cements whereas the lowest value recorded for OCL. To judge whether each company's operating profit ratio is good or not, it was compared with the average operating profit ratio of the industry. The average industry operating profit ratio is 22.87. Companies like Ambuja and Madras cement is above the industry average.

Table 12.8: Details of Gross Profit Margin

Year/ Companies	*Ambuja*	*ACC*	*OCL*	*Indian*	*Madras*	*Birla*	*Prism*
2003	23.19	12.28	14.95	-24.03	14.27	2.35	5.14
2004	25.01	15.54	15.14	-3.11	17.01	6.25	15.14
2005	25.44	17.32	11.95	2.43	16.95	9.79	18.64
2006	33.74	28.97	12.87	8.52	18.06	14.13	23.56
2007	36.26	23.72	17.53	26.82	34.35	31.2	42.81
2008	24.65	20.59	22.66	31.68	32.61	30.98	34.94
2009	22.87	27.68	19.36	21.89	25.31	22.3	23.37
2010	19.93	16.29	19.99	14.22	23.9	30.74	14.61
2011	17.67	13.33	12.4	3.11	15.69	17.86	6.24
2012	19.6	14.41	5.42	15.51	21.77	14.78	2.93
N	10	10	10	10	10	10	10
Range	18.59	16.69	17.24	55.71	20.08	28.85	39.88
Minimum	17.67	12.28	5.42	-24.03	14.27	2.35	2.93
Maximum	36.26	28.97	22.66	31.68	34.35	31.20	42.81
Mean	24.84	19.01	15.23	9.70	21.99	18.04	18.74
Std. Deviation	5.96	5.96	4.95	16.26	7.03	10.54	12.94
Skewness	1.02	.72	-.47	-.76	.84	.05	.63
Kurtosis	.39	-.94	.50	.88	-.52	-1.34	-.24

Source: Compiled & Computed Data.

The value of gross profit ratio reveals excess of sales revenue over and above cost of goods sold in a year. The minimum value of gross profit ratio is recorded for Indian cements and the maximum value for Prism Cements. The average industry gross profit ratio is 18.22. Highest average value of gross profit ratio recorded for Ambuja Cements whereas the lowest value recorded for Indian Cements. Companies like Indian Cements and OCL is below the industry average.

Table 12.9: Details of Net Profit Margin

Year/ Companies	*Ambuja*	*ACC*	*OCL*	*Indian*	*Madras*	*Birla*	*Prism*
2003	12.41	5.93	5.76	-22.52	2.05	0.44	-9.58
2004	16.63	9.59	5.71	-9.39	4.77	3.93	-1.54
2005	17.85	16.85	5.7	0.39	7.5	7.59	5.84
2006	23.86	21.16	6.16	2.92	7.79	10.25	10.83
2007	30.53	20.44	9.38	21.2	19.48	20.56	25.02
2008	22.11	16.29	14.9	20.66	20.21	22.45	27.09

(*Contd...*)

2009	16.78	19.69	10.25	12.44	14.27	17.68	15.09
2010	16.84	14.26	11.78	9.33	12.55	24.9	8.8
2011	14.16	13.78	7.63	1.94	7.97	14.25	2.82
2012	12.86	9.13	2.11	6.93	11.71	10.03	-0.66
N	10	10	10	10	10	10	10
Range	18.12	15.23	12.79	43.72	18.16	24.46	36.67
Minimum	12.41	5.93	2.11	-22.52	2.05	.44	-9.58
Maximum	30.53	21.16	14.90	21.20	20.21	24.90	27.09
Mean	18.40	14.71	7.94	4.39	10.83	13.21	8.37
Std. Deviation	5.62	5.18	3.69	13.25	5.97	8.14	11.63
Skewness	1.19	-.39	.48	-.74	.35	-.06	.34
Kurtosis	1.21	-1.00	.17	.72	-.72	-1.14	-.49

Source: Compiled & Computed Data.

The top three performer of cement industry from net profit ratio point of view is Ambuja Cement, ACC and Birla Cement. The average net profit ratio of these companies is respectively 18.4, 14.71 and 13.21. The average net profit ratio of the cement industry is 11.12. Comparing industry average with individual average it is observes that OCL, Indian Cement, Madras Cement and Prism Cement average is less than industry average.

Table 12.10: Details of Overall Profitability

Year/ Companies	*Ambuja*	*ACC*	*OCL*	*Indian*	*Madras*	*Birla*	*Prism*
2003	3.32	4.43	3.32	-3.33	0.43	0.63	-2.79
2004	4.48	8.11	4.05	-0.86	1.28	6.80	-0.65
2005	8.02	7.55	4.14	0.05	1.90	13.60	3.18
2006	37.76	24.22	4.45	0.61	3.39	13.45	10.34
2007	33.33	278.88	88.28	35.62	478.89	115.98	16.41
2008	40.95	328.20	117.62	63.90	591.16	190.23	25.89
2009	47.54	429.40	107.74	64.80	33.97	217.67	21.74
2010	50.30	389.39	130.15	71.21	37.46	252.41	49.94
2011	57.09	486.52	139.89	61.07	35.87	210.32	37.20
2012	65.65	589.85	142.83	85.88	64.62	209.04	44.96
N	10	10	10	10	10	10	10
Range	62.33	585.42	139.51	89.21	590.73	251.78	52.73
Minimum	3.32	4.43	3.32	-3.33	.43	.63	-2.79
Maximum	65.65	589.85	142.83	85.88	591.16	252.41	49.94
Mean	34.84	254.66	74.25	37.90	124.90	123.01	20.62
Std. Deviation	22.43	225.67	62.43	35.56	218.80	104.22	18.81
Skewness	-.40	.00	-.28	-.12	1.80	-.17	.32
Kurtosis	-1.25	-1.73	-2.14	-2.03	1.76	-2.14	-1.24

Source: Compiled & Computed Data.

The detail of overall profitable ratio is presented in Table 12.10. It is clear from the table that the highest range (590.73), highest individual score (591.16) recorded for Madras Cement whereas highest average value (254.66) and highest deviation (225.67) recorded for ACC. The industry average score in overall profitable ratio is 95.74. ACC, Birla Cement and Madras Cement have mean score better than industry.

Hypotheses Testing

$H_0$1: *Operational efficiency among selected sample is uniform*

The researcher has assumed that operational efficiency among selected sample is uniform. To verify the correctness of the statement an 'F' test was applied among different companies. Operating profit margin, gross profit margin, net profit margin and overall profitability are the variables through which the researcher measures the operational efficiency of selected companies.

Table 12.11: ANNOVA Summary; Variables under Operational Efficiency

	Squares	*Sum of*	*Df Square*	*Mean*	*F*	*Sig.*
OPERATING PROFIT MARGIN	Between Groups	861.075	6	143.513	2.133	.062
	Within Groups	4237.926	63	67.269		
	Total	5099.002	69			
GROSS PROFIT MARGIN	Between Groups	1404.100	6	234.017	2.381	.039
	Within Groups	6191.172	63	98.273		
	Total	7595.273	69			
NET PROFIT MARGIN	Between Groups	1333.634	6	222.272	3.208	.008
	Within Groups	4364.988	63	69.286		
	Total	5698.622	69			
OVERALL PROFITABILITY	Between Groups	400069.542	6	66678.257	4.035	.002
	Within Groups	1041135.191	63	16525.955		
	Total	1441204.733	69			

Source: Computed Data.

The ANNOVA test result in the Table 12.11 discloses the 'F' value is significant at 90 per cent of confidence level. The observed value is less than 0.1 for all the four parameter of operational efficiency (Operating Profit Margin, Gross Profit Margin, Net Profit Margin and Overall Profitability) of different Cement Companies. Further, a detail analysis of 'F' value discloses that only the Operating Profit Margin is not significant at 95 per cent of confidence level. So the null hypothesis *(Operational efficiency among selected sample is uniform)* is to be rejected with 90 per cent confidence.

$H_0 2$: *Managerial efficiency among selected sample is uniform*

Managerial efficiency simply refers to the efficiency in maintaining the sales of the organisation. To establish a relationship between sales and different fixed as well as current assets, the turnover ratio is used. Inventory turnover ratio, Debtors turnover ratio, Investments turnover ratio, Fixed assets turnover ratio, Total assets turnover ratio and Assets turnover ratio are the parameters through which, the researcher measures the managerial efficiency of selected companies.

Table 12.12: ANNOVA Summary; Variables under Managerial Efficiency

	Squares	*Sum of*	*Df Square*	*Mean*	*F*	*Sig.*
INVENTORY TURNOVER RATIO	Between Groups	699.992	6	116.665	2.233	.051
	Within Groups	3290.932	63	52.237		
	Total	3990.924	69			
DEBTORS TURNOVER RATIO	Between Groups	46089.057	6	7681.509	3.222	.008
	Within Groups	150214.227	63	2384.353		
	Total	196303.283	69			
INVESTMENTS TURNOVER RATIO	Between Groups	2269.436	6	378.239	11.419	.000
	Within Groups	2086.731	63	33.123		
	Total	4356.167	69			
FIXED ASSETS TURNOVER RATIO	Between Groups	12.303	6	2.050	9.622	.000
	Within Groups	13.426	63	.213		
	Total	25.728	69			
TOTAL ASSETS TURNOVER RATIO	Between Groups	6.729	6	1.122	9.789	.000
	Within Groups	7.218	63	.115		
	Total	13.948	69			
ASSETS TURNOVER RATIO	Between Groups	4.172	6	.695	9.175	.000
	Within Groups	4.775	63	.076		
	Total	8.948	69			

Source: Computed Data.

Table 12.12 contains ANNOVA summary of different Variables under Managerial Efficiency E for selected cement companies. The results in summary table leads to rejection of null hypothesis for all the Variables under Managerial Efficiency being the significance level is less than 0.1. So the null hypothesis (*Managerial efficiency among selected sample is uniform*) were to be rejected with 90 per cent confidence.

$H_0$3: *There is no impact of Managerial efficiency on Operational efficiency*

Inventory turnover ratio, Debtors turnover ratio, Investments turnover ratio, Fixed assets turnover ratio, Total assets turnover ratio and Assets turnover ratio are the variables under Managerial efficiency. For convenient in measuring impact of Managerial efficiency on Operational efficiency the researcher has spited the six variables into two groups. The first group is consisting of inventory turnover ratio and debtors' turnover ratio which measures the efficiency of management in managing current assets relating to sales. The second group aims at efficiency in managing the fixed assets.

Table 12.13: Correlation Result of Managerial efficiency (Managing Current Assets) and Operational efficiency

	Profit margin	***Operating profit margin***	***Gross profit margin***	***Net profit margin***	***Overall profita-bility***
Inventory	Pearson Correlation	.422**	.363**	.407**	.482**
turnover	Sig. (2-tailed)	.000	.002	.000	.000
ratio	N	70	70	70	70
Debtors	Pearson Correlation	.352**	.360**	.387**	.028
turnover	Sig. (2-tailed)	.003	.002	.001	.821
ratio	N	70	70	70	70

***** & *. Correlation is significant at the 0.01 & 0.05 level (2-tailed).***

Source: Computed Data.

Table 12.13 shows there is positive correlation between different variables under Managerial efficiency on Operational efficiency. This basically means that there is an association between among the variables. While testing the nature of relationship, the correlation is significant at the one per cent level, for all the variables except between debtor turnover ratio and overall profitability. So the hypothesis (*There is no impact of Managerial efficiency on Operational efficiency*) rejected with 95 per cent confidence level.

Table 12.14: Correlation Result of Managerial efficiency (Managing Fixed Assets) and Operational efficiency

	Profit margin	***Operating profit margin***	***Gross profit margin***	***Net profit margin***	***Overall profita-bility***
Investments	Pearson Correlation	.363**	.320**	.213	.306*
turnover	Sig. (2-tailed)	.002	.007	.077	.010
ratio	N	70	70	70	70

(*Contd...*)

Fixed assets turnover ratio	Pearson Correlation	-.143	.096	.160	-.104
	Sig. (2-tailed)	.239	.431	.185	.392
	N	70	70	70	70
Total assets turnover ratio	Pearson Correlation	-.122	.113	.197	.073
	Sig. (2-tailed)	.316	.351	.101	.547
	N	70	70	70	70
Assets turnover ratio	Pearson Correlation	.029	.198	.331**	.293*
	Sig. (2-tailed)	.809	.100	.005	.014
	N	70	70	70	70

** & *. *Correlation is significant at the 0.01 & 0.05 level (2-tailed).*

Table 12.14 contains the correlation result of different variables under Managerial efficiency (Managing Fixed Assets) and Operational efficiency. Positive correlation is indentified between Investment turnover and operating profit margin, gross profit margin, net profit margin, overall profitability. Except the correlation between Investments turnover ratio and Net profit margin rest three correlation result is significant at five per cent level.

The correlation of fixed asset with operating profit margin and overall profitability is negative and the rest two are positive. Further, correlation of total asset with operating profit is negative and the rest three are positive. All these results are very low and not significant at five per cent level.

The correlation between Assets turnover ratio and operating profit margin, net profit margin is positive and very low whereas with rest two profitable ratios is significant at five per cent level. So the hypothesis (*There is no impact of Managerial efficiency on Operational efficiency*) rejected.

Summary of Findings

The key objective behind the research work is to examine the relationship between managerial efficiency and operational efficiency for selected companies over the period of study. Measuring the managerial and operational efficiency the researchers arrived at following points viz:

1. As far as the efficiency in management of current assets is concerned for the selected cement companies in the cement industry, ACC cement has recorded highest inventory turnover ratio whereas Prism cement has recorded highest debtors' turnover ratio.
2. So far as the efficiency in management of current assets is concerned for the selected cement companies in the cement industry, Birla cement has able to manage its fixed assets better

than other selected firms. Out of three ratios tested under long-term asset management, Birla cement has the highest value of ratio in fixed asset turnover ratio, total asset turnover ratio and second highest value of ratio in asset turnover ratio.

3. Out of four ratios of operational efficiency, Ambuja cement has the highest value of ratio in operating profit, gross profit and net profit ratio whereas ACC cement has recorded highest value in overall profitability.

Further, measuring the impact of managerial efficiency on operating efficiency, the following points are indentified by the researcher:

1. As far as the association between inventory and debtors turnover ratio with different profitable ratio, the correlation is not significant at the five per cent level, for the association between overall profitability and debtors' turnover ratio.
2. The association between fixed asset turnover ratio and operating profit margin, overall profitability is negative whereas the association between total asset turnover ratio and operating profit margin is also negative.

Concluding Note

Managerial and operational efficiency are central terms in assessing and measuring the performance of organisations, as well as inter-organisational arrangements such as strategic alliances, joint ventures, sourcing as well as outsourcing agreements. Managerial efficiency refers to efficient management of assets of an organisation whereas operational efficiency refers to profitability of the firm. Profitability is the ability to make profit from all business activities by efficiently managing all the resources available. Dealing with operational efficiency and ignoring managerial efficiency may not focus on issues of competitive advantage through value appropriation and creating new growth opportunities within business networks.

This study develops a theoretical structure that links managerial and operational efficiency and justifies the need with empirical research. The present study attempts to provide answer to following research questions; 'do the fluctuations in efficiency ratio affects the profitability of an organisation? Do these ratios of companies belongs to one industry is similar?' The managerial and operational efficiency of the farms belongs to same industry are not same. The fluctuation in efficiency affects the profitability in a great manner.

References

1. Deloof, M. (2003). "Does Working Capital Management affects Profitability of Belgian Firms?". Journal of Business Finance & Accounting, 30 (3 & 4), pp. 573-587.
2. Dong, H.P and Su, J. (2010). "The Relationship between Working Capital Management and Profitability: A Vietnam Case", International Research Journal of Finance Economy 49, pp. 59-67.
3. Gill, A, Nahum B, Neil M (2010). "The Relationship between Working Capital Management and Profitability: Evidence from the United States". Bus. Econ. J. pp. 1-9.
4. Gopinathan, T. (2009). "Financial Ratio Analysis for Performance Check: Financial Statement Analysis with Ratios Can Reveal Problem Areas". *Journal of financial ratio analysis for performance evaluation.* Retrieved from hv. diva portal.org/smash/get/diva2:323754/FULLTEST01
5. H. W. Collier., T. Grai., S. Haslitt., C. B. McGowan. (2004). "An example of the use of financial ratio analysis: the case of Motorola," Decision Sciences Institute Conference, Florida, 2-6 March 2004, pp. 7-13. Collected from Research Online is the open access institutional repository for the University of Wollongong on 31st July 2014.
6. Ibam, (2008). How to Evaluate a Company before Investing. Stock Exchange News Sat. 22 March 2007 (On-line: freemanskrikesblogspot.com/.../how-toevaluate-company-be) Retrieved on 19th January 1014.
7. Jamali, A. H. and Asadi. A. (2012) Indian Journal of Science and Technology Vol. 5, No. 5, pp. 2779-2781.
8. Jamali. A. H. and Asadi, A. (2012). Indian Journal of Science and Technology Vol. 5 No. 5 pp. 2779-2781
9. James, C. (2009). "Accounting 101 – Income Statement: Financial Reporting and Analysis of Profit and Loss", *Journal of income statement.* Retrieved fromhttp.//en.wikipedia.org/wiki/International_Financial_Reporting_ Standrds.
10. ——(2009). "Basic Accounting 101- Asset Turnover Ratio: Inventory, Cash, Equipment and Accounts Receivable Analysis", *Journal of asset turnover ratio.*
11. Jo, N. (2009). "Inventory Analysis: A Guide to Analyzing Inventory for Small Business Owners", *Journal of inventory analysis.* Retrieved from diva-portal.org.
12. Karaduman, H.A., Akbas, H.E., Ozsozgun, A., Durer, S. (2010). "Effects of Working Capital Management on Profitability: The Case of Selected Companies in the Istanbul Stock Exchange (2005-2008)", International Journal of Finance Study. 2(2): pp. 47-54.
13. Mtetwa, M. (2010). "Fixed Assets: Capital Expenditure", *Journal of fixed assets in accounting.*
14. Okwo, *et.al.,* (2012). "Investment in Fixed Assets and Firm Profitability: Evidence from the Nigerian Brewery Industry" European Journal of Business and Management, Vol. 4, No. 20, pp. 10-17.
15. Paradogonas, T. A. (2007). The Financial Performance of Large and Small Firms, Evidence From Greece. International Journal of Financial Services Management Issues, 2(1).

16. White, D. (2008). "Accounts Receivable: Analyzing the Turnover Ratio", *Journal of account receivable.*
17. Zain, M. (2008). "How to Use Profitability Ratios: Different Types of Calculations that Determine a Firm's Profits", *Journal of profitability ratio analysis*
18. Lazaridis, I. and Tryfonidis, D. (2006). The Relationship between working capital management and profitability of listed companies in the Athens stock exchange. *Journal Financial Management & Analysis.* 19, pp. 26-25.
19. Amritpal Singh Dhillon, A.S. and Vachhrajani, H (2013). "impact of operational efficiency on overall profitability: A case study on Gujarat Industries Power Company Limited" RESEARCH BULLETIN Volume XXXVIII, December 2013.
20. Prasanna Chandra (2001). *Financial Management Theory and Practice,* Tata Mcgraw Hill Publishing Company Ltd., New Delhi.
21. Jain and Khan (2004). Financial Management, Tata Mcgraw Hill Publishing Company Ltd., New Delhi.
22. Gitman, L. J. (2001). Principles of Managerial Finance. New Delhi: Pearson Education Asia.
23. Pandey, I. M. (2010). *Financial Management Tenth Edition.* New Delhi: Vikas Publishing House Pvt Ltd.
24. Brigham, Eugene F. and Joel F. Houston.(2001). Fundamentals of Financial Management, Ninth Edition, Harcourt College Publishers, Fort Worth.
25. www.moneycontrol.com
26. http://financial-dictionary.thefreedictionary.com/return
27. www.ssrn.com
28. www.scholar.google.co.in
29. www.shodhganga.inflibnet.ac.in

Chapter 14

Problems and Prospects for Development of North-Eastern Region of India

Dr Rohini Prasad and Dr Sukanta Sarkar

> *"One of the lessons of leadership worth emphasizing is that you want to get to know other great leaders and take their advice. At some point in your development, it's only people who've been in the seat of having to be leaders who can help you in a deep way."* ***–Jim Yong Kim***

Introduction

Northeast India is the eastern-most region of India. It is connected to East India via a narrow corridor squeezed between independent nations of Bhutan and Bangladesh. It comprises the contiguous Seven Sister States, plus the Himalayan state of Sikkim. Northeast India constitutes about eight per cent of India's size; roughly three-fourth the size of the state of Maharashtra. Its population is approximately 40 million (2011 census), 3.1 per cent of the total Indian population; roughly equal to that of Odisha. The Northeast region can be physiographically categorised into the Eastern Himalayas, Northeast Hills (Patkai-Naga Hills and Lushai Hills) and the Brahmaputra and the Barak Valley Plains. According to 2001 census, the total literacy rate of the population in the region at 68.5 per cent, with female literacy rate at 61.5 per cent, is higher than the country's average of 64.8 per cent and 53.7 per cent respectively. The north-eastern states, having 3.8 per cent of India's total population, are allotted 25 out of a total of 543 seats in the Lok Sabha. This is 4.6 per cent of the total number of seats.

The economy is agrarian. Little land is available for settled agriculture. Along with settled agriculture, jhum cultivation is still practised by a few indigenous groups of people.[1]

North Eastern States

The Northeast region of India comprising of eight states – Assam, Nagaland, Manipur, Arunachal Pradesh, Mizoram, Tripura and Sikkim.

(a) Assam[2]

Assam is a state in Northeast India. Located south of the eastern Himalayas, Assam comprises the Brahmaputra Valley and the Barak Valley along with the Karbi Anglong and Dima Hasao districts with an area of 30,285 square miles (78,440 km^2). Assam tea is produced in the region of Dibrugarh, Tinsukia and Sivasagar. Petroleum is extracted in Digboi, Duliajan. The state is a major producer of Assam silk. Assam is one of the richest biodiversity zones in the world and consists of tropical rainforests, deciduous forests, riverine grasslands, bamboo orchards and numerous wetland ecosystems. Assam has petroleum, natural gas, coal, limestone and other minor minerals such as magnetic quartzite, kaolin, sillimanites, clay and feldspar.

Total population of Assam was 26.66 million with 4.91 million households in 2001. As per 2011 census, total population of Assam was 31,169,272. The total population of the state has increased from 26,638,407 to 31,169,272 in the last ten years with a growth rate of 16.93 per cent. Religious minority-dominated districts like Dhubri, Goalpara, Barpeta, Morigaon, Nagaon, Hailakandi etc. recorded growth rates ranging from 20 per cent to 24 per cent during the last decade. In 2011, literacy rate in the state was 73.18 per cent. According to the 2011 census, 61.5 per cent were Hindus, 34.2 per cent were Muslims. The districts of Dhubri, Goalpara, Barpeta, Morigaon, Nagaon, Karimganj and Hailakandi are Muslim majority districts in absolute terms according to the 2011 census. Assamese and Bodo are the major indigenous and official languages while Bengali holds official status in the three districts in the Barak Valley and is the second most widely spoken language of the state (27.5 per cent).

As of August 2015, the state has 32 administrative districts. On August 15, 2015, five new districts were formed in addition to former 27 districts. The ceaseless illegal influx of Bangladeshi immigrants into Assam has been a great problem for the State. Every year, catastrophic flood caused by Brahmaputra and some other rivers deluges many places of Assam. Unemployment is one of the major problems of Assam which can be attributed to overpopulation, faulty education system and scanty situations for employment. Assam schools are run by the Indian government or by private organisations. Medium of instruction is mainly in English, Bengali or Assamese. Assamese language is the main medium in educational institutions but Nepali language is taught as a major Indian language.

Assam's economy is based on agriculture and oil. Assam produces more than half of India's tea. In Assam, among all the productive sectors, agriculture makes the highest contribution to its domestic sectors, accounting for more than a third of Assam's income and employs 69 per cent of workforce. Assam's proximity to South Asian Association for Regional Cooperation countries such as Bangladesh, Nepal and Bhutan, benefits its trade. Border Trade Centres at Sutarkandi in Karimganj district and Mankachar in Dhubri district have been developed to facilitate border trade with Bangladesh. Assamese culture is traditionally a hybrid one developed due to assimilation of ethno-cultural groups in the past. There are diversified important traditional festivals in Assam. Bihu is the most important and common and celebrated all over Assam.

For the purposes of tourism there are wildlife reserves like the Kaziranga National Park, Manas National Park, Pobitora Wildlife Sanctuary, Nameri National Park, Dibru-Saikhowa National Park etc. It has a rich cultural heritage going back to the Ahom Dynasty which governed the region for many centuries before the British occupation. The major tourist spots of Guwahati are Kamakhya Temple, River Cruise on the river Brahmaputra, Shankardev Kalakshetra, Umananda Temple, Assam State Zoo, Shilpagram etc. The largest freshwater island in South Asia is on the Brahmaputra River. Majuli is famous for its Vaishnavite Satras. Haflong is the only hill station of Assam. It is the headquarters of Dima Hasao. The village of Jatinga is known for mysterious bird suicide on the night of new moon.

(b) Arunachal Pradesh[3]

Arunachal Pradesh borders the states of Assam and Nagaland to the south, and shares international borders with Bhutan in the west, Burma in the east and the country of Tibet in the north. Itanagar is the capital of the state. Most of Arunachal Pradesh is covered by the Himalayas. However, parts of Lohit, Changlang and Tirap are covered by the Patkai hills. Kangto, Nyegi Kangsang, the main Gorichen peak and the Eastern Gorichen peak are some of the highest peaks in this region of the Himalayas. The climate of Arunachal Pradesh varies with elevation. Areas that are at a very high elevation in the Upper Himalaya close to the Tibetan border have an alpine or tundra climate.

The state, on account of its unrivalled aesthetics and diverse cultural heritage possesses a great tourism potential. Popular tourist attractions include Tawang (a town with a Buddhist monastery) at 3000 m elevation, Ziro (which holds cultural festivals), Yomcha (limestone caves called 'tapen uru'), the Namdapha tiger project in Changlang district and Sela Lake near Bomdila with its bamboo bridges overhanging the river. Moving southeast, the Tai Khamti is linguistically distinct from their neighbours and culturally distinct from the majority of other Arunachalese tribes.

Arunachal Pradesh got its first railway line in late 2013 with the opening of the new link line from Harmuti on the main Rangpara North-Murkongselak railway line to Naharlagun in Arunachal Pradesh. On 20 February 2015, the first through train was run from New Delhi to Naharlagun, flagged off from the capital by the Indian Prime Minister, Narendra Modi. India plans to eventually extend the railway to Tawang, near the border with China. Arunachal Pradesh has two highways: the 336 km National Highway 52, completed in 1998, which connects Jonai with Dirak, and another highway, which connects Tezpur in Assam with Tawang. As per 2001 census, out of the 705,158 tribals living in Arunachal, 333,102 are Animist (47.24 per cent), 186,617 are Christian (26.46 per cent), 92,577 are Hindu (13.13 per cent), and 82,634 are Buddhist (11.72 per cent).

Arunachal Pradesh tribes count to more than twenty in number. The tribes of Arunachal Pradesh have an excellent heritage of artistic craftsmanship. Their aesthetic essence of tribal art could be seen in their painting, pottery, wood carving, basket making. Weaving, wood and bamboo crafting are some major professions of these tribes. Another notable feature of these tribes of Arunachal Pradesh is that they are very united and integrated. Every tribe of this state maintains uniformity in them. The occasions celebrated by the tribes of Arunachal Pradesh mirror their culture the best.[4]

(c) Nagaland[5]

Nagaland is a state in Northeast India. It borders the state of Assam to the west, Arunachal Pradesh and part of Assam to the north, Burma to the east and Manipur to the south. The state capital is Kohima, and the largest city is Dimapur. Nagaland became the 16th state of India on 1 December 1963. Agriculture is the most important economic activity and the principal crops include rice, corn, millets, pulses, tobacco, oilseeds, sugarcane, potatoes, and fibers. Nagaland is largely a mountainous. The population of Nagaland is nearly two million people, of which 1.04 million are males and 0.95 million females. The state's population is 1.978 million, out of which 87.92 per cent are Christians. The census of 2011 recorded the state's Christian population at 17,39,651, making it, with Meghalaya, and Mizoram one of the three Christian-majority states in India.

Nagaland is known in India as the land of festivals. The diversity of people and tribes, each with their own culture and heritage, creates a year-long atmosphere of celebrations. The railway network in the state is minimal. Broad gauge lines run 7.98 miles (12.84 km), National Highway roads 227.0 miles (365.3 km), and state roads 680.1 miles (1,094.5 km). Hornbill Festival was launched by the Government of Nagaland in December 2000 to encourage intertribal interaction and to promote cultural heritage of the state. Nagaland has a high literacy rate of 80.1 per cent. Majority of the population in the state speaks English, which is the official language of the state. The state offers technical and medical education. Most of state's population, about 68 per cent of the total, depends on rural cultivation.

(d) Mizoram[6]

Mizoram is one of the states of Northeast India, with Aizawl as its capital. Mizoram was previously part of Assam until 1972, when it was carved out as a Union Territory. It became the 23rd state of India, a step above Union Territory, on 20 February 1987. Mizoram's population was 1,091,014, according to 2011 census. It is the second least populous state in the country. Mizoram is a highly literate agrarian economy. The state has about 871 kilometers of national highways, with NH-54 and NH-150 connecting it to Assam and Manipur respectively. Mizoram has third highest total forest cover with 1,594,000 hectares (3,940,000 acres), and highest percentage area (90.68 per cent) covered by forests, among the states of India, according to 2011 Forest Survey of India. Mizoram has a population of 1,091,014 with 552,339 males and 538,675 females.

The majority (87 per cent) of Mizos are Christian in various denominations, predominantly Presbyterian. Mizoràm population has 8.3 per cent Buddhists making them the largest minority, followed by Hindus at 3.6 per cent according to the 2001 census. Mizo is the official language and the most widely used language for verbal interactions, but English, being important for education, administration, formalities and governance, is widely used. The Mizoram State Legislative Assembly has 40 seats and the Village Councils are the grassroots of democracy and leadership in Mizoram. The state is the southern most in India's far northeast, placing Mizoram in a disadvantageous position in terms of logistical ease, response time during emergencies, and its transport infrastructure. Visitors to Mizoram are required to obtain an 'inner line permit' under the special permit before visiting. Domestic and international visitors face different requirements.

(e) Manipur[7]

Manipur is a state in north-eastern India, with the city of Imphal as its capital. The state covers an area of 22,327 square kilometres (8,621 sq mi).

Its people include the Meitei, Kuki, Naga, and Pangal peoples, who speak different types of Sino-Tibetan languages. Manipur has primarily an agrarian economy, with significant hydroelectric power generation potential. It is connected to other areas by daily flights through Imphal airport, the second largest airport in north-eastern India. The state has four major river basins: the Barak River Basin (Barak Valley) to the west, the Manipur River Basin in central Manipur, the Yu River Basin in the east, and a portion of the Lanye River Basin in the north. Manipur has a population of 2,721,756. Of this total, 58.9 per cent live in the valley and the remaining 41.1 per cent in the hilly regions.

The violence in Manipur extends beyond those between Indian security forces and insurgent armed groups. There is violence between the Meiteis, Nagas, Kukis and other tribal group. The Kuki insurgent groups want a separate state for the Kukis to be carved out from the present state of Manipur. About 41.39 per cent of Manipuri people are Hindus. Christianity is the religion of 41.29 per cent of the people in the state. Muslims, known locally as Pangal, constitute about 8.4 per cent of the state population as per 2011 census. The Manipuri have a rich culture. Theatre has been part of the Laiharaoba festivals since time immemorial. The various festivals of Manipur are Lui-ngai-ni Ningol Chakouba, Yaoshang, Gan-ngai, Chumpha, Christmas, Cheiraoba, Kang and Heikru Hidongba.

(f) Meghalaya[8]

State is bounded to the south by the districts of greater Mymensingh and the Division of Sylhet and the west by the Division of Rangpur of the People's Republic of Bangladesh and the north and the east by India's Assam state. The capital is Shillong, known as the "Scotland of the East". As of 2011, the state has a population of 2,964,007 and is the 23rd most populous in the country. The population of Meghalaya as of 2014 is estimated to be 3,211,474. The state of Meghalaya is mountainous, with stretches of valley and highland plateaus, and it is geologically rich. It consists mainly of Archean rock formations. Tribal people make up the majority of Meghalaya's population. The Khasis are the largest group, followed by the Garos then The Jaintias. Meghalaya is one of three states in India to have a Christian major. English is the official and widely spoken language of the state. The other principal languages in Meghalaya are Khasi and Garo.

The Meghalaya Legislative Assembly has 60 members at present. Meghalaya has two representatives in the Lok Sabha, one each from Shillong and Tura. It also has one representative in the Rajya Sabha.

Meghalaya is basically an agricultural state with about 80 per cent of its population depending entirely on agriculture for their livelihood. Nearly 10 per cent of the geographical area of Meghalaya is under cultivation. Meghalaya has a rich base of natural resources. These include minerals such as coal, limestone, sillimanite, Kaolin and granite among others. Meghalaya has a literacy rate of 62.56 as per the 2001 census and is the 27th most literate state in India. This increased to 75.5 in 2011.

The majority of population and the major tribal groups in Meghalaya follow a matrilineal system where lineage and inheritance are traced through women. The youngest daughter inherits all the property and she is the caretaker of aged parents and any unmarried siblings. All the three major ethnic tribal groups, namely, the Khasis, Jaintias and the Garos also have their own traditional political institutions that have existed for hundreds of years. Meghalaya has a road network of around 7,633 km, out of which 3,691 km is black topped and remaining 3942 km is gravelled. Meghalaya offers many adventure tourism opportunities in the form of mountaineering, rock climbing, trekking and hiking, caving and water sports. The state offers several trekking routes, some of which also afford an opportunity to encounter rare animals. The Umiam Lake has a water sports complex.

(g) Tripura[9]

The third-smallest state in the country, it covers 10,491 km^2 and is bordered by Bangladesh to the north, south, and west, and the Indian states of Assam and Mizoram to the east. The area of modern Tripura was ruled for several centuries by the Tripuri dynasty. Tripura lies in a geographically disadvantageous location in India, as only one major highway, the National Highway 44, connects it with the rest of the country. Tripura is governed through a parliamentary system of representatives democracy, a feature it shares with other Indian states. Universal suffrage is granted to residents. Tripura sends two representatives to the Lok Sabha (the lower house of the parliament of India) and one representative to the Rajya Sabha (parliament's upper house).

Tripura ranks second only to Assam as the most populous state in North East India. According to the provisional results of 2011 census of India, Tripura has a population of 3,671,032 with 1,871,867 males and 1,799,165 females. In the 2001 census of India, Bengalis represented almost 69 per cent of Tripura's population, while the indigenous population amounted to 31 per cent. According to 2011 census, Hinduism is the majority religion in the state, followed by 83.3 per cent of the population.

The diverse ethno-linguistic groups of Tripura have given rise to a composite culture. Football and cricket are the most popular sports in the state.

Bengali people represent the largest ethno-linguist community of the state. Bengali culture, as a result, is the main non-indigenous culture. Tripura is noted for bamboo and cane handicrafts. The state is vulnerable to epidemics of Malaria, Diarrhea, Japanese Encephalitis and Meningitis. Tripura has high incidence of open defecation, especially in the interior hilly and forest areas. The state has extensively implemented Nirmal Bharat Abhiyan and currently the Swachh Bharat Abhiyan and convergence with MGNREGS to address this problem. ONGC and Chambal Fertilizers and Chemicals are jointly building a fertilizer plant to leverage ONGC's natural gas discoveries in Tripura. Tripura State has received the best State Award for Water and Sanitation under the category of Small States in the IBN7 Diamond State Award function for doing commendable work to provide drinking water supply to the people with sparsely distributed tribal population in hamlets of hilly region of the State.

(h) Sikkim[10]

Little is known about Sikkim's ancient history, beyond the fact that its original inhabitants were the Lepcha. In 1947, when India became independent, a popular vote rejected Sikkim's joining the Indian Union. Nestling in the Himalayan Mountains, the state of Sikkim is characterised by mountainous terrain. According to the Constitution of India, Sikkim has a parliamentary system of representative for its governance; universal suffrage is granted to state residents. Sikkim is India's least populous state, with 610,577 inhabitants according to the 2011 census. Hinduism has been the state's major religion since the arrival of the Nepalis; an estimated 57.75 per cent of the total population are now adherents of the religion. Sikkim's Nepalese majority celebrate all major Hindu festivals, including Diwali and Dussera.

Challenges before North-Eastern Region[11]

There are various challenges before the region. Road is an important mode of travel in the hilly areas as other mode of travel is either too expensive or difficult. The road infrastructure is relatively deficient in the NER although the region's road density per capita is significantly higher as compared to the rest of the country. Fragmented land holdings by small and marginal farmers which dominate the landholding pattern in the north east is uneconomical. The region has low proportion of irrigated area and investment in building irrigation capacity has been insufficient and ineffective. Inland water transport can be a viable, cost-effective alternative in the plain areas of NER given the high cost of expanding other mode of transportation. Major river routes in the NER are the Brahmaputra and the Barak in Assam which has a combined navigable length of around 1,000 km.

Regional Conflict

The Northeast region of India comprising of eight states – Assam, Nagaland, Manipur, Arunachal Pradesh, Mizoram, Tripura and Sikkim – a region poorly connected to the Indian mainland by a small corridor. The Naga insurgence, which started in the 1950s, known as the mother of the Northeast insurgencies, is one of the oldest unresolved armed conflicts in the world. Currently, most of the states in the region are affected by some form of conflict, except Arunachal Pradesh, Mizoram and Sikkim in which the situation is at the moment relatively stable. The Indian government's past and ongoing processes of national integration, state-building and democratic consolidation have further aggravated the conflict scenario in the region. The AFSPA (Armed Forces Special Power Act) for instance, shows the inability and reluctance of the government to solve the conflict with adequate political measures. The AFSPA was passed on 18 August, 1958, as a short-term measure to allow deployment of the army to counter an armed separatist movement in the Naga Hills, has been in place for the last five decades and was extended to all the seven states of the Northeast region in 1972 (with the exception of Mizoram).[12]

The recent attacks and killings in Assam, Manipur and Meghalaya by armed non-State groups represent a challenge and test for the Narendra Modi government and the need to understand the frustrating complexities of the North-eastern region. Armed with new weapons which are easily available in the illegal small arms markets in the region, combined with new technology and better connectivity, these groups are demonstrating the seamless manner in which they can move across State borders. The Bodo-Muslim riots in 2012, which displaced nearly half a million people and the incident earlier this year when over 30 men, women and children were butchered by armed men in the Bodo areas, are examples of such violence. All the victims this time were Muslim and the resonance of public anger of minority as well as non-Muslim, non-Bodo groups was visible in the overwhelming victory of a non-Bodo candidate in a Lok Sabha constituency.[13]

Illegal Migration

Migration is a global phenomenon, and will continue to do so in the near future. Every country aspires to regulate migration according to their requirements.[14] An illegal immigrant in India is a person residing in the country without an official permission as prescribed by relevant Indian law. As per 2001 census, there are 3,084,826 people in India who came from Bangladesh. No reliable numbers on illegal immigrants are currently available. Extrapolating the census data for the state of Assam alone gives a figure of two million. The Bangladesh Liberation War and continued political and economic turmoil in Bangladesh in the following decades forced some Bangladeshis to seek refuge in India. During the Bangladesh Liberation War at least 10 million Bangladeshis crossed into India illegal to seek refuge from widespread rape and genocide. In Assam, agitation against immigrants started as early as 1979, led by All Assam Students Union. Their demand was to put a stop on the influx of immigrants and deportation of those who have already settled.

According to M Amarjeet Singh's book, "A Study on Illegal Immigration into North-East India: The Case of Nagaland", Bangladesh is a major source of labour, but mainly of low-skilled and unskilled workers. Over the years, a large number of people have voluntarily migrated for both long and short-term employment, which is an important livelihood strategy for its large population. Such continuing illegal immigration creates tensions between India and Bangladesh, particularly when India's Border Security Force (BSF) tries to push back illegal Bangladeshi immigrants. In 2003, the then Deputy Prime Minister, LK Advani, estimated that about 15 million Bangladeshis were in India. The 'Task Force on Border Management', which submitted its report to the Government of India in August 2000, also estimated 15 million Bangladeshis, with about three lakh entering India illegally every year. In 2007, about 25,712 out of the five lakh Bangladeshis who came to India did not return after the expiry of their visas while in 2006 more than 24,000 went missing from the 4.84 lakh Bangladeshis who had entered India with valid travel documents. About 12 lakh Bangladeshis, who had entered India between 1972 and 2005 with valid documents, have not returned home.

Recently, the Supreme Court of India admitted a petition alleging the presence of 40 lakh illegal immigrants in the voter's list in Assam and issued notices to the central and state governments, and the Election Commission of India. The petition filed by Assam Public Works (APW) seeks the deletion of the names of illegal immigrants from the voter's lists and freezing of the list until names of the foreigners are deleted. The petitioner also demanded that Assembly polls, scheduled for 2011, be kept in abeyance until the voter's list is corrected. In recent times, Nagaland along with Mizoram, Arunachal Pradesh and Manipur has attracted a large number of immigrants. In Mizoram, migration from Bangladesh and Myanmar has become a serious issue. Meghalaya, which shares a 443-km-long border with Bangladesh, has also become another destination for the Bangladeshis. In Arunachal Pradesh and Manipur too, Bangladeshi immigrants has been reported.

Illegal immigration has been taking place in Nagaland, especially in areas bordering Assam, since the early 1970s or even earlier, but it has picked up since the 1980s. While immigration in Assam and Tripura are comparatively well-documented, it has not been done in Nagaland. Immigrants not only provide cheap labour, but are more willing to take up jobs which native workers normally avoid. As a result, unemployment among unskilled and semi-skilled natives has also gone up.[15]

In 2005, a Supreme Court bench ruled Illegal Migrants (Determination by Tribunal) Act (IMDT) as unconstitutional while, with reference to the Sinha Report, maintaining that the impact of the *"aggression"* represented by large-scale illegal migrants from Bangladesh had made the life of the people of Assam "wholly insecure and the panic generated thereby had created fear psychosis" and other north-eastern States.[16]

The Illegal Migrants (Determination by Tribunal) (IMDT) Act[17]

The Illegal Migrants (Determination by Tribunal) Act was an Act of the Parliament of India enacted in 1983 by Indira Gandhi government. It was struck down by the Supreme Court of India in 2005. The Act was pushed through mainly on the grounds that it provided special protections against undue harassment to the "minorities" that were affected by the Assam Agitation. It was applicable to state of Assam only whereas in other states, detection of foreigners is done under The Foreigners Act, 1946. Under the Illegal Migrants (Determination by Tribunal) Act, the burden of proving the citizenship or otherwise rested on the accuser and the police, not the accused. This was a major departure from the provisions of the Foreigners Act, 1946.

The Act was challenged by Sarbananda Sonowal in courts. In 2005, a three-judge Bench of the Supreme Court of India held that the Illegal Migrants (Determination by Tribunals) Act, 1983 and rules "has created the biggest hurdle and is the main impediment or barrier in the identification and deportation of illegal migrants" and struck down the Act.

Terrorism Problem

India's sensitive North Eastern region, especially Assam, is fast emerging as an epicentre of international jihadi networks. The state is increasingly becoming vulnerable to Islamic terrorist outfits largely because of the unabated influx from Bangladesh and presence of several fundamentalist organisations. The presence of Bangladesh-based jihadi outfit JMB has been reported for the first time in Assam. The Union Home Ministry sent directives to the state government in the wake of ethnic violence in BTAD and the resultant polarisation of voters along religious lines during the 2014 Lok Sabha polls that Assam has been figuring in the Islamic terror map.[18]

The United Liberation Front of Assam is the major independentist outfit operating in Assam, North East India. It seeks to establish a sovereign Assam via an armed struggle in the Assam conflict. The ULFA was founded on 7 April 1979 in Sivasagar, Assam by some youths which included Paresh Baruah, Arabinda Rajkhowa, Anup Chetia, Pradip Gogoi, Bhadreshwar Gohain and Budheswar Gogoi. The ULFA is a revolutionary political organisation engaged in a liberation struggle against state terrorism and economic exploitation by India for the establishment of a sovereign, independent Assam. The Government of India (GOI) has classified it as a terrorist organisation and had banned it under the Unlawful Activities (Prevention) Act in 1990. The outlawed group has been using China for shelter following mounting pressure from both Burma and Bangladesh, in turn pressured by India.[19]

The National Democratic Front of Bodoland was formed in 1989 as the Bodo Security Force, aims to set up an autonomous region Bodoland. It is a predominantly Christian armed separatist outfit which seeks to obtain a sovereign Bodoland for the Bodo people in Assam, India. NDFB claims to represent the Bodo people, who form around 10 per cent of Assam's population. The main grievances of the group are the under-development in the region and the influx of immigrants. The promotion of the Roman script for the Bodo language is also a significant demand of NDFB. NDFB has carried out bombings, kidnappings and murders in Assam. The Assam Government has accused it of launching an ethnic cleansing campaign against the Adivasis and Muslim settlers in the region.[20]

The United People's Democratic Solidarity was formed in March 1999 with the merger of two terrorist outfits in Assam's Karbi Anglong district, the Karbi National Volunteers (KNV) and Karbi People's Front. The outfit signed a cease-fire agreement for one year with the Union Government on

May 23, 2002. The outfit's main area of operations is in the Karbi Anglong district, with a relatively minor presence in Dima Hasao district. The outfit held six rounds of peace talks with the State and Union Government representatives between 2002 and 2006. The last round of talks was held on July 26, 2006.[21] Karbi Longri N.C. Hills Liberation Front is a militant group operating in Karbi Anglong district and Dima Hasao district (formerly known as the North Cachar Hills district) of Assam. KLNLF emerged from the United People's Democratic Solidarity, being the anti-peace talk's faction of UDPS. The outfit claims to fight for the cause of Karbi tribes and its declared objective is Hemprek Kangthim, meaning self-rule/self-determination of the Karbi people.[22]

The Dima Halam Daoga (DHD) is a descendant of the Dimasa National Security Force (DNSF), which ceased operations in 1995. They are active mainly in the district of Dima Hasao of Assam. Their presence can be felt in all the territories demanded by them to be included in Dimaraji. The objective of DHD (Nunisa faction) is to include parts of Cachar, Karbi Anglong, and Nagaon districts in Assam, and sections of Dimapur district in Nagaland.[23] The objective of the Kamtapur Liberation Organisation (KLO) is to carve out a separate Kamtapur State. The proposed state is to comprise six districts in West Bengal and four contiguous districts of Assam which are Cooch Behar, Darjeeling, Jalpaiguri, North and South Dinajpur and Malda of West Bengal and four contiguous districts of Assam - Kokrajhar, Bongaigaon, Dhubri and Goalpara.

Nagaland was created in 1963 as the 16th State of Indian Union, before which it was a district of Assam. Insurgent groups classified as active mainly demand full independence. The National Socialist Council of Nagaland was formed in 1980 to establish a Greater Nagaland, encompassing parts of Manipur, Nagaland, the north Cachar hills (Assam). The NSCN split in 1988 to form two groups namely, NSCN (IM) and NSCN (K). Nagaland (NSCN) was formed on 31 January 1980 by Isak Chishi Swu, Thuingaleng Muivah and S.S. Khaplang opposing the Shillong Accord signed by the then Naga National Council (NNC) with the Government of India. The objective of the NSCN was to establish a Sovereign State by unifying all the Naga-inhabited areas in the North East of India and Northern Burma which the organisation and the people of the area proposed as Nagalim. Over the years, the NSCN-IM has tried to develop extensive linkages both within and outside India. It is alleged that Pakistan and China are providing finance as well as arms and ammunition to NSCN in their fight for independence against the Indian Government.[24]

The insurgent groups in Tripura were emerged in the end of the 1970s, as ethnic tensions between the Bengali immigrants and the tribal native population who were outnumbered by the former hailing from other parts of India. The National Liberation Front of Tripura was formed in March 1989. The NLFT seeks to secede from India and establish an independent Tripuri state, and has actively participated in the Tripura Rebellion. The NLFT is currently proscribed as a terrorist organisation in India. In the wake of the expulsion of Biswamohan Debbarma and Nayanbasi Jamatiya, the NLFT divided into two factions in February 2001.[25]

The All Tripura Tiger Force (ATTF) is an isolationist group from the Tripura region of India. It was founded on July 11, 1990, by a group of former Tripura National Volunteer members under the leadership of Ranjit Debbarma. The ATTF is currently considered a terrorist organisation by India. According to South Asian Terrorism Portal, the main objectives of ATTF are: (a) To expel all Bengali-speaking settlers settled in Tripura after 1956; (b) Return tribal lands to their original owners under the Tripura Land Revenue and Land Reforms Act; (c) Purge voter rolls of all immigrants who entered Tripura after 1956.[26]

The state of Meghalaya was separated from the state of Assam in 1971, in order to satisfy the Khasi, Synteng and Garo for a separate state. The first militant outfit to emerge in the region was the Hynniewtrep Achik Liberation Council (HALC), it was formed in 1992, aiming to protect the interests of Meghalaya's indigenous population from the rise of non-tribal immigration. The most active outfit in the state is the Garo National Liberation Army (GNLA) which was formed in 2009. A number of non-Meghalayan separatist groups have also operated in the region, including the United Liberation Front of Assam and the National Democratic Front of Bodoland among others.[27]

Among states in the Northeast, Manipur emerged as the most violent with incidents of violence taking place almost on a daily basis. Despite the heavy presence of security forces and a high police-population ratio, activities of militant groups have further intensified and spread to all nine districts of the state. A common thread running through the use of various tactics is attacks against representatives of the central government, be it paramilitary forces or employees of central government schemes in a bid to oppose their authority in the state and assert their autonomy.[28]

Growth Prospects

India's north-east region is endowed with huge untapped natural resources and is acknowledged as the eastern gateway for the country's

'Look East Policy'. Exploitation of the large hydro potential in the NER could be used for exporting to the power deficit northern and western regions of the country. The spill-over benefits for the region will be the development of infrastructure such as roads, communications, and electricity supply to remote hilly areas, resulting in better quality of life. Recently, the government has taken several steps to overcome these infrastructural bottlenecks to induce sustainable development in the region. All the eight states have different developmental prospects and resources to support their efforts in contributing to the regional as well as national economy. The region is endowed with a varied topography and agro-climactic conditions which offer vast potential for agriculture, horticulture and forestry.

Agriculture provides livelihood to 70 per cent of the region's population. Rubber and bamboo are among the important agricultural produces which can attract a lot of investment opportunities. Tripura is the chief production hub and has been declared as the 'second rubber capital of India' right after Kerala by the Indian Rubber Board. The region's comparative advantages in producing fruits, vegetables and other horticulture products can be tapped by setting up small-scale processing units for the local market which will also boost rural employment. Arunachal Pradesh has taken up the cultivation of horticulture produce especially of sub-tropical fruits on a large scale with assistance from the government. There is also scope for dairy processing and poultry, fishery processing in the region. There is huge demand for dried fish in the region, processing of which is not capital intensive. Private entrepreneurs need to be encouraged to set up storage, distribution and marketing infrastructure such as a cold storage chain along major arterial highways.[29]

North Eastern Council

The Council is an advisory body and may discuss any matter in which the north-eastern states have a common interest and advise the Central Government as to the action to be taken on any such matter. The council has to its credit a lot of achievements mostly in electricity and education sector. The North Eastern Region comprises eight States viz. Arunachal Pradesh, Assam, Manipur, Meghalaya, Mizoram, Nagaland, Sikkim and Tripura. The funding of council mainly lies with the central government with small portions contributed by the state governments as well. The NEC act has been amended in 2002 to add Sikkim and restructure it as the regional planning body for the North Eastern Region.[30]

North Eastern Council under the Ministry of Development of North Eastern Region is the nodal agency for the economic and social development of the North Eastern Region which consists of the eight States of Arunachal Pradesh, Assam, Manipur, Meghalaya, Mizoram, Nagaland, Sikkim and Tripura. Information about NEC, its schemes, beneficiaries under its schemes, supported institutions, monthly progress report, etc. is given. Users can get details regarding North East Rural Livelihood Project (NERLP), guidelines, forms, rules, etc.[30]

The North-Eastern Council (Amendment) Bill, 2013 was introduced in the Rajya Sabha on March 11, 2013 by the Union Minister of State Development of North Eastern Region, Mr. Paban Singh Ghatowar. The Bill seeks to amend the North-Eastern Council Act, 1971. The Act sets up the North-Eastern Council to ensure balanced and coordinated development among the north-eastern states. The membership of the NEC is comprised of Governors and Chief Ministers of the constituent states of Arunachal Pradesh, Assam, Manipur, Meghalaya, Mizoram, Nagaland, Tripura and Sikkim. The Act was amended in 2002 to (i) redefine the functions of the NEC as a regional planning body for the north-eastern region, (ii) include Sikkim as a member state of the NEC and, (iii) provide for three members and the Chairman of the Council to be nominated by the President. The Bill re-introduces the 'conflict resolution' provision to state that functions of the NEC include discussion on matters of common interest to the member states and/or the union government, on issues falling under the fields of: (i) economic and social planning, (ii) inter-state transport and communications, and (iii) power or flood control projects.[31]

Ministry of Development of North Eastern Region

The Ministry of Development of North Eastern Region is a Government of India ministry, established in September 2001, which functions as the nodal Department of the Central Government to deal with matters related to the socio-economic development of the eight States. The current, Minister of Development of North Eastern Region is Jitendra Singh (Minister of state, Independent Charge). The ministry is mainly concerned with the creation of infrastructure for economic development of North-Eastern region.[32]

Tea Plantation

India's largest tea research centre managed by the Tea Research Association is located in Jorhat. This centre, which was started in 1911 at Tocklai (Jorhat), has made significant contributions towards Tea Attributes Assam Tea has a rich, deep-amber colour and is famous for its rich, full-bodied cup. Assam is the single largest tea-growing region in the world.

The low altitude, rich loamy soil conditions, ample rainfall and a unique climate help it to produce some of the finest orthodox leaf teas.[43] Tea requires a moderately hot and humid climate. Climate influences yield, crop distribution and quality. Temperature affects tea yield by influencing rate of photosynthesis and controlling growth and dormancy. Tea grows well on high land well drained soils having a good depth, acidic pH in the range 4.5 to 5.5 and more than two per cent organic matter.[34]

The state of Assam is the world's largest tea-growing region, lying on either side of the Brahmaputra River, and bordering Bangladesh and Burma (Myanmar). Assam has been the second commercial tea production region after southern China. Southern China and Assam are the only two regions in the world with native tea plants. Tea gardens in Assam do not follow the Indian Standard Time, which is the time observed throughout India and Sri Lanka. The Assam tea bush grows in a lowland region, in the valley of the Brahmaputra River, an area of clay soil rich in the nutrients of the floodplain.[35]

Some tea garden owners are trying to plant rubber in tea gardens considering the financial benefits, but the state government will not allow this. Tea garden land cannot be used for any other purposes according to the act concerned. Tripura Industrial Development Corporation chairman Pabitra Kar said that small growers started cultivation of tea in 1994 in the state and they numbered over 7,000 now. Over 10,000 hectare are under cultivation in the state which is six per cent of total tea area in the country. Tripura contributes four per cent of total production in India.[36]

Rubber Plantation

Plantation crops are high-value crops of great economic importance and provide huge employment opportunity, especially to the women throughout the year. The sub-tropical climate of Northeastern India is extremely favourable to the cultivation of many plantation crops. Among the three important crops viz, tea, coffee and rubber, tea was introduced in Assam and Tripura as an industrial crop during the middle of nineteenth century, which has spread to other non-traditional states in the region in recent years.[37]

With limits to the growth of rubber in traditional areas in the hinterlands of the south-west coast comprising Kerala and the adjoining Kanyakumari district of Tamil Nadu, the Rubber Board should actively take up the cultivation of the commercial crop on a larger scale in non-traditional areas. Non-traditional areas so far identified as almost fully or marginally suitable for rubber cultivation are Arunachal Pradesh, Assam, Manipur, lower reaches of hills of Meghalaya, Mizoram, Nagaland and Tripura. Rubber has been identified as one of the thrust areas in Tripura, in view of its suitability to the terrain and the acceptability amongst the people. Studies have shown that about 100,000 hectares of area in the state can be brought under rubber plantation. The area under rubber cultivation at present is estimated to be about 26,500 hectares, which is the second largest, after Kerala.[38]

India's Northeast region is likely to replace Kerala as the country's primary rubber-cultivation zone within the next three decades under the influence of global warming and other factors, scientists have predicted. The scientists at the Rubber Research Institute of India (RRII) in Kottayam and Agartala have used mathematical tools to determine how climate change might increase or decrease land suitable for rubber cultivation in the two hubs for natural rubber.[39]

Challenges to Infrastructure Development

Roads are the underlying foundations for the entire economic development of the North Eastern region. The physical infrastructure includes roads, air-ports, highways, power projects, water supply, urban infrastructure, all of which together hold the key for the growth of this region. The Kaladan River Project envisages a sea route from Kolkata to Sittwe (Myanmar) through Bay of Bengal and traversing 255 kms upsteam on river Kaladan in Myanmar connecting Mizoram. 62 kms of highway road is to be built in Myanmar connecting the India border at Mizoram and finally merging with the National Highway-54. If this route is to be built, it will cut the cost of infrastructure tremendously in the North East.

Communication and transport, health and sanitation, power production and supply, agricultural modernisation, flood control, erosion and land slide, technical education, employment generation, industrialisation, social unity, terrorism are problems of this region which are to be realised by both of governments to solve population and workers problems.

Conclusion

The Northeast region of India comprising of eight states – Assam, Nagaland, Manipur, Arunachal Pradesh, Mizoram, Tripura and Sikkim – a region poorly connected to the Indian mainland by a small corridor. India's north-east region is endowed with huge untapped natural resources and is acknowledged as the eastern gateway for the country's 'Look East Policy'. Agriculture provides livelihood to 70 per cent of the region's population.

Rubber and bamboo are among the important agricultural produces which can attract a lot of investment opportunities.

India's sensitive North Eastern region, especially Assam, is fast emerging as an epicentre of international jihadi networks. The state is increasingly becoming vulnerable to Islamic terrorist outfits largely because of the unabated influx from Bangladesh and presence of several fundamentalist organisations. The road infrastructure is relatively deficient in the NER although the region's road density per capita is significantly higher as compared to the rest of the country.

References

1. Northeast India, https://en.wikipedia.org/wiki/Northeast_India
2. Assam (2015), Available at https://en.wikipedia.org/wiki/Tourism_in_ Assam
3. Arunachal Pradesh (2015), Available at https://en.wikipedia.org/wiki/Arunachal_Pradesh
4. http://www.mapsofindia.com/arunachal-pradesh/society/tribes.html
5. Nagaland (2015), Available at https://en.wikipedia.org/wiki/Nagaland
6. Mizoram (2015), Available at https://en.wikipedia.org/wiki/Mizoram
7. Manipur (2015), Available at https://en.wikipedia.org/wiki/Manipur
8. Meghalaya (2015), Available at https://en.wikipedia.org/wiki/Meghalaya
9. Tripura (2015), Available at https://en.wikipedia.org/wiki/Tripura
10. Sikkim (2015), Available at https://en.wikipedia.org/wiki/Sikkim
11. https://www.pwc.in/assets/pdfs/publications/2013/north-east_summit-2013.pdf
12. Conflict in Northeast India: Issues, Causes and Concern, https://in.boell.org/2009/02/28/conflict-northeast-india-issues-causes-and-concern
13. The Hindu (June 9, 2014), The North-eastern challenge, http://www.thehindu.com/opinion/lead/the-northeastern-challenge/article6095004.ece
14. M. Amarjeet Singh, a Study on Illegal Immigration into North-East India: The Case of Nagaland, http://www.idsa.in/occasionalpapers/AStudy-onIllegal ImmigrationintoNorth-EastIndiaTheCaseofNagaland_masingh_ 2009.html
15. M Amarjeet Singh, A Study on Illegal Immigration into North-East India: The Case of Nagaland, file:///C:/Documents%20and%20Settings/Administrator/My%20Documents/Downloads/OccasionalPaper8_ NagalandIllegal Immigrationl.pdf
16. Illegal immigrant in India(2015), Available at https://en.wikipedia.org/wiki/Illegal_immigration_in_India
17. The Illegal Migrants (Determination by Tribunal) (IMDT) Act, https://en.wikipedia.org/wiki/Illegal_Migrants_(Determination_by_Tribunal)_Act,_1983
18. Rupak Bhattacharjee, Threat of Islamic terror looms large over Assam, Available at http://www.idsa.in/idsacomments/ThreatofIslamicterror-loomslargeover Assam_RBhattacharjee_121114.html

19. United Liberation Front of Assam (2015), Available at https://en. wikipedia.org/wiki/United_Liberation_Front_of_Assam
20. National Democratic Front of Bodoland (2015), Available at https://en.wikipedia.org/wiki/National_Democratic_Front_of_Bodoland
21. United People's Democratic Solidarity (2015), Available at https://en.wikipedia.org/wiki/United_People%27s_Democratic_Solidarity
22. Karbi Longri N.C. Hills Liberation (2015), Available at https://en.wikipedia .org/wiki/Karbi_Longri_N.C._Hills_Liberation_Front
23. Dima Halam Daoga (2015), Available at https://en.wikipedia.org/wiki/Dima_Halam_Daogah
24. Nationalist Socialist Council of Nagaland (2015), Available at https://en.wiki pedia.org/wiki/National_Socialist_Council_of_Nagaland
25. National Liberation Front of Tripura (2015), Available at https://en.wikipedia.org/wiki/National_Liberation_Front_of_Tripura
26. All Tripura Tiger Force (2015), Available at https://en.wikipedia.org/wiki/All_Tripura_Tiger_Force
27. Insurgency in Northeast India (2015), Available at https://en.wikipedia.org/wiki/Insurgency_in_Northeast_India
28. file:///C:/Documents%20and%20Settings/Administrator/My%20 Documents/Downloads/SR71-Final.pdf
29. India's North-East Diversifying Growth Opportunities, Available at https://www.pwc.in/assets/pdfs/publications/2013/north-east_summit-2013.pdf
30. North Eastern Council (2015), Available at https://en.wikipedia.org/wiki/North_Eastern_Council
31. http://india.gov.in/official-website-north-eastern-council
32. The North-Eastern Council (Amendment) Bill, 2013, http://www.prsindia.org/billtrack/the-north-eastern-council-amendment-bill-2013-2677/
33. Ministry of Development of North Eastern Region (2015), Available at https://en.wikipedia.org/wiki/Ministry_for_Development_of_North_ Eastern_Region
34. http://www.indiatea.org/tea_growing_regions.php
35. http://www.tocklai.net/activities/tea-cultivation/
36. Assam tea (2015), Available at https://en.wikipedia.org/wiki/Assam_tea
37. Northeast vies for Kerala rubber crown, http://www.telegraphindia.com/1140805/jsp/nation/story_18688271.jsp#.VhDOauxViko
38. http://www.examrace.com/Study-Material/General-Studies/Economics/Challenges-to-Infrastructure-Development-in-North-East-Region.html
39. http://www.theinternationaljournal.org/ojs/index.php?journal=rjebs&page=article&op=view&path%5B%5D=1679

Chapter 15

Medical Negligence Law in India: An Overview

Dr Parmeshwari Rajyaguru

"The Millennium Development Goals were a pledge to uphold the principles of human dignity, equality and equity, and free the world from extreme poverty. The MDGs, with eight goals and a set of measurable time-bound targets, established a blueprint for tackling the most pressing development challenges of our time."
–Ban Ki-moon

Introduction

One may assert, without compunction, that the inherent disposition of Legal practitioners compels them to wax eloquent upon any given litigious concern! This inimitable peculiarity that some would say is the hallmark of the legal profession however seems to have met its waterloo in the complex and often misunderstood field of medical negligence jurisprudence. Lack of expertise, multiplicity of actors and judicial diffidence in the light of medical difficulties are the prominent reasons that have led to the setting of questionable judicial precedents. In a divisive legal scenario of this nature where one is quick to condemn, it becomes especially necessary to examine the legal principles that are the final arbiter of medical misadventures.

This article seeks to examine the development of medical negligence law in India both in its tortious and criminal variants and attempts to understand the strict framework that judicial interpretation has built around it. This discourse also leads to some ambiguities that judicial material thus far failed to address Part I of the essay attempts to differentiate criminal medical negligence from its civil counterpart within the backdrop of generic tortious principles of liability. Part II seeks to understand the concept of 'gross negligence' and analyses why its judicial interpretation raises more questions than it answers. Part III examines the problem of 'specificity' in cases of medical negligence. The essay in conclusion points out how the Supreme Court in its infinite wisdom having decided the issue accurately has deliberately left the door ajar even for a contrary judicial interpretation.

Negligence – Traversing the Spectrum

Negligence and Its Civil Precept

Negligence in law always relates to a particular fact situation and what is decided in one case is usually little help in deciding later disputes. Yet, as Lord Denning remarked in *Roe v. Minister of Health, '...you will find that the three questions duty, causation and remoteness [run] continually into one another. It seems to me that they are really three different ways of looking at one and the same problem.'*

However, negligence is viewed from different looking glasses in civil and criminal law. The distinction obviously lies in the degree of blameworthiness. The Supreme Court was quick to point this out in *Syed Akbar v. State of Karnataka* where it stated that in civil proceedings, a mere *'preponderance of probability'* is sufficient and the defendant is not necessarily entitled to the benefit of very reasonable doubt but in criminal proceedings the Court must be convinced of the guilt *'as a reasonable man beyond all reasonable doubt'*. That is the negligence established must be culpable or gross and not the negligence merely based upon an error of judgment. This principle of gross culpability was in fact laid down several decades ago by the Apex Court in the landmark three-judge bench decision of *Bhalchandra Bapu v. State of Maharashtra,* within the realm of criminal medical negligence at least the negligence of the doctor should be of such seriousness as to amount to a 'crime against the state.'

Tests for Imputing Liability

Having understood this distinction, fundamental to the discussion at hand, what then are the tests that need to be satisfied in order to establish a case of criminal medical negligence? Within the specific purview of criminal medical negligence vis-à-vis Section 304A of the Indian Penal Code the Supreme Court in *Dr Laxman Balkrishna Joshi v. Dr Trimbak Bapu Godbole* has laid down three determining tests, viz.:

1. A person administering medical advice and treatment impliedly undertakes that he is possessed of skill and knowledge for the purpose.

2. The Doctor then owes certain duties, viz., a duty of care in deciding whether to undertake the case, a duty of care in deciding what treatment to give and a duty of care in the administration of that treatment.
3. A breach of any of those duties gives a right of action for negligence to the patient.

These tests seem to imply that once a Doctor undertakes a particular case he is under a duty to take care and a breach of such duty *ipso facto* gives rise to an action. That however would be oversimplification. One must remember that while judging the actions of a specialist, neither the court nor the victim but another specialist alone is competent. This classic principle, which has been long adopted and very recently confirmed by the Supreme Court, is called the *Bolam Test,* which states that *'Where a situation involves the use of some special skill or competence, then the test as to whether there has been negligence or not, is not the test of the man on the top of a Clapham omnibus, because he has not got this special skill. The test is the standard of the ordinary skilled man exercising and professing to have that special skill.'* It is well-established law that it is sufficient if the Doctor exercises the skill of an ordinary competent man exercising that particular art.

The Bolam Test and its Implications

The full bench of the Apex Court while emphasising upon the *Bolam* test in the *Jacob Mathews* decision was specific in stating that in the future a private complaint may not be entertained unless the complainant has produced prima facie evidence before the Court in the form of a credible opinion given by another competent doctor to support the charge of rashness or negligence on the part of the accused doctor. This precondition however suffers from two obvious albeit divergent repercussions. Either a Doctor from the medical fraternity will be reluctant to give evidence on the conduct of another or this may be used as a tool for settling personal scores. It is assumed that the Court trusts that men of a noble profession such as the one at hand will not resort to such misconduct. However, whether this assumption is a correct one remains to be seen.

Understanding Gross Negligence

In the arena of criminal liability the Supreme Court has been steadfast in applying no standard lower than 'gross negligence'. Prima facie one would wonder how one form of carelessness materially differs from another. The distinction however is real.

Mens Rea in Grossly Negligent Conduct

At first blush the sub-heading above may appear to be a paradox but on further inquiry one finds that it is not so. There are only two states of mind which constitute *mens rea* and they are intention or recklessness. In criminal negligence the concept of 'recklessness' constitutes *mens rea.* The Supreme Court while further elucidating this principle in *Dr Suresh Gupta v. Govt. of N.C.T. of Delhi and Anr* termed it as '*a higher degree of morally blameworthy conduct'.* If the blame-worthiness were to be classified, Recklessness and deliberate wrong doing would be levels four and five of classification of blame, and the courts have been reluctant to impute criminal liability to any conduct falling short of this standard.

Medical Misadventures and the Problem of Specificity

Establishing the Causational Link

A cardinal measure of proof as laid down by the Supreme Court in a plethora of cases pertaining to criminal medical negligence is that the death should have been the *direct result* of a rash and negligent act of the accused, and that act must be the proximate and efficient cause without the intervention of another's negligence. It must be the causa causans; it is not enough that it may have been the causa sine qua non. However, reading the doctrine of causa causans becomes almost impossible when a patient is critically ill and in the advanced stages of a disease, and can only be given palliative treatment. At this juncture it must be noted that a recognised standard of conduct contained in statutory codes and official literature may be used as a practical guide for the standard of care to be aimed for.

Differing Medical Opinion

As in every field of specialisation, medicine is no stranger to varying and sometimes conflicting schools of treatment. Judicial diktats fortunately are very clear on this point and hence the *Bolam* principle withstands the test of doctrinal multiplicity. To quote the Supreme Court, '*Medical opinion may differ with regard to the course of action to be taken by a doctor treating a patient but as long as a doctor acts in a manner which is accepted to the medical profession and that he has acted with due care and diligence and if the patient still does not survive or suffers a permanent ailment it would be difficult to hold the doctor guilty of negligence.'* Simply put a doctor cannot be blamed for making one choice out of two if both are approved practice.

Conclusion

Through the course of this essay it has become abundantly clear that when negligent conduct appears in the course of medical treatment it becomes especially difficult to estimate, given the complexities of the human body and its numerous ailments whether a particular form of treatment will be successful or not. If a patient does not respond to one form of treatment that does not imply that another form should have been used and that the *Bolam* Test of approved practice has failed.

As far as criminal cases are concerned, the Apex Court has stated the ostensible reason for treating medical negligence on a different footing as- not doing so, would be *'doing great disservice to the community at large because if the courts were to impose criminal liability on hospitals and doctors for everything that goes wrong, the doctors would be more worried about their own safety than giving the best treatment to their patients. This would lead to shaking the mutual confidence between the doctor and patient.'* However, the real reason that can be discerned is that an expert in one field can be judged only by another expert in that very field and in emergency situations where risks are in order, doctors must be allowed a margin howsoever small for the possibility of error because often the outcome of the treatment is not in the their hands.

References

1. Oscar Wilde in *the Importance of Being Ernest.*
2. 'Negligence and Duty of Care' *Medical Negligence-A Practical Guide*, Charles J Lewis, Third Edition, Tolley Publishing Company.
3. (1980) 1 SCC 30.
4. AIR 1968 SC 1319 relied upon *Empress of India* v. *Idu Beg* ILR (1881) 3 All 776. See also *S N Hussain* v. *State of Andhra Pradesh* AIR 1982 SC 685.
5. *R* v. *Adomako* (1994) 3 All ER 79.
6. AIR 1969 SC 128.
7. *Dr Laxman Bal Krishna Joshi* v. *Trimbak Bapu Godbole,* AIR 1969 SC 128, *Poonam Verma* v. *Ashwin Patel* AIR 1996 SC 2111.
8. *Jacob Mathew* v. *State of Punjab and Another* AIR 2005 SC 3180.
9. Charlesworth and Percy on Negligence (10th Edn. 2001).
10. Black's Law Dictionary, 6th Edition.

Chapter 16

Women Empowerment and Development: A Study in India

Dr P.K. Ghoshal and Dr Sukanta Sarkar

"There is no single development, in either technology or management technique, which by itself promises even one order-of-magnitude improvement within a decade in productivity, in reliability, in simplicity."

–Fred Brooks

Introduction

Women population constitutes around 50 per cent of the world population. A large number of women around the world are unemployed. The world economy suffers a lot because of the unequal opportunity for women at workplaces. Women are equally competent. Nowadays, women are even ahead of men in many socio-economic activities. Since the older times, women have been treated as second rate citizens of all across the globe. The situation is almost the same everywhere-irrespective of the developed country or the developing country-caste, community, colour or creed a position which is comparable in many ways, with that of racial minorities.[1]

Gender equality is considered a critical element in achieving social and institutional change that leads to sustainable development with equity and growth. Inequalities between men and women manifest themselves in all areas of development. Inequalities are most obvious in: health and education, economic development, violence against women, participation in public life and policymaking and social attitudes and gender stereotyping.[2]

Empowerment is now increasingly seen as a process by which the one's without power gain greater control over their lives. This means control over material assets, intellectual resources and ideology. It involves power to, power with and power within.[3] Women face many social challenges today whether it be making soaps and incence in order to secure an income for her family to raising children amidst the harsh economic crisis. A woman is dynamic in the many roles she plays.[4] The sex ratio in India has improved from 930 in 1971 to 940 as per 2011 census. The female literacy has also increased from 18.3 per cent in 1961 to 74 per cent in 2011, in addition to decrease in male-female literacy gap from 26.6 per cent in 1981 to 16.7 per cent in 2011.[5]

Women's empowerment and the movement toward gender equality is a modern phenomenon that continues to develop around the world. After World War II, international treaties put great focus on human rights; however, as time progressed, it became clear that special attention must be given to women's rights. Therefore, beginning in the 1970s, advocates lobbied for women's rights at greater lengths. Women's empowerment, a major goal of many development projects, formed a basis to foster growth, reduce poverty, and promote better governance. The Beijing Declaration and Platform for Action in 1995 initiated a move to focus on women's empowerment. Drawing attention to women's participation in all realms of society, the document addressed gender inequality gaps in pursuit of guaranteeing women's rights.[6]

The origins of the concept of empowerment go back to the civil rights movement in the USA in the 1960. It has since then been interpreted differently and filled with new meanings and is today used in such different sectors as business, social work, development discourse and by advocates of very different political agendas. The empowerment of women is located within the discourse and agenda of gender equality and is increasingly being taken in the agendas of international development organisations, perhaps more as a means to achieve gender equality than as an end in itself.[7] The United Nations Development Fund for Women includes the following factors in its definition of women empowerment: (a) Acquiring knowledge and understanding of gender relations and the way in which these relations may be changed; and (b) Developing a sense of self-worth, a belief in one's ability to secure desired changes and the right to control one's life.[8]

Meaning of the Concept

Women empowerment is empowering the women to take their own decisions for their personal dependent. Empowering women is to make them independent in all aspects from mind, thought, rights, decisions, etc. by leaving all the social and family limitations. It is the empowerment of women which helps them to take their own decisions by breaking all personal limitations of the society and family.[9]

It refers to increasing and improving the social, economic, political and legal strength of the women, to ensure equal-right to women, and to make them confident enough to claim their rights.[10] It refers to an environment where there is no gender bias and has equal rights in community, society and workplaces.[11] The word women empowerment essentially means that the women have the power or capacity to regulate their day-to-day lives in the social, political and economic terms - a power which enables them to move from the periphery to the centre stage.[12] The empowerment of women is located within the discourse and agenda of gender equality and is increasingly being taken in the agendas of international development organisations, perhaps more as a means to achieve gender equality than as an end in itself.[13]

Importance of Women Empowerment

Women's Empowerment has been an issue of immense discussions and contemplation over the last few decades world-wide. This as an agenda has been on top of the lists of most government plans and programmes as well. Efforts have been made on a regular basis across nations to address this issue and enhance the socio-economic status of women.[14] The main advantage of women empowerment is that there will be an overall development of the society. The money that women earn does not only help them and or their family, but it help develop the society. It leads to more economic benefits not to the individuals but to the society as well. It helps women to stand on their own legs, become independent and also to earn for their family which grows country's economy. It leads to decrease in domestic violence. Uneducated women are at higher risk for domestic violence than educated women. It helps women to get educated and know their rights and duties and hence can stop corruption. It also reduces poverty.[15]

The empowerment of women would result in overall development of society both at micro and macro level. Active participation of women in economic activities and decisions, would contribute towards overall economic development.[16] A host of studies suggest that putting earnings in women's hands is the intelligent thing to do to speed up development and the process of overcoming poverty. Women usually reinvest a much higher portion in their families and communities than men, spreading wealth beyond themselves.[17] The empowerment and autonomy of women and the improvement of their political, social, economic and health status is a highly important end in itself. In addition, it is essential for the achievement of sustainable development.[18]

Empowered women maintain equal mindedness. They act out roles that challenge male dominance. They respond as equals and co-operate to work towards the common good. Empowered women maintain their strength on the face of pressures from the religion and work and contribute towards the empowerment of all women. Empowered women use their talent to live fulfilling lives. They not only survive the harshness of their own subjugation but also transcend their subjugation.[19] Women education in India plays a very important role in the overall development of the country. It not only helps in the development of half of the human resources, but in improving the quality of life at home and outside. Educated women not only tend to promote education of their girl children, but also can provide better guidance to all their children.[20]

Women contribute directly and indirectly for the economic development. Though the nature has given the genetic power of reproduction especially to the women, the socio-economic status of women is so poor and the incidence of poverty is more on woman only. Empowering women is the only solution for all questions.[21]

Women Empowerment in India

According to the provisions of the Constitution of India, it is a legal point to grant equality to women in the society in all spheres just like male. The Department of Women and Child Development is functions well in this field for the proper development of the women and child in India. Women are given a top place in India from the ancient time however they were not given empowerment to participate in all areas.[22] Women's agency is an important constituent of women's empowerment. It can be said to be operative when results into a fundamental shift in perceptions or inner transformation so that women should be able to define self-interest and choice, and consider themselves as not only able, but entitled to make choices.[23]

In India, the customs of purda, female infanticide, child marriage, sati system, dowry system and the state of permanent widowhood were either totally removed or checked to an appreciable extent after independence through legislative measures. Two Acts have also been enacted to emancipate women in India. These are: Protection of Women from Domestic Violence Act, 2005 and the Compulsory Registration of Marriage Act, 2006.

The Domestic Violence Act recognises that abuse be physical as well as mental.[24]

The major policy initiatives undertaken by the Department in the recent past include the establishment of the National Commission for Women (NCW), Rashtriya Mahila Kosh (RMK), adoption of National Nutrition Policy (NNP), strengthening of ICDS, setting up of National Creche Fund (NCF), launching of Indira Mahila Yojana (IMY), Balika Samriddhi Yojana (BSY), and Rural Women's Development and Empowerment Project (RWDEP).[25] Various steps have been taken by the government to prevent such abuses and to empower women. Criminal laws against sati, dowry, female infanticide and foeticide, 'eve teasing', rape, immoral trafficking and other offences relating to women have been enacted in addition to civil laws like the Dissolution of Muslim Marriages Act 1939, the Hindu Marriage Act 1955 and other Matrimonial enactments. The Prevention of Domestic Violence Act has been passed in 2005.[26]

In addition to education, employment can also be an important source of empowerment for women. Employment, particularly for cash and in the formal sector, can empower women by providing financial independence, alternative sources of social identity, and exposure to power structures independent of kin networks. Women who are divorced, separated, deserted, or widowed are much more likely to be employed than currently married women; never married women are least likely to be employed. Women's employment is likely to be affected by residence, since agricultural work, which accounts for most employment in rural areas, is typically more compatible with women's other responsibilities as well as with low levels of education and skill development.[27]

The 73rd and 74th Amendments (1993) to the Constitution of India have provided some special powers to women that for reservation of seats (33 per cent), whereas the report HRD as March 2002 shows that the legislatures with the highest percentage of women are Sweeden 42.7 per cent, Denmark 38 per cent, Finland 36 per cent and Iceland 34.9 per cent. In India, "The New Panchayati Raj is the part of the effort to empower women at least at the village level. The most positive development last few years has been the growing involvement of women in the Panchayati Raj institutions. There are many elected women representatives at the village council level.[28]

Women Entrepreneurship

Female entrepreneurs encompass approximately one third of all entrepreneurs worldwide. Women became more involved in the business world only when the idea of women in business became palatable to the general public. A recent international study found that women from low to middle income countries are more likely to enter early stage entrepreneurship when compared to those of higher income countries.[29] Woman entrepreneur is an adult who owns and runs an enterprise, especially a commercial one, often at personal financial risk. The ILO defined the women's enterprise as a small unit where one or more women entrepreneurs have not less than 50 per cent financial holdings. The concept of women entrepreneurship is becoming a global phenomenon playing a vital role in the business community.[30]

Women have been successful in breaking their confinement within the limits of their homes by entering into varied kinds of professionals and services women entrepreneurs have proved to be on par with their men counterparts in business acumen and are emerging as smart and dynamic entrepreneurs. Women owned businesses are highly increasing in the economies of almost all countries.[31] In India, women entrepreneurship is a recent topic which started only after the 1970s with the introduction of the Womens Decade (1975 to 1985) and which mostly picked up in the late 70s.[32] Women's entrepreneurship encompasses self-employment, income generation, and the management of businesses/ enterprises. Many women in India have attained prominent or leadership positions, rising to the highest echelons in every walk of life — for example, as entrepreneurs, industrialists, civil servants, police officers, airline pilots, scientists, engineers.[33]

Entrepreneurship is the core of economic development. It is a multi-dimensional task and essentially creative activity. Entrepreneur is key factor of entrepreneurship. They play very important role in socio-economic welfare of the country. They identify the needs of the business, purchase the other factors of production and coordinate them for some productive purposes. They are the innovators, researchers and risk-takers of the company. A strong desire to do something positive is an inbuilt quality of entrepreneurial women, who is capable of contributing values in both family and social life. Many women start a business due to some traumatic event, such as divorce, discrimination due to pregnancy or the corporate glass ceiling, the health of a family member, or economic reasons such as a layoff. Women entrepreneurs tend to be highly motivated and self directed, they also exhibit a high internal locus of control and achievement.[34]

The 1991 Industrial Policy has envisaged special training programmes to support women entrepreneurs. Accordingly women entrepreneurs are receiving training through Entrepreneurship Development Programmes (EDPS) conducted by various institutions and organisations both at central and state levels. The Small Industries Development Organisation (SIDO), with its field offices all over the country has been carrying out development programmes for women entrepreneurs and is providing technical schemes for setting up of SSI units.[35]

Challenges before Women Empowerment

There are several constraints that check the process of women empowerment in India. Social norms and family structure in developing countries like India, manifests and perpetuate the subordinate status of women. One of the norms is the continuing preference for a son over the birth of a girl child which in present in almost all societies and communities. The society is more biased in favour of male child in respect of education, nutrition and other opportunities.[36]

The problems and constraints experienced by women entrepreneurs have resulted in restricting the expansion of women entrepreneurship. Women entrepreneurs have to face a stiff competition with the men entrepreneurs who easily involve in the promotion and development area and carry out easy marketing of their products with both the organised sector and their male counterparts. Lack of self-confidence, will-power, strong mental outlook and optimistic attitude amongst women creates a fear from committing mistakes while doing their piece of work. Indian women give more emphasis to family ties and relationships. Women in India lead a protected life.[37]

The financial institutions are skeptical about the entrepreneurial abilities of women. The bankers consider women loonies as higher risk than men loonies. The bankers put unrealistic and unreasonable securities to get loan to women entrepreneurs. Women's family obligations also bar them from becoming successful entrepreneurs in both developed and developing nations.[38]

Government is taking some concrete steps in empowering women by helping women to help themselves and their families. Only 39 per cent of Indian women attend primary schools. Most families pull them out of school, either to help out at home or from fear of violence. While women are guaranteed equality under the constitution, legal protection has little effect in the face of prevailing patriarchal traditions. Women lack power to decide who they will marry, and are often married off before they reach the age of 18. The maternal mortality rate in India is the second highest in the world. India accounts for more than 25 per cent of all maternal deaths in the world.[39]

Women's Reservation Bill

Women's Reservation Bill is a pending bill in India which proposes to amend the Constitution of India to reserve 33 per cent of all seats in the Lower House of Parliament of India, the Lok Sabha, and in all state legislative assemblies for women. The Upper House Rajya Sabha passed the bill on 9 Mar 2010. As of February 2014, the Lower House Lok Sabha has not yet voted on the bill.[40] The Women's Reservation Bill was first introduced in the Parliament in 1996 by the H.D. Deve Gowda government, but no government has successfully passed it yet. The current version of the bill, the 108th Amendment, seeks to reserve 33 per cent of all seats in governing bodies at the Centre, State and Local level. The opponents of the bill propound that reservation would only perpetuate the gender inequality and not solve it. Another major concern of the opponents is that such a reservation will only fill the halls of Parliament with wives and daughters of those unfortunate politicians whose constituencies fell under the reserved category that year.[41]

Self-Help Group

Self-help group is a village-based financial intermediary committee usually composed of 10-20 local women or men. It may be registered or unregistered. It typically comprises a group of micro entrepreneurs having homogeneous social and economic backgrounds; all voluntarily coming together to save regular small sums of money, mutually agreeing to contribute to a common fund and to meet their emergency needs on the basis of mutual help. Self-help groups are started by non-governmental organisations that generally have broad anti-poverty agendas. Self-help groups are seen as instruments for goals including empowering women, developing leadership abilities among poor people, increasing school enrollments, and improving nutrition and the use of birth control.[42]

Self-help groups, also known as mutual help, mutual aid, or support groups, are groups of people who provide mutual support for each other. In a self-help group, the members share a common problem, often a common disease or addiction. Self-help groups may exist separately or as part of larger organisations. They may operate informally or according to a format or programme.[43] Women empowerment is a process in which women challenge the existing norms and culture, to effectively promote their well being. The participation of women in Self Help Groups (SHGs) made a significant impact on their empowerment both in social and economical aspects.

The origin of Self Help Groups is the brainchild of Grameen Bank of Bangladesh, founded by Professor Mohammed Yunus in 1975, who tried out a new approach to rural credit in Bangaladesh. Grameen gave loans without asking borrowers either to provide collateral or engage in paper work. In India NABARD initiated SHGs in the year 1986-87. But the real effort was taken after 1991-92 from the linkage of SHGs with the banks.[44] The main activity of the SHGs is thrift and credit. The SHGs are then trained in different vocations and linked with the banks to start micro enterprises either in groups or individually based on their interests and viability of the vocation. The main thrust of the economic activities is to enhance income from existing resources and create additional opportunities of employment to optimise local resources and skill.[45]

Conclusion

Women's Empowerment has been an issue of immense discussions and contemplation over the last few decades world-wide. This as an agenda has been on top of the lists of most government plans and programmes as well. The empowerment of women would result in overall development of society both at micro and macro level. Active participation of women in economic activities and decisions, would contribute towards overall economic development. There are several constraints that check the process of women empowerment in India. Social norms and family structure in developing countries like India, manifests and perpetuate the subordinate status of women. Government is taking some concrete steps in empowering women by helping women to help themselves and their families.

References

1. Vishal, Essay on omen empowerment in India, Available at http://www.share-youressays.com/2884/1328-words-essay-on-womens-empowerment-in-india
2. Amtul Waris and B. C. Viraktamath, Gender gaps and Women's Empower-ment in India – Issues and Strategies, International Journal of Scientific and Research Publications, Volume 3, Issue 9, September 2013, Available at http://www.ijsrp.org/research-paper-0913/ijsrp-p21116.pdf
3. Dr Rakesh Chandr, Women empowerment in India; Milestones and challenges, Available at http://en.wikieducator.org/images/2/2c/Women_empower-ment.pdf
4. http://www.artofliving.org/in-en/women-empowerment
5. http://www.womenempowermentinindia.com/women-empowerment-essay/
6. Indicators of Women's Empowerment in Developing Nations, Available at https://www.lafollette.wisc.edu/images/publications/workshops/2013-women.pdf

7. Dr Shruti Singh, Women Empowerment in Modern India, Available at http://www.themenplattform-ez.de/wp-content/uploads/2012/07/SSRN-id2361581.pdf
8. Momta Mokta, Empowerment of women in India: A Critical Analysis, Available at http://www.iipa.org.in/New%20Folder/8—Mamta.pdf
9. http://www.indiacelebrating.com/essay/social-issues/women-empowerment/
10. Essay on women empowerment: Its meaning and importance, http://www.import-antindia.com/19050/essay-on-women-empowerment/
11. http://www.importantindia.com/19047/short-paragraph-on-women-empower-ment/
12. Dr Dasarathi Bhuyan (2006), Empowerment of Indian Women: A Challenge of twenty first Century, Orissa Review, http://odisha.gov.in/e-magazine/Orissareview/jan2006/engpdf/Empowerment_of_India.pdf
13. Women Empowerment : A Challenge of 21st Century, Available at http://www.rmttc.com/images/new_pdf/concept_paper.pdf
14. Soumitro Chakravarty, Anant Kumar, and Amar Nath Jha, Women's Empowerment in India: Issues, Challenges and Future Directions, International Review of Social Sciences and Humanities Vol. 5, No. 1 (2013), pp. 154-163.
15. Essay on women empowerment: Its meaning and importance, http://www.import antindia.com/19050/essay-on-women-empowerment/
16. http://www.importantindia.com/19047/short-paragraph-on-women-empower-ment/
17. Why is women's economic empowerment important for development?, Available at http://siteresources.worldbank.org/INTGENDER/Resources/womens_economic_empowerment.pdf
18. http://www.unfpa.org/resources/issue-7-women-empowerment
19. Momta Mokta, Empowerment of women in India: A Critical Analysis, Available at http://www.iipa.org.in/New%20Folder/8—Mamta.pdf
20. M. Suguna, Education and women empowerment in India, International Journal of Multidisciplinary Research, Vol.1 Issue 8, December 2011, http://www.zeni-thresearch.org.in/images/stories/pdf/2011/Dec/zijmr/15_VOL%201_ISSUE8_ZEN.pdf
21. Dr Ravi N. Kadam, Empowerment of Women in India- An Attempt to Fill the Gender Gap (June, 2012), International Journal of Scientific and Research Publications, Volume 2, Issue 6, June 2012, http://www.ijsrp.org/research_paper_jun2012/ijsrp-June-2012-95.pdf
22. Essay on women empowerment, Available at http://www.indiacelebrating. com/essay/social-issues/women-empowerment/
23. Tulika Tripathi, Women's Empowerment: Concept and Empirical Evidence from India, Available at http://www.cdedse.org/ws2011/papers/Tulika% 20Tripathi.pdf
24. Puja Mondal, Essay on Women Empowerment in India, http://www.your-articlelibrary.com/essay/essay-on-women-empowerment-in-india/31317/
25. http://www.megaessays.com/viewpaper/29102.html
26. Empowering Women Rebuilding the Society, Available at http://www.civil serviceindia.com/subject/Essay/empowering-women-rebuilding-the-society.html

27. Sunita Kishor and Kamla Gupta (2009), Gender Equality and Women's Empowerment in India, https://dhsprogram.com/pubs/pdf/OD57/OD57.pdf
28. Dhruba Hazarika, Women Empowerment in India: A Brief Discussion, International Journal of Educational Planning and Administration. Volume 1, Number 3 (2011), pp. 199-202.
29. Female entrepreneur (2015), Available at https://en.wikipedia.org/wiki/Female_entrepreneur
30. Sreenivasa Rao Behara and K. Niranjan, Rural Women Entrepreneurship in India, IJCEM International Journal of Computational Engineering and Management, Vol. 15 Issue 6, November 2012, Available at http://www.ijcem.org/papers 112012/ijcem_112012_02.pdf
31. http://www.ijmra.us/project%20doc/IJPSS_MARCH2012/IJMRA-PSS862.pdf
32. http://shodhganga.inflibnet.ac.in/bitstream/10603/6732/7/07_chapter% 202.pdf
33. Creating an Enabling Environment for Women's Entrepreneurship in India, Available at http://www.unescap.org/sites/default/files/ESCAP-SSWA-Development-Paper_1304_1.pdf
34. http://prj.co.in/setup/socialscience/paper62.pdf
35. http://www.tarj.in/images/download/AJMMR/TAJMMR%20JULY%202013%20COMPLETE%20PDF/7.2,%20T.Vijayakumar1.pdf
36. Dr (Smt.) Rajeshwari M. Shettar, A Study on Issues and Challenges of Women Empowerment in India, IOSR Journal of Business and Management, Volume 17, Issue 4.Ver. I (Apr. 2015), pp. 13-19.
37. http://www.zenithresearch.org.in/images/stories/pdf/2011/Sep/14. Vol_01_Issue_05%20MEENU%20GOYAL%20women%20paper.pdf
38. Arakeri Shanta V., Women Entrepreneurship in India, Available at http://www.abhinavjournal.com/images/Arts_&_Education/Mar12/1.pdf
39. Women Empowerment: Challenges and Prospects, Available at http://www.civilserviceindia.com/subject/Essay/women-empowerment-challenges-and-prospects.html
40. Women's Reservation Bill (2015), Available at https://en.wikipedia.org/wiki/Constitution_of_India
41. Women's Reservation Bill, Available at http://www.lokniti.org/women-reservation-bill.php
42. Self Help Group (2015), Available at https://en.wikipedia.org/wiki/Self-help_group_(finance)
43. http://psychcentral.com/lib/what-is-a-self-help-group/
44. S.Thangamani, and S.Muthuselvi, A Study on Women Empowerment through Self- Help Groups with Special Reference to Mettupalayam Taluk in Coimbatore District, IOSR Journal of Business and Management, Volume 8, Issue 6 (Mar. - Apr. 2013), pp. 17-24.
45. http://www.vedantaaluminium.com/pdf/yagna-vol3.pdf

Chapter 17

Foreign Direct Investment in India: An Overview

Dr Suman Kalyan Chaudhury,
Manoj Kumar Panda and Professor A.K. Sahu

"The consuming desire of most human beings is deliberately to plant their whole life in the hands of some other person. I would describe this method of searching for happiness as immature. Development of character consists solely in moving toward self-sufficiency." **–*Quentin Crisp***

Introduction

India is the country of potentiality and that is the one of the most prominent and striking feature for today's globalised world, but have a scarcity of resources. When scarcity meets with resources, then scope of growth and development emerges. In the last two decades, the pace of FDI flows is rising faster than almost all other indicators of economic activity worldwide. Developing countries considered FDI as the safest type of external finance, as it not only supplement domestic savings, foreign reserves but promotes growth even more through spillovers of technology, skills, increased innovative capacity, and domestic competition. Now-a-day, FDI has become an instrument of international economic integration.

Located in South Asia, India is the seventh largest, and the second most populated country in the world. India has long been known for the diversity of its culture, for the convergence of geography. Today, the world's largest democracy has come to the forefront as a global resource for industry in manufacturing and services. Its pool of technical skills, its base of an English-speaking populace with an increasing disposable income and its burgeoning market has all combined to enable India emerge as a viable partner to global industry.

Significance of FDI

Developing countries, which invite FDI, can gain access to a wider global and better platform in the world economy. Economic growth is one of the major factors, which is enormously benefited from foreign direct investment. Foreign direct investments have opened a wide spectrum of opportunities in the trading of goods and services in India both in terms of import and export production. Products of superior quality are manufactured by various industries in India due to greater amount of FDI inflows in the country. FDI apparently helps in the outsourcing of knowledge from India especially in the Information Technology sector.

Developing countries by inviting FDI can introduce world-class technology and technical expertise and processes to their existing working process. Foreign expertise can be an important factor in upgrading the existing technical processes. The civilian nuclear deal led to transfer of nuclear energy knowhow between the USA and India. FDI increases the level of competition in the host country. Other companies will also have to improve on their processes and services in order to stay in the market. FDI enhanced the quality of products, services and regulates a particular sector.

Linkages and spillover to domestic firms- various foreign firms are now occupying a position in the Indian market through Joint Ventures and collaboration concerns. The maximum amount of the profits gained by the foreign firms through these joint ventures is spent on the Indian market. Employees of the country get acquainted with the globally valued skills through these industries where FDI is used. FDI has also ensured a number of employment opportunities by aiding the setting up of industrial units in various corners of India.

Genesis of FDI flow to India

The historical background of FDI in India can be traced back to the establishment of East India Company of Britain. British capital came to India during the colonial era of Britain in India. After Second World War, Japanese companies entered Indian market and enhanced their trade with India, yet U.K. remained the most dominant investor in India. Further, after Independence issues relating to foreign capital, operations of MNCs, gained attention of the policy makers. Keeping in mind the national interests, the policy-makers designed the FDI policy which aims FDI as a medium of acquiring advanced technology and to mobilise foreign exchange resources. With the passage not time and as per the changes in economic and political regimes, there have been changes in the FDI policy too.

The industrial policy of 1965, allowed MNCs to venture through technical collaboration in India. Government adopted a liberal attitude by allowing more frequent equity participation to foreign enterprises, and to accept equity capital in technical collaborations. But due to significant outflow of foreign reserves in the form of remittances of dividends, profits, royalties etc, the government has to adopt same stringent foreign policy measures in 1970s. During this period the government adopted a selective and highly restrictive foreign policy as far as foreign capital, type of FDI and ownerships of foreign companies was concerned.

Government setup Foreign Investment Board and enacted Foreign Exchange Regulation Act in order to regulate flow of foreign capital and FDI flow to India. The soaring oil prices continued, as a result there is low exports and deterioration in Balance of Payment position during 1980s which forced the government to make necessary changes in the foreign policy and this resulting in the partial liberalisation of Indian Economy. The government introduces reforms in the industrial sector, aimed at increasing competency, efficiency and growth in industry through a stable, pragmatic and non-discriminatory policy for FDI flow.

In this critical face of Indian economy the Government of India with the help of World Bank and IMF introduced the macro-economic stabilisation and structural adjustment programme. As a result of these reforms India open its door to FDI inflows and adopted a more liberal foreign policy in order to restore the confidence of foreign investors. Further, under the new foreign investment policy Government of India constituted FIPB (Foreign Investment Promotion Board) whose main function was to invite and facilitate foreign investment through single window system from the Prime Minister's Office. The present study aims at fulfilling the following objectives: (a) to study the sector-wise role of foreign direct investment in India; (b) to discuss the various problems about the foreign direct investment in India; and (c) to suggest some recommendations with reference to foreign direct investment in India.

The study is confined to role of foreign direct investment in different sectors. The functional scope of the study is to suggest remedial measures for the successful growth and development of FDI. The study is purely descriptive in nature and all the data used for conducting research were taken from secondary sources.

Analysis of Empirical Data

Table 17.1: Foreign Investment Inflows (FDI and FII) and GDP of India from 2000 to 2012

Year/ Details	*Foreign Investment in Rs Billion*			*GDP in Per cent*	*GDP in Rupee Billion*
	Direct investment	*Portfolio investment*	*Total investment*		
2000	9338	13112	22450	3.1	20865.69
2001	18406	12609	31015	3.9	22399.05
2002	29235	9639	38874	4.6	23930.30
2003	24367	4738	29105	6.9	24352.97
2004	19860	52279	72139	8.1	27987.47
2005	27188	41854	69042	9.2	31822.56
2006	39674	55307	94981	9.7	37795.10
2007	103367	31713	135080	9.9	39243.86
2008	140212	109741	249953	6.2	53889.52
2009	192268	-63618	128650	6.6	59252.44
2010	178974	153516	332490	10.6	62434.55
2011	158821	143435	302256	7.2	79851.64
2012	223095	83434	306529	6.9	104715.71

Source: Directorate General of Commercial Intelligence and Statistics and *Hand book of statistics RBI 2000-2013.*

Table 17.1 discloses the foreign capital inflow to India as well the position of GDP of India. Over a period of 13 years starting from 2000 to 2012, it was clear from the table and graphs that there was a similar trend observed in case of total foreign capital inflow and portfolio inflow. Both these inflows increases year over year upto 2008. There was a heavy decline in 2009 in the inflow of both total foreign capital inflow and portfolio inflow whereas year 2010 has witnessed a further increase in the same. The FDI has shown a clear increasing trend over the study period. From the year 2000 to 2003 the FDI was more than the portfolio inflow to India whereas up to 2006 it was less than the portfolio inflow. From 2007, it was more than portfolio inflow up to 2012 whereas in 2009 the FDI was more than the total foreign capital inflow. The Gross Domestic Product of India was 3.1 per cent in the year 2000 which was increased to 9.9 per cent by the end of 2007. In the year 2008, it was declined to 6.2 per cent. From 2009, it was again increased and reached to the top (10.6 per cent) in 2010.

Table 17.2: Inflow/ Outflow under Various NRI Deposit Schemes

(Rupees Billion)

Year/ Source	*FCNR(B)*	*NR(E)RA*	*NR(NR)RD & NRO*	*Total Flow*
2000	14.60	38.35	13.78	66.73
2001	41.30	39.29	25.26	105.85
2002	28.33	77.55	24.23	130.11
2003	25.46	299.81	-181.24	144.03
2004	35.02	215.74	-83.45	167.31
2005	22.11	3.77	-69.10	-43.22
2006	71.37	52.11	41.17	164.65
2007	93.51	82.87	19.29	195.67
2008	-38.63	4.39	41.45	7.21
2009	-43.94	115.16	125.72	196.94
2010	49.65	-3.37	92.27	138.55
2011	61.03	-12.76	99.36	147.63
2012	-30.19	409.12	192.31	571.24

Source: Directorate General of Commercial Intelligence and Statistics and Hand book of statistics RBI 2000-2013.

Table 17.3: Details of Receipt and Payment from the Invisibles Category of Transactions

(Rupees Billion)

Year/Details	*Invisibles Receipts*	*Invisibles Payments*	*Net Invisibles*
2000	1314.49	744.21	570.28
2001	1477.78	1026.39	451.39
2002	1751.08	1037.27	713.81
2003	2027.57	1204.00	823.57
2004	2454.13	1180.44	1273.69
2005	3115.50	1719.59	1395.91
2006	3976.60	2117.33	1859.27
2007	5171.46	2815.67	2355.79
2008	5981.00	2939.00	3042.00
2009	7704.00	3506.00	4198.00
2010	7746.00	3944.00	3802.00
2011	9025.00	5170.00	3855.00
2012	10535.00	5173.00	5362.00

Source: Directorate General of Commercial Intelligence and Statistics and Hand book of statistics RBI 2000-2013.

As would be observed from Table 17.4 and corresponding Figure-3 that the invisible receipt, payment as well as net invisible has shown an increasing trend. The receipt from invisible transactions has grown year over year from 2000 to 2012. But, in case of invisible payments, it was declined in the year 2004 as compared to 2003. Further, the analysis of net

Invisibles disclosed that it was more than the payment in the year 2009. The net invisible was declined in the year 2001 as compared to 2000 and also in 2010 as compared to 2009.

Table 17.4: Details of Primary Products Export

(*Rupees Billion*)

Year	*Agriculture and Allied Products*	*Share of Agriculture and Allied Products*	*Ores and Minerals Ores*	*Share of and Minerals*	*Primary Products*
2000	243.012	85.96	39.698	14.04	282.709
2001	272.882	83.82	52.674	16.18	325.556
2002	281.440	82.38	60.206	17.62	341.646
2003	324.733	77.07	96.599	22.93	421.333
2004	346.157	76.08	108.846	23.92	455.004
2005	380.781	62.53	228.188	37.47	608.969
2006	452.201	62.37	272.883	37.63	725.084
2007	573.920	64.43	316.860	35.57	890.780
2008	742.090	66.90	367.169	33.10	1109.260
2009	806.489	69.21	358.770	30.79	1165.260
2010	841.363	67.18	410.976	32.82	1252.339
2011	1102.961	73.70	393.527	26.30	1496.488
2012	1793.312	82.11	390.729	17.89	2184.041

Source: Directorate General of Commercial Intelligence and Statistics and Hand book of statistics RBI 2000-2013.

Export details of Primary products from year 2000-2012 can be observed from the Table 17.4 and Figure-4. It was clear from the data that the contribution of Agriculture and Allied Products to total Primary products export were more than the contribution of Ores and Minerals each year. The contribution of Agriculture and Allied Products was 85.96 per cent in the year 2000 which was decreased to 62.37 per cent by the end of 2006. Further, it increased from 2007 and reached to 82.11 per cent in 2012.

Concentrating on exports from 2000 to 2012, it would be seen from the above Table that, 'B' Chemicals and Related Products, 'C' Engineering Goods, showed a steady growth rate. So far as "G" Other Manufactured Goods was concerned, it also showed relatively increasing growth rate. Similarly, considering sectors like; 'A' Leather and Manufactures, 'D' Textile and Textile Products, 'E' Gems and Jewellry and 'F' Handicrafts (excluding Handmade Carpets) were witnessed a declining trend in growth trajectory.

Table 17.5: Sector-wise Details of Export Products of India

(Rupees Billion)

Year	A		B		C		D		E		F		G
2000	282.71	9.71	1287.61	44.25	1.69	0.06	23.61	0.81	1595.61	54.83	1314.49	45.17	2910.10
2001	325.56	9.27	1568.58	44.64	85.42	2.43	56.15	1.60	2035.71	57.94	1477.78	42.06	3513.49
2002	341.65	8.89	1591.46	41.43	101.07	2.63	56.00	1.46	2090.18	54.41	1751.08	45.59	3841.26
2003	421.33	9.20	1947.65	42.53	124.69	2.72	57.70	1.26	2551.37	55.72	2027.57	44.28	4578.94
2004	455.00	8.45	2228.29	41.36	163.97	3.04	86.40	1.60	2933.67	54.45	2454.13	45.55	5387.80
2005	608.97	8.87	2728.72	39.73	314.04	4.57	101.66	1.48	3753.40	54.64	3115.50	45.36	6868.90
2006	725.08	8.49	3212.61	37.61	515.33	6.03	111.16	1.30	4564.18	53.44	3976.60	46.56	8540.78
2007	890.78	8.18	3842.61	35.29	845.20	7.76	139.20	1.28	5717.79	52.51	5171.46	47.49	10889.25
2008	1109.26	8.85	4145.99	33.06	1141.92	9.11	161.47	1.29	6558.64	52.30	5981.00	47.70	12539.64
2009	1165.26	7.23	5664.02	35.16	1233.98	7.66	344.29	2.14	8407.55	52.18	7704.00	47.82	16111.55
2010	1252.34	7.73	5464.56	33.73	1328.99	8.20	409.45	2.53	8455.34	52.19	7746.00	47.81	16201.34
2011	1496.49	7.32	7198.61	35.19	1887.79	9.23	846.33	4.14	11429.22	55.88	9025.00	44.12	20454.22
2012	2184.04	8.69	8951.25	35.62	2658.19	10.58	799.33	3.18	14592.81	58.07	10535	41.93	25127.81

Source: Directorate General of Commercial Intelligence and Statistics and Hand book of statistics RBI 2000-2013.

A-Primary Products B- Manufactured Goods

C-Petroleum Products D-Others

E- All Commodities F- Invisibles Receipts

G- Total Export %- Share of each sector to total

Analysing export profile (Primary Products, Manufactured Goods, Petroleum Products others and receipt from Invisibles) from 2000 to 2012, it would be seen that amount of export of primary products, manufacturing goods and invisibles showed a increasing trend but, considering the ratio of both the sectors towards total export were declined. Other two sectors viz. *'Petroleum'* and *'Others'* remarkably showed increasing trend in amount of export as well as in ratio towards total export.

Positive Impact of FDI

Following are the some of positive impact through FDI:

1. Foreign corporations bring new technical know-how and managerial skills into target country.
2. Foreign corporations can help to change the economic structure of host country as governments can attract companies from promising and innovative sectors.
3. The foreign corporations often bring additional investors into the target country.
4. Foreign corporations improve the business environment of the target country.
5. Foreign corporations bring new clean technologies that help to improve the conditions.
6. Foreign corporations usually help increase the level of wages in the target economy.
7. Foreign corporations usually have positive effects on the trade balance.

Negative Implications of FDI

Here we have listed some negative impacts of FDI.

1. Foreign corporations may buy a local company in order to shut it down and gain monopoly.
2. The foreign corporations target the domestic market and sometimes the domestic corporations are not able to compete with these corporations.
3. The working positions of host country are also affected because of privatisations deals or merger and acquisition transactions.
4. Foreign corporations have a tendency to use their usual suppliers which can lead to increased imports and thus make negative impact on balance of payments.

5. The high growth of wages in foreign corporations can influence a similar growth in the domestic corporations which are not able to cover this growth with the growth of productivity.
6. There can be an emergence of the problem of dual economy because of a developed foreign sector and an underdeveloped host sector.
7. There is negative effect on environment also.

General Suggestions

There are some suggestions for more inflow of FDI.

1. Indian infrastructures must be developed to capture more FDIs.
2. Present reforms for FDI must be continued for the desired economic growth.
3. It is advised to the government that service charges should be reduced to encourage FDI and allied foreign investments.
4. It is better to give special benefits to NRI for investments in India that will strength the image of Indian economy in the world community.
5. Government can encourage FDI investors to park their funds in sectors like cultivation, energy, communication, infrastructure and other essential sectors.

Conclusion

The growth of FDI gives opportunities to Indian industry for technological up gradation, gaining access to global managerial skills and practices, optimising utilisation of human and natural resources and competing internationally with higher efficiency. FDI plays an important role in economic growth of an economy. The study observes that FDI is a significant factor influencing the level of economic growth in India. It provides a sound base for economic growth and development by enhancing the financial position of the country. It also contributes to the GDP and foreign exchange reserves of the country.

Despite India offering a large domestic market and low labour costs due to restricted FDI regime, high imports tariffs, exit barriers for foreign firms, stringent labour laws, poor quality infrastructure, centralised decision-making process make India an unattractive investment destination for FDI. However, there are different views in this context. Under the new economic policy of LPG adopted in 1991 the FDI inflow to India in the last thirteen years made the country to grow both in quantitative as well as qualitative way. India has been ranked at the second place in global foreign direct investments in 2010 and will continue to remain among the top five attractive destinations for international investors during 2010-12, according to United Nations Conference on Trade and Development in a report on world investment prospects titled, 'World Investment Prospects Survey 2009–2012'.

To sum up, it can be said that government have been simplifying and relaxing entry barriers for business activities and providing investor-friendly laws and tax system for foreign investors. Somewhere, a restriction related to the track record of Sub-Accounts is also to be made on the investors who withdraw money out of the Indian stock market. Similarly, the laws should be such that it protects domestic investors and also promote trade in country through FDI.

References

1. Agarwal, J, Khan MA (2011). Impact of FDI on GDP: A comparative study of China and India, International Journal of Business Management 6(10): pp.71-79.
2. Kumar Gajendran Lenin, Karthika S (2010). Sectoral performance through inflows of foreign direct investment (FDI).
3. Singh, S (2009). Foreign direct investment (FDI) and growth of states of India. VISION 2020 - Managerial Strategies and Challenge, Wisdom Publications, Delhi.
4. Devajit Mahanta, (2012). Impact of foreign direct investments on Indian Economy, Research Journal of Management Sciences, 1(2): pp. 29-31.
5. Ministry of Finance (2005-06). Report of the economic survey, Government of India, New Delhi.
6. Nayak D.N (1999). "Canadian Foreign Direct Investment in India: some Observations", Political Economy Journal of India, Volume 8, No. 1, pp. 51-56.
7. Basu, P., Nayak, N.C, Archana (2007). "Foreign Direct Investment in India: Emerging Horizon", Indian Economic Review, Vol. XXXXII. No.2, pp. 255-266.
8. Agrawal, G. and Khan, M.A. (2011). "Impact of FDI on GDP: A Comparative Study of China and India", International Journal of Business and Management, 6(10): pp.71-79.
9. Guech Heang, L. and Moolio, P. (2013). "The Relationship between Gross Domestic Product and Foreign Direct Investment: The Case of Cambodia", *KASBIT Business Journal*, 6: pp. 87-99.
10. Hossain, A. and Hossain, M.K. (2012). "Empirical Relationship between Foreign Direct Investment and Economic Output in South Asian Countries: A Study on Bangladesh, Pakistan and India", *International Business Research*, 5(1): pp. 9-21.

11. Karimi, M.S. and Yusop, Z. (2009). "FDI and Economic Growth in Malaysia", *Munich Personal Re PEc Archive*, Paper No. 14999.
12. Kaur, M., Yadav, S.S. and Gautam, V. (2012). "Foreign Direct Investment and Current Account Deficit- A Causality Analysis in Context of India", *Journal of International Business and Economy*, 13(2): pp. 85-106.
13. Durham, J. B. (2004). "Absorptive Capacity and the Effects of Foreign Direct Investment and Equity Foreign Portfolio Investment on Economic Growth" *European Economic Review,* 48, pp. 285-306.
14. Bende-Nabende, A., Ford, J., Santoo, B. and Sen, S. (2003). "The Interaction between FDI, Output and the Spillover Variables: Cointegration and VAR Analysis for APEC, 1965-99", *Applied Economics Letters*, 10, pp.165-172.
15. Kohpaiboon, A. (2006). "Foreign Direct Investment and Technology Spillover: A Cross-Industry Analysis of Thai Manufacturing", *World Development*, 34, pp. 541-556.
16. Bengoa, M. and Sanchez-Robles, B. (2003), "Foreign Direct Investment, Economic Freedom and Growth: New Evidence from Latin America", *European Journal of Political Economy*, 19, pp. 529-545.
17. www.imf.org
18. www.rbi.org
19. www.worldbank.org

Chapter 18

Growth and Composition of Population in Karnataka State Spatio-Temporal Analysis from 1991-2011

Dr D. Rajasekaran

"The higher mental development of woman, the less possible it is for her to meet a congenial male who will see in her, not only sex, but also the human being, the friend, the comrade and strong individuality, who cannot and ought not lose a single trait of her character." **–Emma Goldman**

Introduction

Generally speaking the history of demography may be traced since about three centuries back. However, it may in quantitative as well as qualitative. Its development may be observed only in the twentieth century. Today demography is being considered as an independent branch of knowledge. According to Peter R. Cox 'it is sometimes argued that certain branches of population analysis should be distinguished from others by a separate title'. In this connection the word 'demology' has occasionally been suggested as an indicator of the more learned branches of the subject. But this has not come into general use. Rather more commonly the expression population studies are used to indicate the simpler and more descriptive demographic work. There is however no sharp dividing line between the various parts of demography and these expressions are used if at all without much consistency.

In the beginning demography was concerned only with the enumeration of population gradually it began to study population from empirical, statistical and mathematical viewpoints. Today it studies the size, composition and distribution of population. The size includes the population at a place in different periods. The composition of population includes measurable characteristics of population such as age, sex, marital status, education, religion, caste, health etc. These characteristics of population organisation are always changing. Distribution of population may be studied according to communities and religious groups or according to fields of population. Demography studies the patterns and causes of the changes in the size, composition and distribution of population.

In this regard the study of the population growth and composition in Karnataka during the period of 1991 to 2011 was taken to analyses the decadal growth and composition of population within the past two decades. (1991 to 2011).

Study Area

Karnataka is located in the western part of the Deccan plateau. Larger part of the state belongs to the Mysore plateau which is one of the three segments of larger Deccan plateau. The state has both lands as well as water frontiers. It is surrounded by Maharashtra in the North, Andra Pradesh in the East, Tamil Nadu in the South and South East, Kerala in the South West and Goa in the North West, in the western part is flanked by the Arabian Sea.

The state extends from 11°-31′ to 18°-45′ North latitudes. The state has maximum latitudinal extent of 7°-14′. Longitudinally the state extends from 74°-12′ to 78°-40′ east, thus the state has a longitudinal extent of 4°-28′. From North to South 750 km. long and west to east the state is about 400 km. The total Geographical area of the state is about 191791 Sq. km, which contributes 5.83 per cent of total area of the country, and a population of 61130704, as per 2011 census. It contributes 5.05 per cent of the total population of the country.

It is the eighth largest state in terms of area and ninth in terms of population in the country. The density of population per square km. is about 300. It is below the national average. The state has a growth rate of about 15 per cent which is the 22nd highest growth rate in the country. The population of the state is rising considerably due to rapid efforts towards development and progress. The literacy rate in the state is about 75 per cent which is a cause for concern and a statistic. The authorities must take notice and look to correct in the years to come. The sex ratio in the state is stands about 20 points higher than the national average. The statistics in the Karnataka census 2011 reveal the facts that can be taken into consideration by the government in a bid to further development. The state is moving towards development at a rapid rate and has emerged as one of the prime economical contributors to the revenue of India as a whole. The objectives of the study are: (a) to analyse the changes in district-wise population in Karnataka for the decades of 1991 to 2011; and (b) To trace the major changes in growth rates, literacy, male female ratio, density of population during 1991 to 2011.

Data and Methods

To study the decadal variation in population growth and composition in Karnataka State during the period of 1991 to 2011 secondary data have been obtained from census publications for the three different periods of census years for 1991, 2001 and 2011. District-wise population and also decadal growth rates have also been computed for the study. A comparative analysis has been done for the study to trace the major changes in growth rate and decadal variations in population composition in two decades. In understanding the demographic shift and its impact on the changes in proportion and growth of population in Karnataka a district-wise analysis has been done for the study. In the context of increasing population growth, literacy, urban population, density in modern society in India. A special emphasis has been laid to understand the growth rate, density, male-female ratio, literacy, rural urban ratio in Karnataka between two decades of 1991 to 2001 and 2001 to 2011.

Table 18.1: Trend of Population Growth in Karnataka 1901-2011

Years	*Population (in Lakhs)*	*Decadal Variation (in Lakhs)*	*Decadal Variation (in percentage)*
1901	130.5	—	—
1911	135.2	+4.70	+3.60
1921	133.8	-1.47	-1.40
1931	146.3	+12.55	+9.34
1941	162.5	+16.22	+11.07
1951	194.0	+31.46	+19.38
1961	235.8	+41.84	+21.56
1971	292.6	+47.12	+24.22
1981	370.4	+77.44	+26.75
1991	448.2	+71.33	+21.12
2001	527.3	+77.56	+17.25
2011	611.3	+79.10	+15.93

Source: Census Karnataka 1991-2011.

The trend of population growth in Karnataka clearly reveals large variations over the past Eleven decades. The growth of population in first three decades was either small or negative. It was due to many epidemics like plague and influenza. In the first 30 years between 1901 to 1931 the net addition was only 16.3 lakh. The second stage between 1931 to 1961 between three decades the growth of population was steady with a decadal growth of 9.35 per cent in 1931, 19.36 per cent in 1951, and 21.57 per cent in 1961. The total population in the state during these three decades has increased to 16.25 million, 19.40 million and 23.58 million respectively. In these decades the state has witnessed a rapid growth of population from 1961.

In the history of population growth in the state the period 1961 to 1981 is most important. It has recorded highest growth rate. The decadal growth of population in 1971 was 24.22 per cent, and it was increased to 26.75 per cent in 1981. The growth rate of 1981 was a record in the state because of medical facilities availability throughout the state and other healthcare measures, the government initiated were so effective and have caused rapid decline in the death rate. The phenomenal growth in this period is described as population explosion.

The decades 1991, 2001 and 2011 is quite interesting in the census history both in the state as well as India. It is because that a ray of hope has appeared in the horizon in controlling growth of population. The decadal population growth rate has started declining from 21.12 per cent in 1991, to 17.25 per cent in 2001, and to 15.93 per cent in 2011. Actual increase of population was 77.8 lakhs between 1981 to 1991, 79.1 lakhs in 1991 to 2001 and 84.0 lakhs in 2001 to 2011. The difference in the actual increase was only marginal. Thus there are very strong positive evidences to believe declining trend of population in the coming census.

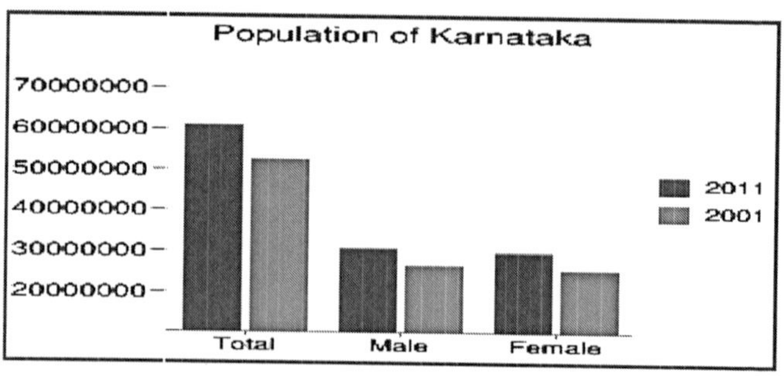

The Table 18.1 shows, the decadal growth of population has wide variation in the districts of Karnataka. The average growth rate was 17.25 in 2001 and 15.7 per cent in 2011 comparatively the decadal growth was declined. Even there are large variations in the growth rate of urban and rural areas. Among the districts, Bangalore urban district has register a highest growth rate of 35.09 in 2001 and 46.10 per cent in 2011, followed by Koppal (24.84 per cent) in 2001 and Bellary 24.9 per cent in 2011. In contrast, some of the districts have recorded lowest decadal growth such as Udupi 7.15, Mandya 7.26, Mysore 5.75 per cent in 2001 census and Chikmagalur -0.3 per cent, Kodagu 1.1, Mandya 2.2, Tumkur 3.7, Hassan 3.2, Ramanagar 5.1, Chamarajanagar 5.1, Udupi 5.9, Uttara Kannada 6.2, Shimoga 6.9 per cent in 2011 census.

Density

Density is the most important criteria in analysing distribution of population. Usually number of people per Sq. K.M. or a mile is called density. The mean the population density of the state is 235 in 1991, 275 in 2001 and 319 in 2011. That is lower than the mean density of India, relief pattern of rainfall, urbanisation, irrigation, climatic conditions are the influencing factors for the density of population?

Table 18.2: District-wise density of population in Karnataka 1991-2011

Sl. No.	*Districts*	*Density per Sq. k.m.*		
		1991	*2001*	*2011*
1.	Bangalore Urban	2210	2979	4378
2.	Bangalore Rural	298	323	441
3.	Bagalkot	—	251	288
4.	Belgaum	267	314	356
5.	Bellary	191	240	300
6.	Bidar	231	276	312
7.	Bijapur	172	172	207
8.	Chamarajnagar	—	189	200
9.	Chikmagalur	141	158	158
10.	Chitradurga	201	179	197
11.	Davanagere	—	302	329
12.	Dharwad	255	376	434
13.	D. Kannada	319	416	457
14.	Gadag	—	209	229
15.	Gulbarga	159	193	233
16.	Haveri	—	298	331
17.	Hassan	220	253	261
18.	Kolar	270	307	384
19.	Koppal	—	166	250
20.	Kodagu	119	133	135

(Contd...)

21.	Mandya	231	355	365
22.	Mysore	285	383	437
23.	Raichur	165	241	228
24.	Shimoga	181	193	207
25.	Tumkur	218	243	253
26.	Udupi	—	286	304
27.	U. Kannada	119	132	140
28.	Ramanagar	—	—	303
29.	Chikballapur	—	—	298
30.	Yadagiri	—	—	224
	Karnataka	**235**	**275**	**319**

Source: Karnataka census 1991, 2001, 2011.

The Table 18.2 has shows an analysis of density of population of the districts reveals that the costal districts, urbanised districts and the districts which have irrigation facilities have more density. In contrast, the Malnad districts, Hyderabad-Karnataka, North Karnataka and also drought prone central districts of the state have lower density of population. The lowest density of population is in Kodagu, Uttara Kannda, Chittradurga, Chamarajnagar, Bijapur, Shimoga, Yadagiri, Gadag, Raichur, Hassan. These are Malnad and Semi-Malnad and drought prone areas. Kodagu is the lowest density district in the state. The highest population density in the state is found in Bangalore Urban, Bangalore rural, Mysore, Mandya, Kolar, Dharwad, Davanagere and Belgaum districts. These are urban areas well irrigated, and good agriculturally developed districts. The Bangalore urban district has highest density in the state with 2210, 2979, 4378 per sq.k.m. in 1991, 2001 and 2011 census respectively.

Literacy

Literacy is one of the important features of demographic composition and it is an indicator of the levels of human development. It reflects socio-economic development to a large extent. Improvement of literacy helps to improve people's productivity by strengthening their income. It is an established fact that there is a positive relationship between the levels of literacy and income. At the same time, literacy rate also influences much on sex ratio and the status of women. This is apparent from the situation prevailing in Dakshin Kannada, Udupi, and Kodagu districts which have highest sex ratio in the state as well as very high female literacy.

The literacy rate in the state has continuously increased and has always remained much above the literacy rates of the country. Not only the total literacy has even the male and female literacy remained higher than the national average. It is increasing rapidly in the recent decades. Since 1971, the decadal growth of literacy is always remaining higher than 10 per cent. Even between 1991 to 2001 (66.6), and 2001 to 2011 (75.6), it has increased by 10 per cent and 9 per cent respectively.

Table 18.3: District-wise Male and Female Literacy 1991 to 2011

Sl. No.	Districts	Literacy 1991			2001			2011		
		Male	Female	Total	Male	Female	Total	Male	Female	Total
1.	Bangalore Urban	72.1	59.22	65.94	87.92	77.48	82.70	91.82	84.80	88.48
2.	Bangalore Rural	52.5	32.87	47.71	73.99	54.99	64.49	85.44	70.73	78.29
3.	Bagalkot	—	—	—	70.88	43.56	57.22	80.16	58.55	69.39
4.	Belgaum	55.26	32.45	44.10	75.70	52.32	64.01	82.90	64.74	73.94
5.	Bellary	47.84	26.21	37.21	69.20	45.28	57.24	77.24	58.28	67.85
6.	Bidar	47.60	24.74	36.44	72.46	48.81	60.63	79.94	61.66	71.01
7.	Bijapur	57.37	33.60	45.70	69.94	43.47	56.70	77.41	56.54	67.20
8.	Chamarajnagar	—	—	—	59.03	42.48	50.75	67.88	54.32	61.12
9.	Chikmagalur	60.48	43.99	52.32	80.29	64.01	72.15	85.66	72.88	79.24
10.	Chitradurga	56.03	36.24	46.41	74.66	53.78	64.22	81.37	66.05	73.82
11.	Davanagere	—	—	—	76.37	58.04	67.20	83.02	69.39	76.30
12.	Dharwad	59.46	37.58	48.83	80.82	61.92	71.37	86.88	73.57	80.30
13.	D. Kannada	72.29	59.14	65.51	89.70	77.21	83.45	93.31	84.04	88.62
14.	Gadag	—	—	—	89.32	52.52	65.92	84.89	65.29	75.18
15.	Gulbarga	41.75	19.87	31.02	61.77	37.90	49.83	75.11	65.87	65.65
16.	Havery	—	—	—	77.61	57.37	67.49	84.22	70.65	77.60
17.	Hassan	58.45	38.44	48.44	78.37	59.00	68.68	83.55	68.30	75.89
18.	Kolar	53.09	32.02	42.74	73.17	52.23	62.70	81.93	66.56	74.33
19.	Koppal	—	—	—	68.43	39.61	54.02	78.21	56.21	67.28
20.	Kodagu	64.26	52.66	58.49	83.70	72.26	77.98	87.24	77.91	82.52
21.	Mandya	50.46	31.56	41.18	70.50	51.53	61.01	78.14	62.01	70.14
22.	Mysore	47.67	32.09	40.06	70.88	55.81	63.39	78.44	66.59	72.53
23.	Raichur	39.54	17.81	28.78	61.52	35.93	48.72	71.35	49.56	60.44
24.	Shimoga	60.22	43.48	52.01	82.01	66.88	74.44	86.11	74.89	80.50
25.	Tumkur	56.76	33.77	46.47	76.78	56.94	66.86	82.05	66.45	74.32
26.	Udupi	—	—	—	88.23	75.19	81.71	91.69	81.41	86.29
27.	U.Kannada	64.49	48.12	56.44	84.53	68.47	76.50	89.72	78.21	84.03
28.	Ramanagar	—	—	—	—	—	—	76.92	61.30	69.20
29.	Chikballapur	—	—	—	—	—	—	78.36	61.55	70.08
30.	Yadagiri	—	—	—	—	—	—	63.33	41.31	52.36
	KARNATAKA	**67.26**	**44.34**	**56.04**	**76.10**	**56.90**	**66.64**	**82.85**	**68.13**	**75.60**

Source: Karnataka census 1991, 2001, 2011. (Total per cent calculated by author).

The Table 18.3 shows that the literacy rates of men and women in Karnataka 67.2 per cent, 44.3 per cent in 1991, 76.1 per cent, 56.9 per cent in 2001, 88.8 per cent, and 68.1 per cent in 2011. And also the average literacy is also increased. Thus, the women literacy has increased from 44.3 per cent in 1991 to 56.9 per cent in 2001 and 68.1 per cent in 2011 census.

The male and the average literacy also increase in the recent decades. A district-wise comparison of literacy is more interesting to analyse its growth in the last two census decades. The literacy rate between different districts varies.

The highest male literacy recorded in Bangalore urban, Bangalore rural, Dakshin Kannada, Udupi, Uttar Kannada, Dharwad districts. In Dakshin Kannada there is highest male literacy rates, and Yadagir district records lowest male literacy rate in 2011 census. The highest female literacy recorded in the districts of Bangalore urban, Dakshin Kannada, Udupi, Uttar Kannada, Dharwad according to 2011 census, and Raichur district records lowest female literacy in the state.

The male literacy rate is much higher than the state average and also in female and rural urban literacy also. The state needs to take immediate steps to increase female rural literacy in the state. Koppal, Raichur, Gulbarga, Bagalkot and Gadag districts are highly depressed in terms of rural female literacy. The overall view of the male, female, rural, urban literacy among the districts of Karnataka is increased by nearly 10 per cent in every census decades, because of the several literacy programmes, initiated by the state government.

Sex Ratio

Sex ratio is one of the important attributes of population composition. The sex ratio is expressed as ratio of women per thousand male populations. It is one of the indicator of socio-economic development, it also indicate several other social conditions of the society. The status of women, role of women in decision-making, general equality, rate of literacy particularly female literacy the impact of women empowerment programmes of literacy have all been reflected in the sex ratio of the society.

The Table 18.3 below represents the district-wise sex ratio, the sex ratio in the state highly variable as it is an indicator of social development to a large extent. Udupi has highest sex ratio in the state with 1134, 1127, 1093 in 1991, 2001 and 2011 census accordingly, followed by Dakshin Kannada, Kodagu, Hassan, Chikmagalore, these five districts are have higher levels of sex ratio in the state. Among 176 taluks 25 taluks have 1000 or more female population per thousand males. These are two in Uttar Kannada, two in Shimoga, seven in Dakshin Kannada, one in Chikmagalor, two in Tumkur, three in Mandya, six in Hassan, one each in Kodagu and Gulbarga districts. The trend of urban and rural sex ratio is almost same. The lowest sex ratio in the state is in Bangalore urban, which has 908 female populations per thousand males, it is followed by Bangalore rural 945, Haveri 951, Bidar 952, Bijapur 954 and Gulbarga 962 districts.

Lower sex ratio is related to several factors; it is largely caused by poor reproductive healthcare and gender bias. These have caused women and girls not to get adequate nutrition and healthcare, there is preference of male child in the society. However in the recent years with increasing literacy and public health care the female sex ratio has registered a modest improvement. Sex determination is one of the worst situations in the society which has to be tackled with proper programmes which are already implemented by the government.

Table 18.4: District-wise sex ratio in Karnataka 1991-2011

Sl. No.	*Districts*	*Sex ratio*		
		1991	*2001*	*2011*
1.	Bangalore urban	903	906	908
2.	Bangalore rural	945	953	945
3.	Bagalkot	—	933	984
4.	Belgaum	954	959	969
5.	Bellary	966	969	978
6.	Bidar	952	948	952
7.	Bijapur	948	948	954
8.	Chamarajnagar	—	968	989
9.	Chikmagalore	977	984	1005
10.	Chitradurga	951	955	969
11.	Davanagere	—	951	967
12.	Dharwad	935	948	967
13.	Dakshin Kannada	1020	1023	1018
14.	Gadag	—	968	978
15.	Gulberga	962	964	962
16.	Haveri	—	942	951
17.	Hassan	999	1005	1005
18.	Kolar	965	970	976
19.	Koppal	—	982	983
20.	Kodagu	996	996	1019
21.	Mandya	963	985	989
22.	Mysore	953	965	982
23.	Raichur	978	980	992
24.	Shimoga	964	977	995
25.	Tumkur	959	966	979
26.	Udupi	—	1127	1093
27.	Uttar Kannada	966	970	975
28.	Ramanagar	—	—	976
29.	Chikkaballapur	—	—	968
30.	Yadagir	—	—	984
	Karnataka	**960**	**965**	**968**

Source: census report Karnataka 1991, 2001, 2011.

Child Sex Ratio

The child sex ratio (CSR) signals, the fourth coming sex ratio to a large extent, it is thus a projected sex ratio of the society in the coming decades. At all India level, the child sex ratio in 1991 was 945 which drastically declined to 927 in 2001 and 928 in 2011 which is the serious problem of the country. It clearly indicates the preference for male child. A notion is that has strong economic and cultural routes in India. A son is viewed as an economic asset where as a daughter is insensitively considered as a burden on the resources of the family.

Table 18.5: District-wise child sex ratio in Karnataka 1991-2011

Sl. No.	*Districts*	*Child Sex ratio (0-6yrs)*		
		1991	*2001*	*2011*
1.	Bangalore urban	957	943	940
2.	Bangalore rural	950	942	946
3.	Bagalkot	—	940	928
4.	Belgaum	955	921	930
5.	Bellary	957	947	953
6.	Bidar	962	941	934
7.	Bijapur	956	928	930
8.	Chamarajnagar	—	964	941
9.	Chikmagalore	978	959	962
10.	Chitradurga	970	946	933
11.	Davanagere	—	946	930
12.	Dharwad	952	943	942
13.	Dakshin Kannada	966	952	945
14.	Gadag	—	952	943
15.	Gulberga	959	938	935
16.	Haveri	—	957	945
17.	Hassan	967	958	964
18.	Kolar	971	959	954
19.	Koppal	—	953	952
20.	Kodagu	957	977	976
21.	Mandya	959	934	933
22.	Mysore	966	962	956
23.	Raichur	965	964	949
24.	Shimoga	961	956	959
25.	Tumkur	670	949	952
26.	Udupi	—	958	954
27.	Uttar Kannada	949	946	946
28	Ramanagar	—	—	960
29	Chikkaballapur	—	—	944
30	Yadagir	—	—	942
	Karnataka	**960**	**946**	**943**

Source: census report Karnataka 1991, 2001, 2011.

The Table 18.5 shows the district-wise child sex population under the age 6, in Karnataka from 1991 to 2011. The child sex ratio in the state is only 943; even the child sex ratio has also large variations among the districts of Karnataka. Kodagu district has registered highest child sex ratio with 976, followed by Hassan 964, and Chikmagalore 962. And also the lowest child sex ratio registered in Bagalkot with 928, followed by Belgaum 930, Chitradurga and Mandya 933, remaining districts are registered moderate child sex ratio in between 976 and 928.

Conclusion

In the past 20 years there has been a continuous decline in population growth in Karnataka. The decades of 1991, 2001 and 2011 is quite interesting in the census history both in the state as well as in the country. It is because that a ray of hope has appeared in the horizon in controlling growth of population. The decadal population growth rate has started declining from 21.12 per cent in 1991 to 17.25 per cent in 2001 and to 15.93 per cent in 2011. It indicates the positive evidences to believe declining trend of population in the coming census.

This study summarise the decadal growth how is different among the districts, the Hyderabad Karnataka region records highest growth rate comparatively to the Mysore region. The Mumbai region and remaining districts have registered moderate growth. The density is also varies among the districts, the southern, coastal, and the Mumbai region has high density, and remaining northern, Mysore region has moderate density, in the Malnad districts have registered low density.

The literacy is also varies among the districts, the costal districts Udupi, Uttar Kannada, Dakshin Kannada, Kodagu, Bangalore urban, Dharwad have registered highest literacy more than 81 per cent, the northern part of Karnataka has below 70 per cent, and remaining district of Mumbai and Mysore region has 71 to 80 per cent, especially the Raichur and Yadagir registered very low literacy rates in the state. The sex ratio also variably distributed among the districts of Karnataka, the highest sex ratio registered in coastal and Malnad districts. The lowest sex ratio is in Bangalore urban, Bidar, Dharwad, Haveri districts, the remaining districts have moderate sex ratio. The overall view of the study is to understand the growth, composition, of population in Karnataka during the period of 20 years from 1991 to 2011.

References

1. Dr. R.C.Chandana (2004-2005). "A Geography of Population" – Kalyani Publishers, New Delhi.
2. G.T. Trewartha (1953-1969). "A Geography of Population- World pattern", New York.
3. H.R. Jones, "Population Geography New London"-Harper and Row.
4. Gosh, B.N. (1985). "Fundamental Population Geography-Sterling Publishers, New Delhi.
5. Census Karnataka-1991, 2001, 2011.
6. Chandana, R.C. "Principle of population geography", Kalyani Publishers, New Delhi.
7. Dr Suryanath U. Kamath. Concise history of Karnataka, 2001, MCC, Bangalore.
8. Mohammad Izhar Hassan (2005). Population geography, Rawat Publication, Jaipur.
9. Karnataka State Gazetteer.
10. www.censusindia2011.

Bibliography

1. A. Venkat Raman, James Warner Bjorkman (2008), *Public-Private Partnerships in Health Care in India: Lessons for developing countries,* Taylor & Francis.
2. Akintola Akintoye, Matthias Beck, Cliff Hardcastle (2003), *Public-Private Partnerships: Managing Risks and Opportunities*, Wiley.
3. Albert N. Link (2006), *Public/Private Partnerships: Innovation Strategies and Policy Alternatives*, Springer.
4. Alberto Paloni, Maurizio Zanardi (2005), *The IMF, World Bank and Policy Reform,* Taylor & Francis.
5. Ambuj Gupta (2010), *Non-Performing Assets (Npas) in Indian Banks,* Lambert Academic Publishing.
6. Anders Åslund, George De Menil (2000), *Economic Reform in Ukraine: The Unfinished Agenda,* M.E. Sharpe.
7. Anne O. Krueger (2002), *Economic Policy Reforms and the Indian Economy,* University of Chicago Press.
8. Arpita Mukherjee, Nitisha Patel (2005), *FDI in Retail Sector, India,* Academic Foundation.
9. B. S. Bhatia, G. S. Batra (2006), *Management of Financial Services*, Deep and Deep Publications.
10. Bishwa Nath Singh, Mohan Prasad Shrivastava, Narendra Prasad (2003), *Economic Reforms in India,* APH Publishing.
11. C. H. Chai, K. C. Roy 2006), *Economic Reform in China and India: Development Experiences in a Comparative Perspective*, Edward Elgar Publishing.
12. Charles Gibson (2012), *Financial Reporting and Analysis*, Cengage Learning.
13. Dale R. Weigel (1997), *Foreign Direct Investment,* World Bank Publications.

14. Darrin Grimsey, Mervyn Lewis (2004), *Public Private Partnerships: The Worldwide Revolution in Infrastructure Provision and Project Finance*, Edward Elgar.
15. David Williams (1984), *Financial Astrology*, American Federation of Astr.
16. Debaprosanna Nandy (2010), *Banking Sector Reforms in India and Performance Evaluation of Commercial Banks,* Universal-Publishers.
17. Dr Vibha Jain (2007), *Non-performing assets in commercial banks,* Regal Publications.
18. E S Savas (2000), *Privatisation and Public-Private Partnerships*, CQ Press.
19. E. R. Yescombe (2011), *Public-Private Partnerships: Principles of Policy and Finance,* Butterworth-Heinemann.
20. Ellen Marie Pint (2001), *Public-private Partnerships: Background Papers for the U.S.-U.K. Conference on Military Installation Assets, Operations, and Services*, Issue 1309, Rand.
21. Ernest Aryeetey, Jane Harrigan, Machiko Nissanke (2000), *Economic Reforms in Ghana: The Miracle and the Mirage,* Africa World Press.
22. Eugene Brigham, Michael Ehrhardt (2010), *Financial Management: Theory & Practice*, Edition 13, Cengage Learning.
23. Franklin Allen, Douglas Gale (1994), *Financial Innovation and Risk Sharing,* MIT Press.
24. Gogula Parthasarathy (2003), *Economic Reforms and Rural Development in India,* Academic Foundation.
25. Graeme A. Hodge, Carsten Greve (2005), *The Challenge of Public-Private Partnerships: Learning from International Experience*, Edward Elgar Publishing.
26. H. K. Yong (2010), *Public-Private Partnerships Policy and Practice: A Reference Guide,* Commonwealth Secretariat.
27. Howard A. Frank (2006), *Public Financial Management,* CRC Press.
28. I.M. Pandey (2009), *Financial Management*, Vikas Publishing House Pvt Ltd.
29. Jae K. Shim, Joel G. Siegel (2000), *Financial Management*, Barron's Educational Series.
30. John Williamson (1994), *The Political Economy of Policy Reform,* Peterson Institute.

31. José María Fanelli, Lyn Squire (2008), *Economic Reform in Developing Countries: Reach, Range, Reason,* Edward Elgar.
32. Justin Nelson Michael (2011), *Non Performing Assets in Co-operative Banks*, LAP Lambert Acad. Publ.
33. Justin Yifu Lin, Fang Cai, Zhou Li (2003), *The China Miracle: Development Strategy and Economic Reform,* Hong Kong Centre for Economic Research and the International Center for Economic Growth.
34. K. Seeta Prabhu (2001), *Economic reform and social sector development: a study of two Indian states,* Sage Publications.
35. Kenneth A. Froot (2008), *Foreign Direct Investment*, University of Chicago Press.
36. Larry Jay Diamond, Marc F. Plattner (1995), *Economic reform and democracy*, Johns Hopkins University Press.
37. Manmohan Singh, Isher Judge Ahluwalia, Ian Malcolm David Little (1998), *India's economic reforms and development: essays for Manmohan Singh*, Oxford University Press.
38. Marco Neuhaus (2006), *The Impact of FDI on Economic Growth: An Analysis for the Transition Countries of Central and Eastern Europe,* Springer Science & Business Media.
39. Margaret M. Pearson (1997), *China's New Business Elite: The Political Consequences of Economic Reform,* University of California Press.
40. Menjor Singh (2001), *Economic Reforms in India: Problems & Prospects,* Mittal Publications.
41. Mirjam Bult-Spiering, Geert Dewulf (2007), *Strategic Issues in Public-Private Partnerships: An International Perspective,* Wiley.
42. Nicholas Avery *et. al.* (2006), *Public-Private Partnerships: A Practical Analysis*, Globe Law and Business.
43. Organisation for Economic Co-operation and Development (2002), *Foreign Direct Investment for Development: Maximising Benefits, Minimising Costs: Overview,* OECD.
44. Paolo Urio (2010), *Public-Private Partnerships: Success and Failure Factors for In-Transition Countries*, University Press of America.
45. Parmatam Parkash Arya, B. B. Tandon (2003), *Economic Reforms in India: From First to Second Generation and Beyond,* Deep and Deep Publications.
46. Pauline Vaillancourt Rosenau (2000), *Public-Private Policy Partnerships*, MIT Press.

47. Philipp H. Pattberg (2012), *Public-Private Partnerships for Sustainable Development: Emergence, Influence and Legitimacy*, Edward Elgar Publishing.
48. Philippa Dee (2012), *Economic Reform Processes in South Asia: Toward Policy Efficiency,* Routledge.
49. Pradip Baijal (2008), *Disinvestment in India: I Lose and You Gain*, Pearson Education India.
50. R. Charles Moyer, James McGuigan, Ramesh Rao, William Kretlow (2011), *Contemporary Financial Management*, Cengage Learning.
51. R. K. Mishra, Bulusu Navin (2002), *Restructuring Public Enterprises in India: Privatisation and Disinvestment*, Mittal Publications.
52. R. K. Uppal (2005), *Economic Reforms in India: A Sectoral Analysis,* New Century Publications.
53. Ricardo Ffrench-Davis (2002), Economic Reforms in Chile: From Dictatorship to Democracy, University of Michigan Press.
54. Ronald W. Melicher, Edgar A. Norton (2011), *Introduction to Finance: Markets, Investments, and Financial Management*, Edition 14, John Wiley & Sons.
55. Roy E. Bailey (2005), *The Economics of Financial Markets,* Cambridge University Press
56. S.N. Bidani (2005), *Managing Non-Performing Assets in Banks,* Vision Books Private Limited.
57. Stephen Osborne (2002), *Public-Private Partnerships: Theory and Practice in International Perspective*, Taylor & Francis.
58. Stephen W. Perl (2010), *Public-Private Partnerships: Costs, Benefits and Efficiencies,* Nova Science Publishers.
59. Steven Heydemann (2004), *Networks of Privilege in the Middle East: The Politics of Economic Reform Revisited,* Palgrave Macmillan.
60. Sudhindra Bhat (2008), *Financial Management*, Excel Books India.
61. Sudhir Naib (2004), *Disinvestment in India: Policies, Procedures, Practices*, SAGE Publications India.
62. Sultan Singh (2007), *Banking Sector Reforms in India*, Kanishka Publication.
63. Susan L. Shirk (1993), *The Political Logic of Economic Reform in China,* University of California Press.

64. Susan Robertson, Karen Mundy, Antoni Verger (2012), *Public Private Partnerships in Education: New Actors and Modes of Governance in a Globalising World,* Edward Elgar Publishing.

65. T.V. Gopalakrishnan (2004), *Management of Non-performing Advances: A Study with Reference to Public Sector Banks*, Northern Book Centre.

66. Uma Kapila (1996), *India's Economic Reforms*, Academic Foundation.

67. World Bank. Independent Evaluation Group (2008), *Public Sector Reform: What Works and Why? : an IEG Evaluation of World Bank Support*, World Bank Publications.

Index